SHELLS
Treasures from the Sea

SHELLS
Treasures from the Sea

James A. Cox

Foreword by J. R. H. Lightbourn

Special photography by F. H. Roberts

A Rutledge Book
Larousse & Co., Inc.
New York, New York

Copyright 1979 by Larousse & Co., Inc.,
and Rutledge Books, Inc., in all countries
of the International Copyright Union.
All rights reserved.
Published by Larousse & Co., Inc.
572 Fifth Avenue, New York, New York 10036
Prepared and produced by Rutledge Books, Inc.
Library of Congress Cataloging in Publication Data
Cox, James A
    Shells treasures from the sea.
    "A Rutledge book."
    1. Shells. I. Title.
QL405.C68   594'.04'7   79-7520
ISBN 0-88332-118-1

Printed in Italy by Mondadori, Verona.

Contents

For my wife, JoAnne, who deserves more than a dedication

Pages 6 –7 left: Mitra vulpecula *Linné, the little fox miter, 1 to 2 inches, Indo-Pacific.*

Pages 6 –7 right: Chlamys australis *Sowerby, the southern scallop, 4 inches, Australia.*

Pages 10 –11: Epitonium scalare *Linné, the precious wentletrap, 2 ½ inches, of the southwest Pacific. Wentletrap is a corruption of the German word for winding staircase,* wentletreppe. *This shell was once thought to be extremely rare. An emperor in antiquity reportedly paid the equivalent of £10,000 for a specimen, and at a shell auction in London in 1753, another specimen brought the equivalent of £250. So rare and valuable were wentletraps, the story goes, that clever Chinese entrepreneurs molded counterfeits out of rice paste and sold them for hundreds of dollars apiece, but the bottom dropped out of the market when real shells were found in abundance off Australia. No one has been able to establish the truth of that story, and no one has ever admitted to owning a forged wentletrap; if one did show up, it would undoubtedly be worth far more as a curiosity than it sold for as a counterfeit in the eighteenth century.*

Pages 14 –15: *Polished specimen of* Turbo sarmaticus *Linné, 4 inches, from South Africa.*

Foreword

My interest in mollusks started when, as a very young boy, I accompanied my grandfather in his search for seashells and coral in the shallow waters and bays of Bermuda. This early beginning gave me a deep interest in this fascinating hobby, and through the years my love for seashells has allowed me to travel to many countries and has brought me into contact with many of the world's leading collectors and authorities in the field of malacology.

Bermuda is not an outstanding collecting area, and this prompted my experiments in deep-water trapping and dredging carried out jointly with my close friend Arthur T. Guest. These excursions into the deep have brought to light many interesting specimens, many of them hardly known—others never before reported in the Bermuda area.

From depths to two thousand feet, the rare Perotrochus adansonianus *Crosse and Fisher 1861 and the* Perotrochus quoyanus *Fisher and Bernardi 1856 remain outstanding finds. The great prize, however, was a* Murex pterynotus, *new to science, which will soon be named.*

In addition to these local efforts, I have also accumulated a collection of foreign mollusks of all types, including nearly eight hundred specimens of my two favorite species, cones and cowries.

I was very pleased when I was asked to provide the foreword for this book. Neither a textbook nor an authority on any particular family or species, this book is meant to meaningfully display some of the most beautiful of nature's creations. I'm sure that readers will benefit from the beauty and design of these shells, and while observing their symmetry of line and color will share with me some of the great thrill and delight that the study of shells can provide.

It is my hope that this book will help open up new worlds to those people who collect and enjoy these treasures from the sea, which have been an inspiration to man through the ages.

J. R. H. LIGHTBOURN
"Shellbourn"
Hamilton Parish
Bermuda

The Animal Inside

Shells have fascinated people since the dawn of time, but little scientific attention was paid to them except for the work of Aristotle and Pliny the Elder until after the Renaissance. Even then, the emphasis was on describing the shell—the external skeleton of the animal inside—as is evidenced by the name given the study, *conchology* (from the Latin word *concha*, "shell"). Eventually, naturalists began to examine more closely the shell dweller, and in 1832, the distinguished French zoologist, H. M. de Blainville, suggested *malacology* (from a Greek word meaning "soft") as a better name for a science dealing with invertebrate animals.

De Blainville had his adherents in England: "This branch of Natural History," wrote a commentator named Wood in 1857, "has leaped at once out of the mere childish toy of conchology into the maturer science of malacology." Nevertheless, conchology remained the preferred term in England, as did malacology in France, and for a long time the two names were used interchangeably. In some quarters and for some usages they still are, but in recent years it has become common practice to use *malacology* when referring to the study of animals and their biology, and *conchology* for the study of shells.

For reasons similar to those of de Blainville, another great French naturalist, Georges Cuvier, earlier had proposed calling the boneless creatures *mollusca*, from the Latin adjective *mollis*, which also means "soft." From this we get, in English, mollusc, or, more frequently, mollusk, the name applied to a group containing between sixty and seventy thousand species—second in number only to the insects. Although they are most numerous in the sea, mollusks also live on land and in fresh water, and can be found all over the world, from above the snow line in the Himalayas to ocean depths where water pressure amounts to tons per square inch; from scorching deserts to boiling hot springs; and even in the solid ice of frozen ponds. They range in size from microscopic sea slugs to the sixty-foot giant squid, and include such familiar and diverse creatures as snails, clams, oysters, and octopuses.

To make some order out of nature for the purpose of studying it, scientists have developed a process of classification in which all the "things" of nature are bunched into systems of groups, generally based on common or like properties. There are three kingdoms: animal, vegetable, and mineral. Next come the phyla (from the Greek word *phylon*, meaning "tribe"), the primary divisions of each kingdom. These are followed by ever more finely graded classifications and closely related groupings: classes, orders, families, genera, species, and, occasionally, subspecies.

Because of the great diversity within the phylum Mollusca, it is difficult to define the characteristics its members have in common that put them together in the same "tribe." Generally speaking, mollusks are characterized by a soft, unsegmented body; a protective external shell; a muscular, solelike organ called the foot; a rasplike "tongue" fitted with many rows of hooked teeth, called the radula; and a fleshy mantle, a fold or curtain of tissue that lines the shell and secretes the calcium carbonate with which the shell is built. The mantle is one feature common to all mollusks, even octopuses and squids, which do not have external shells; the squid, however, has a delicate, vestigial, lance-shaped shell under the mantle, known as the pen shell, and the octopus forms a shell in its embryonic state, but loses it on the way to maturity.

Still, to the eyes of the layman, there is little resemblance between a clam and an octopus, and because of their many anatomical variations the mollusks have been divided into six main classes.

Monoplacophora—the gastroverms—*mono* (one) *placos* (plate) *phora* (bearing): These are the most primitive forms of mollusks, and also the most recent addition to the list of mollusk classes. They had been known from fossil remains, but were considered extinct. Then, in 1952, the Danish research vessel *Galathea*, dredging in two-mile depths off the western coast of Mexico, brought up some small limpetlike shells. No one paid much attention to the shells, and it wasn't until 1957 that zoologists examining them suddenly realized that they were participating in one of the most exciting biological events of the century—the rediscovery of a form of life that had flourished during the Paleozoic era, from more than 500 to 350 million years ago, and had been assumed extinct. Since the initial discovery of *Neopilina galatheae*, as it was christened, six other species of gastroverms, the popular name adopted in 1960, have been taken in deep water in the Gulf of Aden, off the coasts of Peru and California, and in the South Atlantic.

It was not the thin, simple shell of the

Chitons

gastroverms that stirred up all the excitement but the animal inside—especially the fact that it was segmented like annelid worms, with each segment containing duplicate kidneys, ovaries, testes, gills, and excretory organs. This seemed to verify a suspicion long entertained by zoologists—an evolutionary relationship between mollusks and segmented worms.

Polyplacophora—the chitons—*poly* (many) *placo* (plate)—until recently called Amphineura: The chitons, most primitive of the familiar mollusks, are easily recognized by the eight overlapping plates arranged along the back, which account for their most popular nicknames—coat-of-mail shells and armadillos of the sea. The plates are encircled by a leathery or fleshy girdle that is part of the mantle and is often decorated with spicules, spines, scales, or hairy bristles. There are six hundred living species, the largest of which, the foot-long giant Pacific chiton, inhabits the western coast of North America. Most chitons live attached to rocks between the tide marks, clinging tenaciously with a large, powerful foot. They move about at night seeking food, which for the most part consists of algae and seaweeds. Only a few species are predatory.

Unable to withdraw into its shell like a snail or snap its valves shut like a bivalve, a chiton will roll up into a ball to protect its soft underside if it is pulled from its rocky resting place. These animals are found in all parts of the world, usually in shallow water, but some deep-water species have been dredged from the ocean floor more than twelve thousand feet down. They are used as fish bait in many areas, and in the West Indies the sturdy foot is eaten raw or tenderized by pounding and cooked in a dish called sea beef.

Scaphopoda—the tusk or tooth shells—*scapho* (boat) *pous* (foot): These animals get their scientific name from the shape of the foot and their popular names from their resemblance to tiny curved elephant tusks. They have the simplest anatomy of all the mollusks, possessing neither eyes, gills, nor heart. They "breathe" with the entire surface of the body, spreading the mantle and keeping water circulating through the opening at the narrow end of the shell by expanding and contracting the muscular foot. The ribbed shells, which are usually white or ivory, but with pink, green, yellow, and other colors occurring in some species, are open at both ends. The foot extends through the larger opening at the front; there is no head, but a short snout located just above the foot contains a mouth, equipped with a radula, and a cluster of long, threadlike tentacles, called *captacula*, each of which is tipped by a tiny, sticky pad. The animal lives partially buried head-down in the sandy or muddy bottom, with the narrow end of its shell thrust up into clear water and

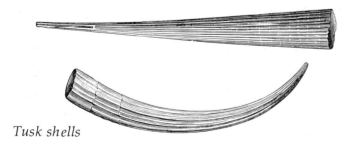

Tusk shells

its tentacles stretched out on the sea floor, ready to seize the microscopic organisms upon which it feeds.

Only a hundred or so species of scaphopods remain of the rich variety that populated Tertiary seas, but the number of individuals in that relatively few species is enormous. Exclusively marine, the tusk shells are found in all seas, from the shallows to depths of more than 2,600 fathoms. In size, they can be as small as a grain of rice or as long as five inches; in shape, they range from slender hollow

Bivalve scallops

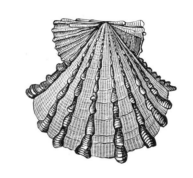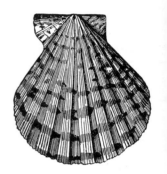

needles to swollen cucumbers.

The most interesting species is undoubtedly *Dentalium pretiosum*, the money tooth shell of the Pacific Northwest. Long before the coming of the white man to the shores of North America, the western Indians were converting these little white shells, about an inch long, polished, and perforated by nature as if intended for stringing, into necklaces and *haik-wa*, the wampum of the Pacific coast. In some areas of the Northwest, tusk shell wampum was still being used as currency as late as the nineteenth century.

Bivalvia—the clams—until recently designated Pelecypoda, *pelecy* (hatchet) *pous* (foot): With the bivalves—second largest of the molluscan classes with ten thousand species—we reach more familiar territory, especially in the gastronomic sense, for here we find many of the most popular edible mollusks: oysters, clams, scallops, and mussels. As the name Bivalvia suggests, all members of this class possess two valves, or shells, which the animal closes tightly when under threat. The valves are hinged at the side with an elastic ligament, held open by a rubberlike wedge called the *resilium*, and closed by two strong adductor muscles. Some species, notably the scallops, have only one adductor muscle, a regrettable circumstance from the human point of view, since that is the most edible part.

The mantle of the bivalve is divided into two lobes, which hang down on either side of the body like curtains. The edges of the mantle, often bearing sense organs or tentacles, are rarely uniform; they contain several openings, one for the foot to pass through, and two smaller ones, one to bring in fresh water and food particles, the other to expel used water and waste. In some species, the mantle lobes form siphons for inhaling and exhaling water.

The size of the bivalve's foot, which in most species is the only means of locomotion, largely determines the animal's life habits and habitat. In mobile mollusks and those that burrow in sand and mud, the organ is large and developed. In species that live fixed or largely sedentary lives, such as oysters and mussels, the foot is much reduced in size and contains a gland that secretes a mucus substance. This substance solidifies in water and forms chitinous filaments, known as byssus, by which the animal attaches itself solidly to rocks or other underwater objects.

Of all the mollusks, only the bivalves and a few gastropods lack a radula. Neither does the bivalve have a head, but it does possess a mouth. It feeds by drawing in seawater, which passes over the gills, where any fine food particles, animal or vegetable debris and plankton, are trapped in mucus and moved by thousands of cilia, microscopic hairs, toward a pair of leaflike growths, or palps, which push the food into the mouth. The gill plates are attached at the top and free at the bottom, and the cilia on the gill surfaces keep water circulating through the mantle cavity. Since most bivalves do not go seeking either food or mate, all things must come and go to and from them by way of this water current.

Gastropod

Many bivalves are best looked at through a microscope; the largest, the giant clam, *Tridacna gigas*, of Australian waters, measures four feet or more at its extremes and weighs over five hundred pounds. Other remarkable bivalves include the razor clams, cousins to the common long clam but far swifter, capable of burrowing through sand faster than man and shovel can follow. They also rank with scallops and file shells as the few bivalves able to swim.

Gastropoda—the snails—*gaster* (belly) *pous* (foot): The gastropods, known as the univalves because of their single, usually coiled, shells, are the largest class of mollusks, with thirty thousand species. They include such well-known creatures as whelks, winkles, conchs, limpets, abalones, freshwater snails, and garden slugs, as well as some lesser-known, such as sea slugs and the curious free-swimming sea butterflies, or pteropods. In addition to their diversity, gastropods must be considered the most successful of all mollusks, since they are the only ones to have invaded the land.

The anatomy of gastropods is complicated by a remarkable twisting, or torsion, of both body and shell. In their earliest phase, the larvae have bilateral symmetry; the mantle and shell are cap-shaped, the intestine is straight, and the mouth and anus are at opposite ends, with the foot between. Then an extraordinary thing happens—the front edge of the conical shell, together with the body

Saucerlike abalone shell

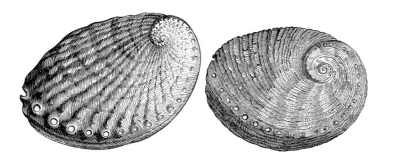

and organs of the animal, twists 180 degrees to the right, bringing the anus and reproductive organs up front to a new position above the back of the head. As the shell continues to twist with the growth of the animal, the organs on the outside of the spiral grow forward unretarded, but those on the inside become compressed. As a result, one of each paired structure, such as the gills, the kidneys, and the auricles of the heart, degenerates and disappears, while the other develops fully, changing a symmetrical animal into an asymmetrical one.

A few of the gastropods, notably the limpets and abalones, have shallow, saucerlike shells rather than coiled ones. Others, like the garden slugs and nudibranchian sea slugs, have fragile vestigial shells or no shell at all. It is interesting to note that in the gastropods that have evolved out of their shells, the body has become untwisted, with front and back having meaning again.

Gastropods have recognizable heads, usually with two eyes, one on each side, which are sometimes located on stalks. Tentacles projecting from the head carry well-developed olfactory organs. The foot is robust or rudimentary, depending upon the species. Most univalves "walk" in typical snail fashion, extending the foot and then gliding forward on it. Scientists studying their migration habits report that some marked specimens traveled as far as sixty miles from where the experiment began—a long trek to cover at a snail's pace. Most species are equipped with the radula, an extremely efficient tool for shredding vegetable matter or flesh, or for drilling through another mollusk's shell. A retractable proboscis, serving the digestive apparatus, shows thickening at the base, suggesting vestigial jaws.

An interesting feature of many univalves is the operculum, or trapdoor, a tough and often colorful "plug" that grows on the back part of the foot and seals the mouth of the shell when the animal retreats inside. In some species the operculum is composed of a heavy, shell-like substance; in others, it is thinner, more like a chitinous or horny material; and in still others, such as the cowries, with long, narrow apertures, it does not occur at all.

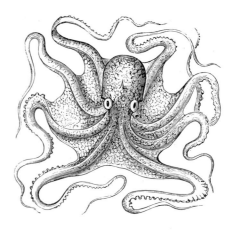

Octopus, one of the shell-less mollusks

Cephalopoda—the squids and octopuses—
cephalon (head) *pous* (foot): It may be difficult to
believe that squids and octopuses—among the most
agile creatures in the sea, and possessors of
surprising intelligence, as well—are related to
sedentary oysters and creeping snails. But mollusks
they are, say the biologists, properly equipped with
the basic requirements of mantle, radula, and foot,
even though the latter has evolved into sets of arms.

Exclusively marine, the cephalopods—a class
that also includes the cuttlefish, the argonaut or
paper nautilus, and the chambered nautilus—are
the most highly developed of all mollusks. They
can be found in any ocean, from the tropics to the
polar regions, and at any depth. Squids from the
depths off Newfoundland and New Zealand attain a
length of sixty feet and even more; an eighty-five-
footer is the largest ever recorded. Although its
reputation in literature is more than a little
exaggerated, the giant squid, the dreaded kraken of
Scandinavian tales, is not an adversary to be taken
lightly. Huge sperm whales captured by whaling
vessels often bear circular scars "as big as dinner
plates" on their tough hides, mementos left by the
giant squid's suckers during some epic battle in the
dark depths of the sea. Whales, which consider
squids of all sizes a preferred food, invariably win
these one-on-one encounters; in fact, some ten
thousand parrotlike squid beaks once were found in
the stomach of a bottle-nosed whale. Sometimes the
whale has to pay the glutton's price, however, for
the sharp, indigestible beaks can cause trouble in
the intestines. To isolate the source of discomfort,
the whale will encase the offending beak in a
protective waxy substance known as ambergris,
treasured since the ninth century for use in
medicines, as a spice for wines, as an aphrodisiac,
and as a base for perfumes.

Squids and octopuses are no slouches themselves
when it comes to eating. The octopus will creep
along behind a crab or swim above it, then swoop
down and seize it, often holding the victim helpless
with its suckers while it pursues other prey. Once
captives disappear under the mantle, the end comes
quickly as the powerful beak crunches off crab claws
and the suckered arms wrench apart the shells of
bivalves. In addition to these formidable tools,
many octopuses secrete a venom that is so toxic and
fast-acting that it paralyzes and then kills crabs
within forty-five seconds. And not only crabs—a
tiny Australian species on the Great Barrier Reef has
lately been credited with killing several human
beings who were thought to have died of heart
attacks.

Large squids, so streamlined for speed that some
members of the family are called sea arrows, are
often seen in swarms, swimming swiftly with fins
foremost and arms trailing out behind, and
sometimes leaping fifteen feet and more out of the
water. Squids may be the fastest swimmers in the
sea; they use jet propulsion, expelling water from a
funnel under the mantle with such force that they
shoot through the water like torpedoes—forward or
backward or off to the sides, for the funnel can be
directed in any direction. They are swift killing
machines when they swoop down on a school of
herring or mackerel, striking out this way and that to
grasp fish with their sucker-clad arms, and with
their cruel beaks instantly biting a triangular chunk
of flesh out of the back of their victim—deep
enough to sever the spinal cord and always in the
same place. They may continue killing even after
eating their fill, and are capable of destroying a huge
school of fish in a matter of minutes.

The key to the anatomy of the cephalopods is in
the name, which literally means "head-footed
animal." The foot has been divided into arms that
surround the head and mantle cavity, with the
visceral organs extending behind—a body extension
pointed or cigar-shaped in the squids and bulbous in

the octopuses. Only the chambered nautilus of the tropical Pacific retains a visible shell, beautiful creamy white objects with orange brown stripes that English sailors several hundred years ago mistook for drowned tortoiseshell cats. Most of the squids have the long internal pen shell; most of the octopuses have no shell at all. Cuttlefish have a flat internal bone of calcareous material—the "cuttlebone" still useful for making polishing powders and for providing pet birds with calcium. Since antiquity the cuttlefish has been the chief source of a dark brown fluid called sepia ink, and in fact is called the sepia squid in the Mediterranean.

All cephalopods have a gland for secreting "ink," a liquid so strong that a few drops can cloud a large amount of water, which they use to confuse an attacker or screen their escape. Some observers have reported that the inky cloud "hangs" in the water unless disturbed and takes on roughly the size and shape of the animal producing it. The coloring agents in the ink are copper and iron, drawn from the cephalopod's blood. These creatures, especially the octopuses, also have the ability to change color to blend with their background.

Most people think of a tangle of tentacles when they visualize cephalopods, but that picture is inaccurate. The appendages are arms, not tentacles, and both the octopus and squid have eight; the squid, in addition, has a pair of real tentacles, much longer than the arms, which shoot out to seize prey and retract into the body again as soon as the arms, taking over, have a secure hold. The little nautilus, usually four to six inches long, with specimens up to ten inches, completes the picture, at least in terms of tentacles. The female has almost one hundred of the slender appendages arranged in rows around her mouth and eyes, the male about sixty. Otherwise these animals bear small resemblance to the other cephalopods. The argonaut is sometimes called the paper nautilus because of the paper-thin egg case

that it builds; it is not a nautilus, however, but a member of the octopus family.

All cephalopods have highly developed eyes, those of the squid and octopus being remarkably similar to those of man and the other vertebrates. The strangest eyes belong to the nautilus. Like miniature bowls, they are covered by a thin skin, with a tiny opening in the center; water filling the cavity acts as a lens. These simple eyes are constructed on the principle of the pinhole camera, and have no known parallel in nature.

One of the most remarkable things about mollusks is their ability to construct shells from calcium carbonate, a limy material extracted from seawater, using only the fleshy mantle, certainly one of nature's most unusual building tools. The mantle is pitted with a network of microscopic tubes through which the animal secretes tiny particles of lime that solidify as they adhere to a base of conchiolin, a hornlike material composed largely of protein, which the mollusk also manufactures. As additional courses of calcium carbonate and, sometimes, conchiolin, are laid—often cross-grain to those preceding—the shell grows in dimension and thickness.

The shell is composed of three main layers: a skinlike outer coating of conchiolin called the periostracum; a hard, chalky, middle layer of calcium carbonate, with crystals shaped like prisms and arranged at right angles to the surface; and an inner layer of calcium carbonate with the crystals arranged parallel to the surface, overlapping with each other somewhat in the manner of roof shingles. This inner layer is smooth and shiny, and may be porcelainlike or pearly (nacreous), depending upon the mineral content. Shells with nacreous linings generally belong to the more primitive species, such as the paper oysters. Light bouncing from the edges of the crystal "shingles" produces the iridescent luster known as mother-of-pearl. Oysters produce pearls by secreting layer upon layer of nacre over a particle of sand or other foreign material that becomes trapped in their tissues. Mollusks with porcellaneous inner layers react to irritants in much the same way, but the pearls that result are dull and lifeless.

The top and middle layers of the shell are secreted by the edge of the mantle; the innermost layer by the entire outside face of the mantle. In some species, such as cowries and olives, there is no periostracum and the mantle completely envelops the shell. There is some debate among malacologists as to whether, in such cases, the mantle builds new layers all over the outside surface of the shell, or merely covers the shell protectively while building only along the edge. In other species, such as the cones, the animal has the amazing ability to dissolve the calcium carbonate crystals in certain areas of the inner layer, reabsorb them, and deposit them on the outside surface, thereby making room inside for body growth. Through the same system, the mollusk can repair cracks, chips, and other damages to its shell.

Although some mollusks cease to grow after reaching sexual maturity, most continue growing throughout their lives. Size is no positive indicator of age, however, since many other factors, including water temperature, type of food and quantities available, affect the rate of shell growth. An unusual growth problem occurs with bivalves that become embedded in coral; they must grow at least as fast as the coral to prevent themselves from being overwhelmed and smothered.

Shell shapes, especially among the univalves, show an almost infinite variety. "Mankind has always been astonished," wrote Paul A. Zahl, senior natural scientist of the National Geographic Society, "by the fantastic structures that the mantle can produce—the frozen starlight of the Venus comb murex, the gleaming marble mound of the cowrie, the ivory minaret of the auger, the massive alabaster embattlements of the conch, the petrified flowers of the thorny oyster. Only a highly sophisticated and biologically successful animal could create such magnificent architecture."

Magnificent architecture, yes, but on a basically simple plan. Even among the gastropods, there are only a few fundamental shapes. For in all the bewildering variety of forms, the flat caps of the

Some of the vast variety of gastropod shell shapes

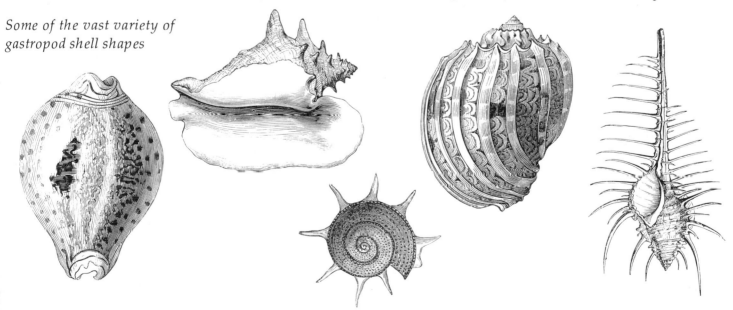

limpets and cup-and-saucer shells, the narrow pointed spires of the turrets, the splendidly spined murices, there is but one basic structure—a tube coiled about an imaginary axis. In most instances, the coiling is clockwise when the apex is up and the mouth of the shell opens to the right; these are right-handed, or dextral, shells. A few shells, such as Florida's lightning whelk, coil naturally counterclockwise, or sinistrally; but any shell that coils to the left in a normally right-handed species is a rarity. No one knows why a few species go against the norm, or why freak individuals occasionally occur.

The gastropod builds its spiral castle as it grows, and the final whorl, the largest and the one containing the aperture, is called the body whorl. Leonardo da Vinci, inspired to design a spiral staircase through his study of shells, wrote appreciatively: "The creature that resides within the shell constructs its dwelling with joints and seams and roofing, and the other various parts, just as a man does in the house which he inhabits; and this creature expands the house and roof gradually in proportion as its body increases and as it is attached to the sides of these shells."

In addition to shape, many shells are distinguished by ornamentation—ridges, knobs, spines, and the like. Ridges and grooves usually indicate periods during which the lime-producing cells in the mantle were inactive. The more bizarre pieces of sculpture are formed when the edge of the mantle, following the genetic code of the species, divides into sections, each following its innate program. If some of the lime tubes are injured or destroyed, the tubes that continue to function will create freak shells with distorted shapes.

It is not known why mollusks grow knobs and spines. The most obvious explanation is that they are grown to discourage predators, but starfish are the worst enemies and they can come up with a shellfish dinner just about whenever they set their minds to it. It has also been pointed out that if protection from predators were the reason for the odd protuberances, then spined and knobbed mollusks would be more numerous than those not similarly equipped—and they're not.

Perhaps the reason advanced by Edward Step, a Victorian naturalist, comes as close to the truth as any: "This diversity of form is, no doubt, determined by the habit of the mollusc and the situation it inhabits. For example, those species that adhere to rocks in shallow water (such as the ordinary limpet) and are therefore subjected to the heavy beating of the breakers, have their shells broad, smooth, and free from sculpturing that might catch the water and so result in the mollusc being swept away from its hold. Closely related species that live on sandy or gravelly bottoms appear, in many cases, to find the advantages in angles and knobs; probably because of their being precarious, when they are detached by waves, their irregular

Highly ornamented thorny oyster

surface prevents them from being swept from the spot."

Just as the ornamentation of the shell species is predetermined by genetic programming, so is the basic coloring, not only of the shells, but of the soft parts, such as mantle, foot, and head, which sometimes are more brilliant than the shell. The pigments that provide these sometimes spectacular colors are manufactured from the food the mollusk eats and are concentrated in cells along the mantle edge, where they are mixed with the structural material before it hardens into crystals. The position of the color glands determines the pattern produced on the shell. If they are in continuous series, produce only one pigment, and are steadily active, the shell will be one solid color. Any variation in the arrangement of the color glands, the type of pigment they lay down, and the rhythm of their operation, constant or intermittent, results in color patterns—spiraling stripes, vertical or horizontal bands, dashes, dots, spots, triangles, and other odd figures. One writer draws a graphic illustration of the process by likening the arrangement of the color tubes on the mantle to the holes in a player piano roll.

Coloration is amazingly identical in some species, and in others it varies from one individual to another. The factors affecting shell coloring include sunlight, warmth, abundance of food, and, to an extent, type of food. Researchers report that young abalone snails feeding on red seaweeds produce red shells; that grayish-white dogwinkles turn yellow on a diet limited to barnacles, and develop purple and brown markings if they feed on blue mussels. The general rule, however, is that the brightest shell colors are found in tropical waters, with a paling out as distance from the equator increases; thus, shells from frigid polar waters are usually uniformly white or gray.

The majority of shell colors result from two large groups of pigments: the melanins, ranging from tan to brown and black, and the carotenoids, which provide shades of yellow and orange. Red and violet occur fairly frequently, and although blue is a striking feature of the columella and operculum of *Astraea stellaris*, there are few shells that are really blue. Green also is rare, usually being limited to the periostracum when it does occur. In fact, the blue and green hues found in shells usually are produced by light refraction, as in the pearly inner linings, rather than by pigmentation. This phenomenon generally holds true throughout nature: the blue in feathers, iridescent beetle wings, and fish scales usually results from light refraction, and green is the result of a combination of refracted blue and a yellow pigment.

Most single-colored shells are white, and although most shells have more than one color, five colors seem to be the limit. Shades of brown predominate, but this does not mean that the colors are drab, for the shades range from tan to chestnut to cinnamon. Yellows, pinks, and oranges run the full scale, too, along with brilliant reds and glossy blacks, which, in concert with pure white, cream, and gray, offer an endless variety of striking combinations and patterns.

Biologists cannot explain this lavish display of color. It has been ascertained that some of the pigments in the shells of some mollusks are waste products, but that information doesn't help explain why such products should end up in the shell. There is no evidence to suggest that colors and patterns play a role in sex recognition—in fact, most bivalves do not have eyes and most snails are incapable of perceiving complicated images. Color cannot serve as a warning to predators, either, since just as many bright-shelled mollusks get eaten as dull ones; nor is camouflage the purpose of the coloration—indeed, some of the most vividly colored and fantastically marked shells hide their glory beneath a drab periostracum or fleshy mantle. Concerning the latter, modern biologists find it difficult to accept the explanation, offered by an eighteenth-century naturalist, that "the Almighty so covered them that we might have the pleasure of discovering their underlying beauties ourselves."

Although scientists have not been able to determine the meaning of colors and patterns, less-inhibited interpreters have been at work on the problem. Some collectors are convinced, for example, that there is a message in the hieroglyphlike markings of the lettered olive, *Oliva sayana*. An even finer display of credulity concerns the music volute, *Voluta musica*, which was named for the five thin bands and scattered spots, suggestive of a musical staff marked with notes, that follow the spiral of its whorls. Fair enough—but not long ago a misguided musician sat down at the piano and played, in all seriousness, the song of the shell.

Variety seems to be the spice of molluscan sex life. The sexes are separate in scaphopods, chitons, cephalopods, most bivalves, and most marine gastropods. Land and freshwater snails, however, are hermaphrodites, as are the duck clams, sea hares, and nudibranch sea slugs. Bivalves do not have copulatory organs, but are often equipped with both male and female glands and produce both eggs and sperm cells, or gametes. Self-fertilization is rare, even among bivalves, but it is not unknown; neither is parthenogenesis (production of offspring without benefit of male contributions—in essence, virgin birth).

In some instances, sex distinctions are not altogether clear. All common oysters, for example, begin life as males, turn into females after breeding, then change back to males. They continue this commuting between the sexes throughout their breeding life, always reverting to male after shedding their eggs. The common slipper shell,

Crepidula fornicata, lives an equally full life. R. Tucker Abbott tells the fascinating story succinctly: It "lives in clusters with one shell clinging on top of its neighbor. The four or five larger individuals at the bottom of the pile are all females. The younger and smaller ones at the top are males. Very often the middle ones are in the process of changing sex from male to female. Sexuality is controlled by a hormone that is constantly being produced by the females and exuded into the water. As long as the level of this hormone is high enough, it will prevent the males from turning into females. Should the females die or cease to function because of old age, the hormone disappears and the snails at the top of the pile begin to lose their testes, the penis shrinks away and ovaries begin to develop. In a week, the males have become females."

Because of the variety of reproductive methods, molluscan reproductive organs also vary considerably. Marine univalves, which usually have separate sexes, have simple genital organs. In the male, the testis is embedded in the liver and is connected by a duct called the vas deferens to the penis, which may be inserted in the right tentacle, or may be similar to a third tentacle. The female's ovary is also embedded in the liver, and the long oviduct generally opens in the left part of the body, just below the head. Fertilized eggs are enclosed in a gelatinous substance in the oviduct and released. Sometimes, in viviparous species, the female has a copulatory sac in which the eggs are incubated until the young develop and emerge.

The genital organs of the hermaphroditic freshwater and land snails are far more complex. Generally there is a single genital orifice, or pore, on the head, containing both male and female copulatory organs. Although these organs are closely linked in some species, individuals cannot fertilize themselves. Reproduction in these snails is often preceded by a courtship rite, and some species have a special organ, called a dart sac, which produces small chalky shafts that the individuals shoot at each other, presumably for sexual stimulation. The mating performance is a head-to-head matter, during which each partner fertilizes the eggs of the other by inserting its copulatory organ into the genital pore of the other. Each snail then goes its own way to lay its clutch of eggs.

Bivalves without copulatory organs utilize the most primitive of reproduction methods, spewing eggs and sperm directly into the sea. The eggs and sperm float about in the water until fate, currents, or tide bring them together and fertilization takes place. Some bivalves discharge only sperm, some only eggs, and some, with both organs, discharge both products. The latter, in order not to fertilize their own eggs, generally release the sperm first. Some bivalves don't discharge their eggs, but hold them in the mantle to be fertilized by sperm carried into the body cavity on the normal water intake. Some wood-boring clams, says Abbott, store live sperm in a special sac and release them when their eggs mature, thus ensuring "a lone female adrift at sea in a log a supply of male gametes."

Broadcasting the seeds of tomorrow's generations into the sea is a chancy way of assuring survival of the species, but nature has tried to compensate for all the obvious disadvantages. The broadcasting types of mollusks produce enormous quantities of eggs and sperm cells, all at the same time and as quickly as possible. Oysters belong to this group, and their production is so prodigious that the waters over oyster beds become cloudy during reproduction cycles. Biologists studying *Crassostrea gigas*, an oyster found on the Pacific Coast and in Japan, estimate that one female will discharge 1,000,000,000,000,000,000,000,000 eggs into the water in the course of a single year. Obviously, if all the eggs from all the females of just this species reached maturity, the world would soon become one huge oyster bed. Few of the many billions survive to fulfill their mission, however, and fewer still reach maturity; the vast remainder serve as food for the many other creatures in the sea.

The cephalopods, most highly developed of the mollusks, have separate sexes but a curious method of mating. The male produces cigar-shaped packets of sperm, called spermatophores, which he removes from his genital opening and transfers to the female's oviduct with one of his arms, the tip of which is modified into a sex organ known as the hectocotylus. In the octopus, the third arm on the right side is hectocotylized. Many go through a period of courtship, the male, displaying a series of color changes, caressing the female with the tip of his hectocotylized arm, then inserting it into her mantle cavity. The partners may remain this way for hours, the female quiescent, the male shifting his arm slightly as the sperm packets move down a groove in the hectocolyte.

The romance of the squids is usually somewhat more exciting. In the common American squid, *Loligo pealii*, the left arm of the fourth, or lowest,

Egg case of argonaut, or paper nautilus

pair modifies into a hectocotylus during breeding periods. The same pair of squids may mate several times within a few hours, and sometimes an especially ardent male kills the female with the violence of his caress. In one case observed in an aquarium, a hungry male retained his hold on a female after copulating with her and killed her by eating a considerable portion of her mantle. Cannibalism is not unknown among octopuses and squids, however, and if hungry enough they will eat even their own young.

The most remarkable sex story of all the cephalopoda, and perhaps of all the mollusks, belongs to the small, octopuslike argonaut, the misnamed paper nautilus. The names nautilus and argonaut both stem from the fact that the animal's paper-thin shell floating on the water looks like a sail. Aristotle called it *nautilos*, which means "little sailor," and later, when the chambered nautilus of the East Indies was discovered, the adjective "paper" was added to prevent confusion. But the two are entirely different animals, so in his great eighteenth-century taxonomy work, Linnaeus changed the name of the paper nautilus to *Argonauta argo*, in honor of the Argonauts of fable who sailed in the *Argo* with Jason in search of the Golden Fleece.

Even though argonauts had been observed since antiquity, scientists as late as the middle of the nineteenth century knew little more about them than the observations that Aristotle had put down some four centuries before Christ. The ancients, and later observers, noting that the animal was not connected to its shell, assumed that it had no shell-secreting glands and, like a hermit crab, had appropriated some other creature's shell, such as the unfinished shell of the chambered nautilus, which has a similar shape.

This was the commonly accepted belief in 1839, when Mme. Jeannette Power, studying argonauts

over a long period of time at a marine aquarium in Messina, Italy, watched argonaut eggs hatch into tiny shell-less creatures. After ten or twelve days, Mme. Power noted, certain individuals began to form shells with secretions from glands in a pair of webs that spread out from the ends of the two rear arms. The shell, keeled in the center and delicately sculptured with parallel ridges as new sections were added, grew with the animal, who rested in the mouth of it, clasping it tightly with the two webbed arms. When the argonauts reached maturity, they laid eggs in the parchmentlike shell. This answered one question: the argonaut's shell was not a proper shell at all, but an egg cradle.

But another mystery still tantalized the naturalists. All the argonauts seen so far had been females. Where was the male? How were the female's eggs fertilized?

Earlier in the century, small creatures that looked like parasitic worms had been discovered in the mantles of female argonauts. Because they resembled the arm of a cephalopod, they were given the scientific name hectocotylus, which means "arm of a hundred suckers," and a new genus of worms was officially born. Later, a Swiss zoologist named Albert Kolliker, after making a detailed study of the "worm," pointed out that almost everything about it, including sperm cells carried in a small cavity, connected it directly to the cephalopoda. Kolliker, poised at the threshold of truth, now made a wrong turn. The alleged parasitic worm, he announced, was really the male argonaut, which bodily entered the female to fertilize the eggs. In his enthusiasm, he even described and drew the heart and digestive organs of the newly identified animal—an incredible feat, since other scientists could find no evidence of them.

Finally, in 1853, the German zoologist Heinrich Muller solved the mystery. Studying some very small argonauts at the aquarium in Messina, he discovered, coiled in a sac hidden among the arms, a hectocotylus. Here were the long-sought male argonauts—tiny animals little more than a half inch long; and here, too, was a striking example of dimorphism, for they compared with the female about as a pea does with a soccer ball.

But the marvels were not over. Later studies showed how the argonaut's hectocotylus works. Bursting out of its sac, it uncoils to a length of about five inches—almost ten times the length of the male—and breaks away from the arm on which it grew. Then it swims *under its own power* (looking much like a worm, as a matter of fact) until it reaches a female and fixes itself in her mantle cavity with its suckers. How does it find the female? Part of the mystery of the argonaut lives on.

Although a number of snails and clams give birth to live young, retaining the eggs and hatching them inside the mantle chamber, most marine mollusks lay their eggs directly in the sea. Some deep-sea species rise almost to the surface to leave their eggs in a light, warm zone. Some wrap them in a protective membrane or gelatinous capsules; some secure them to the bottom with a sticky mucus;

others place their eggs in an ootheca, a tough-skinned egg case. Sometimes the egg cases from a number of females are stuck together in masses, occasionally forming a ribbon more than a yard long.

As a general rule, aside from trying to find a safe place to deposit their eggs, most mollusks do not take care of them—or of the young that hatch out, either. There are exceptions, of course. Female cowries sit on their egg clusters to protect them from predators. The female octopus not only hides her eggs in empty bivalve shells, but remains beside them for weeks, fanning the water to keep silt and predators away and ensure a fresh supply of oxygenated water.

Newly hatched cephalopods, apart from being stumpy and short-armed, resemble their parents. When some univalve eggs hatch, the occupants emerge as free-swimming "veligers," the second larval stage; in others, the veligers remain in the egg capsule until developing all the parts that make them full-fledged, if miniature, snails. They may then eat their way out of the capsule or, as in the case of some whelks, eat each other, until only the strongest and biggest is left.

Egg case

The eggs of the more primitive bivalves tend to be smaller than those of other mollusks, though much more numerous. Because they are not protected by an egg case or provided with a food reserve, the time lapse between fertilization of the eggs and development into the larval stage is amazingly short—sometimes less than twenty-four hours. The animal starts life as a trochophore larva, a tiny, top-shaped creature with a ring of cilia around its middle that beat the water like oars, providing it with a means of locomotion. When the trochophore grows a pair of long ciliated arms, or lobes, and develops in rudimentary fashion some of the basic features of the adult, it becomes a veliger. In this two-phase larval stage, the animals—in immense numbers—live as members of the plankton, feeding on diatoms and other minute organisms, and themselves providing nourishment at the beginning of the ocean's food chain.

The ciliary phase ends when the foot develops into a locomotor organ and the hard shell begins to form on the soft body of the larva. Now the aquatic mollusks fall to the seabed to begin life as recognizable miniature versions of their parents. Mobility is very important at this stage, especially for the sedentary species, because if the young are to complete the metamorphosis into adults, they must find a suitable environment—or die. An excellent example is the teredo, the dreaded shipworm; unless it finds a piece of wood suitable for boring into, it cannot survive.

The duration of the youthful stage varies greatly with the species, but its end is signaled in all cases by sexual maturity, which often shows itself as a swelling of the shell's external lip. Some shells stop growing at this point; others resume their growth after a pause for the onset of the reproductive phase. In either case, sexual maturity also brings to the shell its most beautiful colors and striking ornamentation.

As old age creeps up and reproductive activity slows to a halt, pigmentation and ornamentation of the shell diminish, and the brilliant colors fade. The mantle still works, though at a reduced rate, at laying on its secretions, but since the mollusk is no longer growing, this activity merely thickens the walls of the shell. The shells of very old mollusks sometimes become so thick and cumbersome that the animals inside find it difficult to manage them—a condition not without its human parallel.

Only a few bivalves can be considered in the same league with the univalves, universally admired as the most attractive of shells, and of these the scallop is certainly the favorite. But members of the pecten

Scallop

family are more than just beautiful shells, for in gastronomic appeal and economic importance they rank on a par with their tasty but duller cousins: clams, oysters, and mussels. It seems both proper and fitting, therefore, to take a close-up look at a creature that appeals to our senses in so many delightful ways.

There are almost four hundred species of scallops living in warm and temperate seas the world over, descendants of animals that developed in prehistoric waters some 300 million years ago. The shells of most of them have a rounded triangular form, with pairs of projecting "ears" or "wings" at the apex, and a series of ribs radiating outwards.

The similarity of this shape with that of a Roman comb prompted Pliny to call Mediterranean specimens *pecten*, but Carolus Linnaeus lumped the scallops and many other bivalves with oysters, and named them after that family. Near the end of the eighteenth century, however, another taxonomist, Denmark's Otto Müller, rescued scallops from the oyster clan, to which they are but remotely related, and gave them independence and respectability with their own family name—none other than Pliny's descriptive *Pecten*. Since then, various differences among the members of the family have prompted further refinements in classification, with the result that many genera of pectinids no longer carry the official family name. This does not, however, endanger their membership in what has been called the aristocracy of mollusks—a scallop by any scientific name is still a scallop.

In appearance, the scallop is undeniably the most attractive of bivalves, and some of its members rival even the handsome volutes and cones. The brilliance of its colors, the range of its hues, and the variety of patterns seem almost endless. Shapes and types come in interesting varieties, too. Some are fat and some are flat; some are delicately sculptured and some are gnarled; some are glassy and some are opaque. And some—the moon scallops—seem to incorporate all the general exceptions to the rule: their shells are almost circular, extremely smooth, and so flat that the adductor muscle holding the valves together has no commercial food value.

In many of the better-known species—the great scallop, *Pecten maximus*, which reaches a diameter of more than five inches; the common bay scallop of Massachusetts, *Argopecten irradians*; the zigzag scallop, *Pecten ziczac*, of Florida, Bermuda, and the West Indies; and the famous Jacob's scallop, *Pecten jacobaeus*, of the Mediterranean—one valve is deep and dishlike, the other flat. At rest on the bottom, the normal position for adult scallops is flat valve on top, convex valve beneath. This position raises the opening of the shell clear of the bottom so that the animal can draw in clear water for breathing and feeding.

Scallop shells are lighter in weight and considerably more brittle than the shells of such sedentary bivalves as oysters, much as sprinters are trimmer and leaner than weightlifters. The analogy is valid, at least in the case of the scallop, for it is one of the few bivalves capable of swimming, which it does in a lively but unusual zigzag fashion, using a jet propulsion system that sends it darting through the water several yards at a time. The thinning down of the shell does mean a corresponding reduction in strength—finding an intact scallop shell on the beach is a challenge—but nature has tried to compensate for the shell's thinness by designing radial ribs that add to structural stability.

The scallop's two valves are connected at the hinge line by an external ligament. Inside, on the hinge, another ligament, triangular in shape and elastic in consistency, acts as a door-opener: it compresses when the adductor muscle pulls the valves closed, and expands to pop them open when the muscle relaxes. This muscle, a large, creamy white chunk of tender flesh, is the comestible sold as "scallop" in fish markets in the United States—although there are occasions when the so-called scallops are in reality short cylinders of meat cut from the wings of skates. In the West Indies and South America, the entire animal, with the possible exception of the black-green digestive gland, is considered not only edible, but delicious. In Europe, on the other hand, the gills, mantle, and foot, known collectively as the "beard," are discarded, along with the digestive gland, the "black mark" of older recipes, while the reproductive glands are counted a rare delicacy, especially during the spawning period.

"Their plump bodies, white as mother of pearl,"

wrote Paul Gaultier of France's Academie des Gastronomes some years ago, "and their roes shaped like scarlet beans containing the eggs, when simply scalded or poached have a delicate taste of incomparable subtlety. As a treat they vie with lobster and particularly crawfish, which are tougher and rougher than the tender flesh fragrant with marine flavors that hides between the valves of a scallop, to the surprise and joy of gourmets. For this reason, no restaurant in Paris or the French provinces forgoes the honor of including on its menu scallops prepared according to its own recipe. For there are thirty-six ways and a few more of preparing these succulent shellfish by plain cooking. . . . Blessed therefore be the scallops that allow our chefs and cooks, those venerated *cordon bleus*, jealous guardians of our culinary traditions, to

exercise their talents for the delight of connoisseurs."

In hermaphroditic species of scallops, the reproductive glands, usually creamy white (male) and orange red (female), are immediately below the adductor muscle. Below them are the delicate, crescent-shaped gills, which filter incoming water and food particles. Above the adductor, and between it and the hinge, lie the digestive gland and the animal's mouth and foot. The alimentary canal, after winding through the digestive and reproductive glands, doubles back and opens behind the adductor muscle roughly one hundred and sixty degrees from the mouth.

The mantle, often pinkish, often mottled with darker colors, edges each valve like a pair of curtains. Around the circumference, where each is

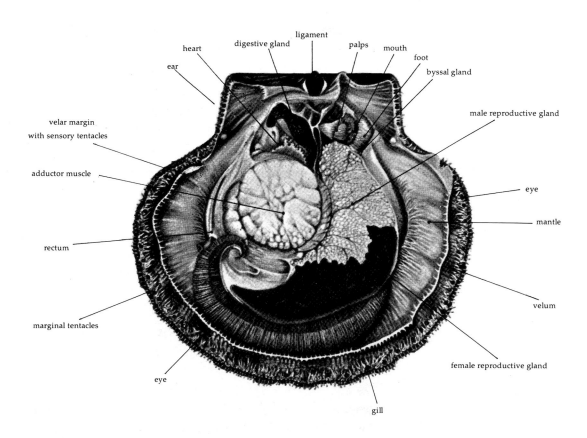

The great scallop, Pecten maximus, *with the flat right valve removed to show the animal inside.*

attached to its respective valve, the curtains are fringed with hundreds of threadlike tentacles. These cells, called marginal tentacles to distinguish them from another set which we shall discuss later, are in constant motion as the scallop extends them beyond the edge of its shell, waving them slowly in all directions. They are the animal's advance warning system; the slightest disturbance in the water will cause them to retract and bring the valves snapping together.

But not all the way closed. A narrow opening remains, a space so slight that it is all but unnoticeable. But it is large enough for a hundred or so tiny eyes, as bright as gems and often a brilliant blue in color, to peer out and see—what? The scallop's eyes, each equipped with lens, retina, and optic nerve, are better developed than those of any other bivalve, but it is doubtful that they can register images clearly. They are, however, particularly sensitive to light and movement. In an aquarium experiment, the shadow of one of the investigators crossing the scallop's line of vision caused the valves to snap shut immediately; the reaction was just as swift when a three-by-five-inch white file card was moved across a dark background—and this more than a foot away outside the tank.

Eyes and marginal tentacles do not exhaust the scallop's arsenal of sense organs. In addition to numerous small sensory cells scattered over its skin, it possesses another set of tentacles, an inner guardline located on a fold of the mantle called the velum. These tentacles form a screen through which food and water drawn in have to pass, and seem to have a sense of smell, or at least a sensitivity to minute chemical changes in the water. Experiments conducted in the United States revealed that a piece of crushed flesh from a starfish, the scallop's worst enemy, elicited no response from the marginal tentacles, but caused

the valves to slam shut when brought near the velar tentacles.

The scallop's diet consists mainly of microscopic plants, suspended in the water. Because of its structure, the animal does not go hunting for food but lies on the bottom, waiting for its next meal to come drifting by. It does help matters along, however, by creating currents in the water with its gills. These organs are composed of filaments through which water can pass. The filaments, in turn, carry thousands of microscopic cilia that beat in the water, creating a current that enters the scallop between the velar tentacles, passes through the gills, and exits on either side near the ears of the hinge. The gills extract the oxygen necessary for life from the water as it passes through, and trap food particles in bands of mucus. Other cilia shuttle the mucus and its cargo of edibles to the lower edges of the gills and from there up to the mouth—in essence, an automated but pot-luck cafeteria line.

If the water is overloaded with food or silt, the gills drop the strings of mucus into the mantle cavity. Here, another group of cilia picks them up and passes them along to the shell's exhalant openings, where foreign particles are expelled. If, in particularly dirty water, the gills become smothered with particles, they can perform a writhing movement to free themselves. The scallop also is able to quickly flush away accumulations within the mantle cavity by swimming.

Like many mollusk families, the pectens include both species with separate sexes and species that are hermaphroditic. Studies undertaken on the Isle of Man in the Irish Sea have shown that the great scallop becomes sexually mature at the age of two to three years, with the male half of the reproductive organs achieving pubescence slightly ahead of the female portion, a situation not uncommon among hermaphroditic mollusks. Spawning takes place between January and August, reaching a peak in

2

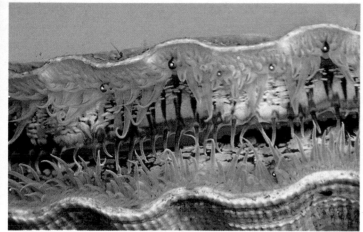

3

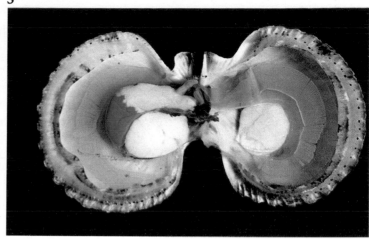

1: Pecten maximus *Linné, the great scallop, 4 to 6 inches, northeast Atlantic. In Great Britain it is also called the edible scallop or the clam. Some confusion exists over the historical roles played by P. maximus and P. jacobaeus, the St. James scallop, because both are known as the pilgrim shell and the shell of St. James. There is no doubt that P. maximus was the shell worn by pilgrims to the shrine of the saint at Compostela, in the northwestern corner of Spain, for it is the only scallop occurring along the Atlantic coast there. P. jacobaeus is similar, but it is a Mediterranean scallop. The confusion began when Linné named the Mediterranean scallop jacobaeus (or James), an error that can be accounted for only by assuming that Linné's geography was weak—he must have thought that Compostela was on Spain's Mediterranean coast. The confusion was compounded by the fact that the Crusaders picked up specimens of P. jacobaeus from the shores of Palestine and wore them as badges of "having been there," just as pilgrims to the shrine of St. James did with P. maximus.*

2: Aequipecten opercularis *Linné, the queen scallop, 2 inches, Atlantic coast of Europe. This close-up and enlarged view shows the scallop's many-tentacled mantle edge and some of its many beady eyes.*

3: *A freshly opened queen scallop displays the large white adductor muscle that opens and closes the animal's valves. This chunk of tender flesh is the "scallop" sold in fish markets in the United States. In the West Indies and South America, the entire animal, with the exception of the black-green digestive gland, is considered not only edible, but delicious. In Europe, this gland, along with the*

mantle, gills, and foot, is usually discarded, but the red-and-white reproductive glands are considered a rare treat, especially during the spawning period.

4: *In swimming, scallops utilize a water-jet propulsion system, suddenly expelling a stream of water by rapidly snapping shut their valves. The dotted lines in the diagram denote the propelling jets of water, the solid arrows show the direction in which the shell moves. By its ability to form the muscular edges of its mantle into a jet "nozzle" anywhere around the margin, the scallop has considerable control over the direction it takes. The normal progression is forward, in the direction of the free margins of the shell; the "escape movement," used when the scallop is under threat, is to the rear, hinge first.*

4

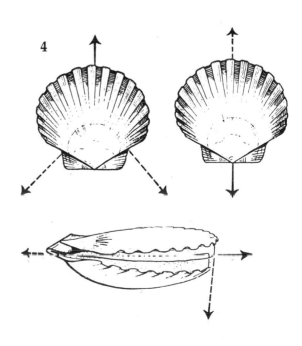

March. In addition, each month has its own peak, which occurs about the time of the full moon. In all months, water temperature must reach at least ten degrees centigrade or the great scallop will not spawn.

The queen scallop, another hermaphrodite, breeds from January to June, and also experiences heightened activity during the full of the moon. Like the oysters, it sheds its eggs directly into the water, where they are fertilized by current-borne sperm cells. The larva that develops is fitted out with a swimming membrane and a thin, transparent shell. It lives near the surface in the shallows for several weeks, then drops to the bottom, where it settles on a rock or other hard substance, discards the swimming membrane, and begins changing into a miniature duplicate of the adults in its species.

At this point in its development, the young scallop uses its foot to move about on the sea bottom in search of a suitable homesite. The mechanics of this operation bring to mind the progress of the inchworm: the scallop extends its foot, gripping the seabed with the tip, then contracts the foot, so that the after part catches up with the forward part. While creeping along this way it carries its bivalve shell on its back, hinge uppermost, in much the same manner that its cousins, the snails, carry their univalve dwellings.

Finding a spot to its liking, the scallop anchors itself to the site with a number of special threads, collectively called the byssus, which it secretes from its body. For sedentary species, such as some of those in the *Chlamys* genus, this is the beginning of a lifetime spent in one place, unless some danger or condition forces the animal to move, in which case it will cast off its mooring lines and seek a new location. But for mobile types like the great and queen scallops, the attachment is only temporary. When they are ready to step into maturity, the byssal cables break away, sometimes through the increased weight of the shell, but often through the animal's decision to start swimming.

Now ready to take up adult life, the young scallops prepare to migrate to deeper water, where their mature fellows, gregarious creatures, congregate in the thousands on beds of clean, firm sand at depths ranging downwards from sixty feet. But first they apparently enjoy an interlude of free swimming near the shore, for they have been spied there at low water and in tidal pools.

One of these observers was the Scottish naturalist, David Landsborough. Meandering along the coast in Ayrshire some years ago, he noted "the fry of *Pecten opercularis* skipping quite nimbly through the pool. Their motion was rapid and zigzag, very like that of ducks in a sunny blink rejoicing in the prospect of rain. They seemed, by the sudden opening and closing of their valves, to have the power of darting like an arrow through the water. One jerk carried them some yards, and then by another sudden jerk they were off in a moment on a different tack. We doubt not that, when full grown, they engage in similar movements, though, as Pectens of greater gravity, they choose to romp unseen, and play their gambols in the deep."

Scallops are not unique among mollusks for their ability to swim, but their natatory habits place them in a definitely select group—with squids and octopuses, pteropods, sea hares, a few nudibranchs and snails, and only three or four other bivalves. All the swimming bivalves utilize the same water jet-propulsion system, suddenly expelling a stream of water by rapidly clapping shut their valves, but none of them is livelier in the water than such expert swimmers as the giant scallop, the queen, and the aptly named zigzag scallop of the Caribbean.

Scallops sitting on the ocean bottom, placidly sifting the passing currents for their vegetative dinners, will explode into action, beating their

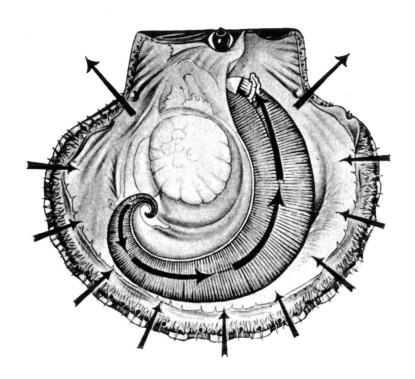

How the scallop breathes and feeds. The inner arrows show the direction of water currents bringing in oxygen and food; the outer arrows show the movement of food particles through the filtering gills to the mouth.

valves frantically and swiftly zigzagging away when threatened by predators, especially their mortal enemies the starfish. The fate of a slow-moving scallop is not pleasant to behold (see page 38). The starfish wraps its arms around the shell, gripping it with the suction cups on its tube feet, and exerts a strong, continuous pull until eventually the scallop's adductor muscle wearies. The victorious starfish then forces the valves open, extrudes its stomach around the soft parts of the mollusk, and ingests them.

Other enemies have their own ways of dining on scallop. The whelk, for example, slips the thin part of its shell between the victim's valves and attacks the adductor muscle with its slender proboscis. And pity the poor scallop whose upper valve becomes an anchorage for barnacles, serpulid worms, sponges, and other hitchhikers. The combined weight seriously hampers the bivalve's ability to swim, and in severe cases can ground it permanently—which will not be a very long time since the unfortunate is now a sitting duck for the first hungry predator that happens by.

Strangely enough, when a scallop is beating a hasty retreat from an enemy, it swims backward—that is, hinge first. This so-called escape movement was observed and first described by naturalist Philip Gosse in 1852: "I perceived the lips of the mantle (which were held in contact, though the valves were considerably separated) suddenly open to a partial extent, *as if by a blowing from within*. At this instant there was a leap in the opposite direction, attended with a considerable agitation in the water. With this clue, I observed more definitely. . . . The mode of proceeding is as follows: when the Pecten is about to leap, it draws in as much water as it can contain

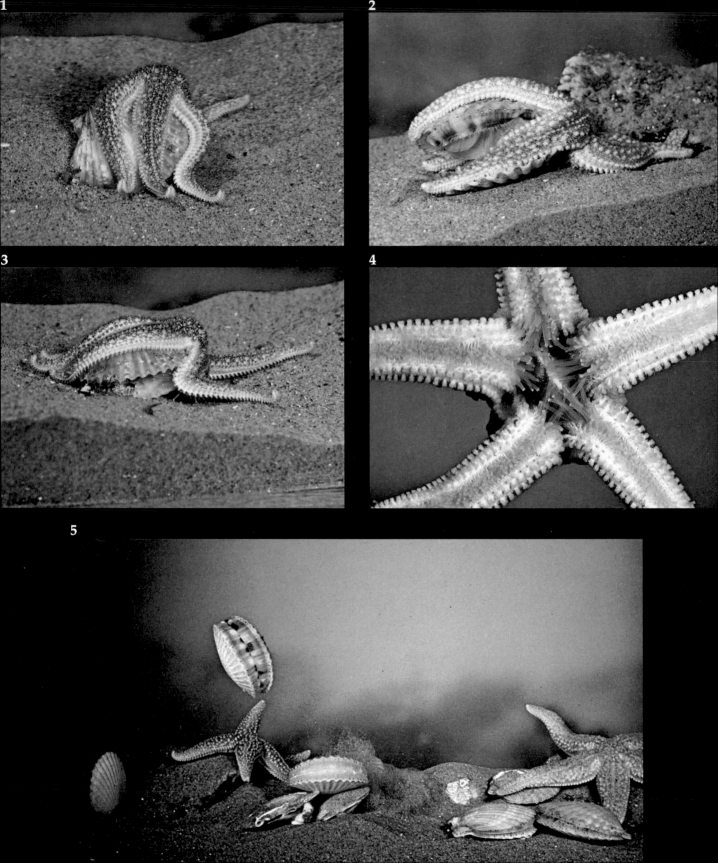

1: *The opening scene in a life-and-death drama of the sea: A scallop is caught in the deadly embrace of a starfish, its mortal enemy.*

2: *By exerting a continuous pull with its sucker-clad arms, the starfish puts a tremendous strain on the scallop's adductor muscle. Eventually the scallop tires, and its valves gradually begin to open.*

3: *Forcing the valves apart, the starfish extrudes its stomach around the soft parts of the scallop and proceeds to ingest them.*

4: *From below, a starfish with a small scallop in its stomach.*

5: *Valves beating rapidly, scallops flee approaching starfish. The mollusks' only hope for safety lies in flight; in the unequal contest of strength, the starfish never loses.*

6: *There are about eighty species in the family Phasianellidae, the pheasant shells, most of them tropical, herbivorous, and nearly always highly colored in intricate designs.*

7: Strombus costatus *Gmelin, the ribbed stromb, 4 to 6 inches, Florida to the West Indies. A shallow water dweller, the ribbed stromb has a solid shell of about ten whorls, with the body whorl greatly expanded. Series of nodes mark the body whorl and twist up the spire. In older specimens, the outer lip becomes considerably thickened.*

8: Spondylus americanus *Hermann, the Atlantic thorny oyster, Florida to the West Indies. Crowded conditions sometimes produce irregularly shaped specimens.*

9: Cypraecassis testiculus *Linné, the reticulated cowrie helmet, 3 inches, Caribbean.*

within the mantle, while the lips are held firmly in contact. At this instant, the united edges of the lips are slightly drawn inward. . . . The moment after this is observed, the animal, doubtless by muscular contraction, exerts a strong force upon the contained water, while it relaxes the forced contact of the lips at any point of the circumference, according to its pleasure. The result is the forcible ejection of a jet of water, *from that point*; which, by resilience of its impact upon the surrounding fluid, throws the animal *in the opposite direction*, with a force proportioned to that of the *jet d'eau*."

Under more salubrious conditions, the scallop's normal swimming mode is in a horizontal position, with the hinge to the rear. Dr. W. J. Rees of the British Museum has described that action this way: "In the typical swimming movement, speed depends upon the vigorous clapping together of the shell valves and the associated strength of the jets of water which are expelled. As the animal prepares to swim, the valves open more widely than in the resting condition and the mantle curtains appear to be drawn inwards as if by water flowing in. Just as the valves of the shell reach their maximum gape, the mantle tentacles are suddenly retracted all round and the shell shuts with a snap. Simultaneous with this the mantle curtains become closely pressed together, preventing the escape of water except where they do not meet—that is, on either side of the hinge line. Thus, with the sudden closure of the shell, two jets of water are forced out between the ears and the scallop moves forward. Meantime, some water escapes, to a lesser and controlled extent, around the free margins of the valves (where the upper curtain of the mantle can be adjusted to overlap the lower one) and so between them they produce a downward jet all round, which initiates the take-off from the bottom and maintains the upward movement of the shell. The animal then moves upwards and forwards in the direction of the free margins of its shell in an erratic motion which looks as though it were taking a series of bites out of the water as it claps its valves together."

The scallop can even right itself if, through some mishap, it becomes overturned on the seabed. To accomplish this feat it adjusts its mantle curtains, forcefully expels water downward all around the free margins of its valves, and somersaults over its hinge to a right-side-up position. It also can spin on its axis without leaving the bottom, much like a child's pinwheel, by discharging water at one point only. Its ability to swim is so highly developed, in fact, that it can execute twisting motions and can take any direction it wishes, left or right or up or down. It accomplishes this by controlling the muscles of the mantle and expelling water from any selected point along the edges of the mantle curtain. This natatory prowess helps to explain why large beds of edible deep-sea scallops off the coast of New England have gradually disappeared from one area and gradually reformed in another—the animals apparently *migrated*, either to escape unfavorable conditions or to find richer feeding grounds!

A wonderful swimmer, the scallop:
It zigs and it zags at a gallop.
—author unknown

One of many: the lion's paw

1: Chlamys pallium *Linne, the mantle scallop,* from the Indian and Pacific oceans.

2: Excellichlamys spectabilis *Reeve, the spectacular scallop, found in the western Pacific and Indian oceans.*

3: Aequipecten reevei *A. Adams, Reeve's scallop, named after the naturalist, western Pacific.*

4: Decatopecten striatus *Schumacher, the striate scallop, found off the coasts of Japan.*

5: Pecten maximus *Linné, the magnificent scallop, 6 inches, eastern Atlantic and Europe.*

6: Chlamys swifti *Bernardi, Swift's scallop, marked by only a few, but bold, ribs, and wide color variations, Japan.*

7: Lyropecten subnodosus *Sowerby, the Pacific lion's paw scallop, a ponderous species, west coast of tropical America.*

8: Chlamys nobilis *Reeve, the noble scallop, with a strongly ribbed shell and equal valves, Japanese waters.*

9: Amusium pleuronectes *Linné, the Asian moon scallop, smooth, flat, and almost circular; Japanese waters.*

10: Pecten ziczac *Linné, the zigzag scallop, 5 inches, North Carolina through the Caribbean to Brazil.*

11: Lyropecten nodosus *Linné, the lion's paw scallop, a favorite with collectors, Caribbean and southeastern U.S.*

12: *Another example of* Chlamys pallium *Linné, the mantle scallop.*

13: Aequipecten vexillum *Born, the flag scallop, a striking shell from the southwest Pacific.*

14: Argopecten circularis *Sowerby, the circular scallop, common in the eastern Pacific from the Gulf of California to Ecuador.*

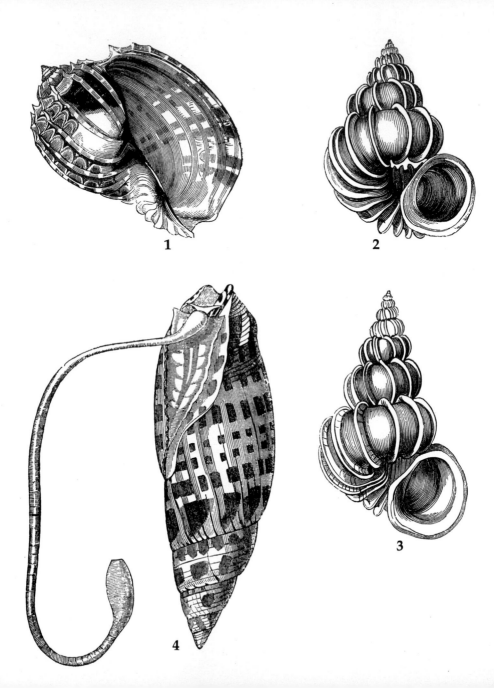

1

2

3

4

A Shell Galaxy

Part I

"A Galaxy of Shells," divided into two parts (Part II begins on page 204), is intended to be both useful and enjoyable, used to identify shells, and to be read and enjoyed visually. There are both full-color and black-and-white illustrations in "A Galaxy of Shells." Most of the black-and-white illustrations are from Nicolaus Gaulterius's Index Testarum Conchyliorium, published in 1742. These etchings display the eighteenth-century love for natural form. Rather than merely outlining shapes—as do many contemporary illustrations—these drawings revel in the unanticipated, incredible beauty of shells.

1: Harpa ventricosa *Lamarck*, *the ventricose harp*,3 to 4 *inches, Indo-Pacific.*

2,3: Epitonium scalare *Linné*, *the precious wentletrap*, 2½ *inches, southwestern Pacific.*

4: Mitra mitra *Linné*, *the episcopal miter*, 6 *inches, Indo-Pacific.*

1: Lepas anatifera *Linné, goose-neck barnacles, 1 inch, worldwide distribution. Like the early biologists, most people today assume that barnacles are members of the mollusk family because they have a mollusklike calcareous shell. They are not mollusks, however, but relatives of crabs and other arthropods. One of the strange beliefs in parts of Europe during the Middle Ages held that certain types of wild geese hatched from barnacle shells. This caused a great controversy among theologians as to whether these geese should be considered fish or fowl—in other words, could they be eaten on Fridays and other fast days, or not? The common folk, as you might have guessed, were strongly on the side of the fish adherents.*

2: Octopus vulgaris *Cuvier, the common octopus, 2 feet, European waters. This animal, known as* polypus *in ancient times, was accurately described by Aristotle. It is one of a family numbering between one hundred fifty and two hundred species and ranging in size between the 2-inch O.* arborescens *and the large O.* hongkongensis *of the Pacific. One of the latter, taken off Alaska, measured 32 feet, but the body was only 18 inches long and the arms were extremely slender toward the tips. O.* vulgaris *lives along rocky shores, usually in caves at moderate depths. Its favorite foods are fish and bivalves, and it is itself a dietary staple, along with squid, for people in many areas of the world.*

3: Argonauta nodosa *Lightfoot, one of the paper nautiluses, 6 inches, circumtropical, South Africa to Australia. The beautiful but fragile "shell" of the argonaut is really an egg cradle manufactured by the female; neither she nor the much smaller male has the molluscan external shell. They are often confused with the pearly, or chambered, nautilus because of a superficial similarity of shape between*

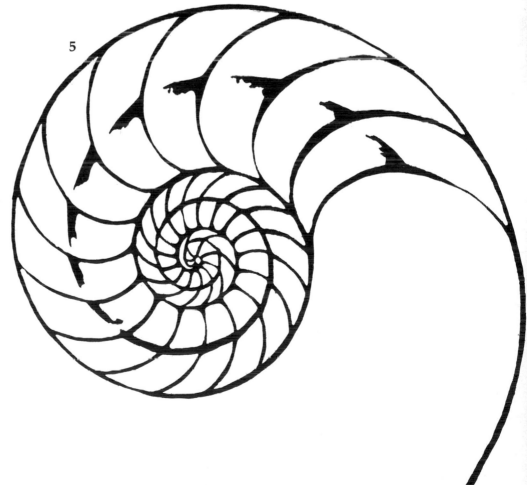

the egg cradle of the one and the shell of the other, but argonauts are more closely related to octopuses.

4, 5: Nautilus pompilius *Linné, the chambered nautilus, 7 to 8 inches, Indo-Pacific, particularly in the area of the Philippines. The nautiluses are the only cephalopods with an external coiled shell. As the animal grows, it moves forward into the new outer section it has built, sealing off the previous living quarters with a nacreous partition, but leaving a hole so that all the chambers are connected. These chambers contain a gas that the nautilus uses to control the buoyancy of its shell. The drawing shows the interior of a nautilus shell.*

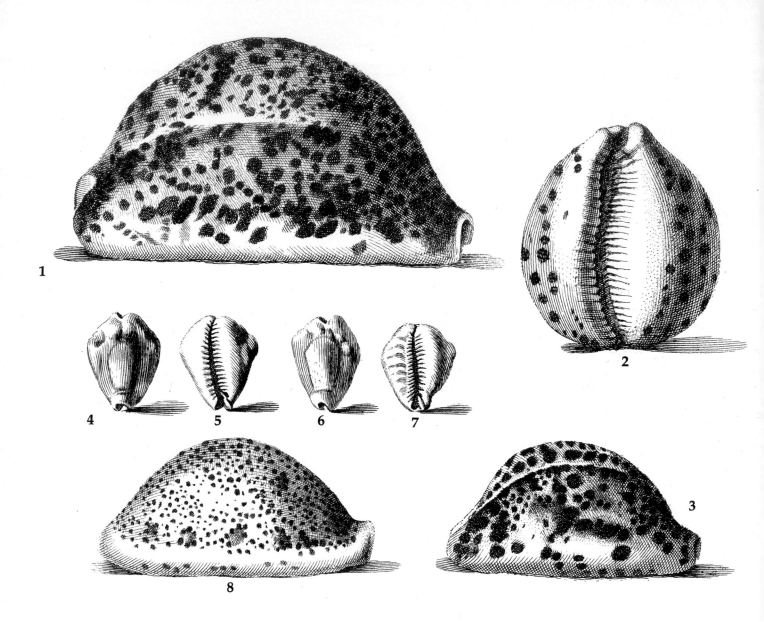

1-3: Cypraea tigris *Linné, the tiger cowrie, 2 to 4 inches, Indo-Pacific. Among the most abundant shells of the Indo-Pacific, the large, handsome tiger cowrie, with black spots on a background that ranges from almost-white to dark brown (only immature specimens wear the "tiger" stripes), can be found in novelty shops and souvenir stands all over America. They were a favorite of seamen in the great days of sail, and were later imported in large quantities by Yankee skippers and merchants, who engraved their glossy backs with the Lord's Prayer or sentimental poems, strung several of varying sizes together with bits of wire to make head-nodding turtles, and subjected them to other indignities to supply a national fad.*

4-7: Cypraea moneta *Linné, the money cowrie, 1 inch, Indo-Pacific. Even more abundant than the* tiger cowrie, this little shell served as currency for primitive peoples all over the world for many years.

8: Cypraea pantherina *Lightfoot, the panther cowrie, 2 to 3 inches, Red Sea. Like the tiger cowrie, this is one of several in the family named after land animals; the others include the rat, the lynx, the serpent's head, the stag, the leopard, and the rhinoceros cowries. To the peoples living along the shores of the Indian Ocean and the Red Sea, the panther and other large cowries were sex symbols.*

9: Thatcheria mirabilis *Angas, the miraculous thatcheria, 2½ to 4 inches, Japan and Taiwan. A resident of the depths four hundred to six hundred feet down, this beautiful shell has a mysterious attraction for many collectors.*

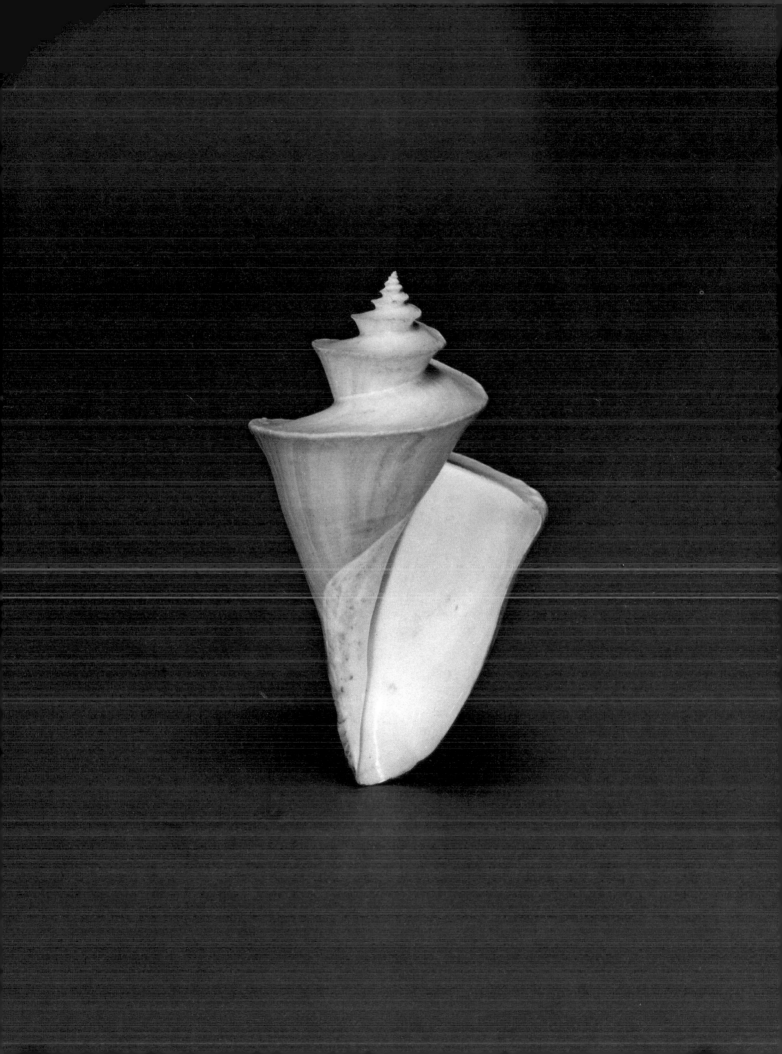

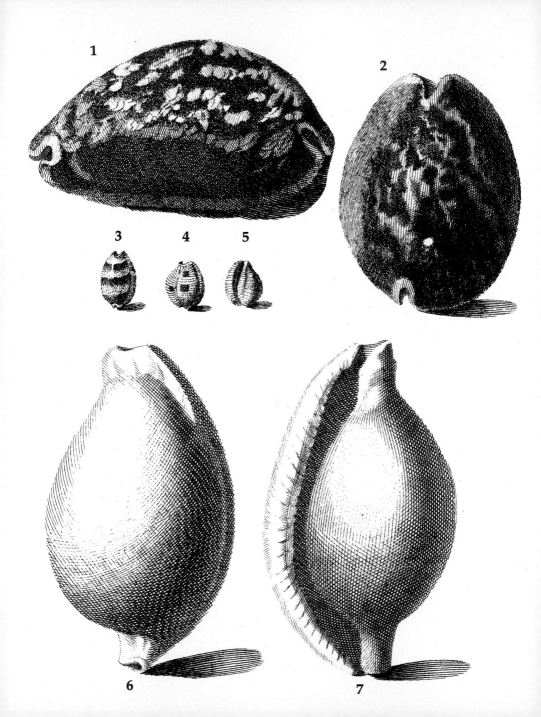

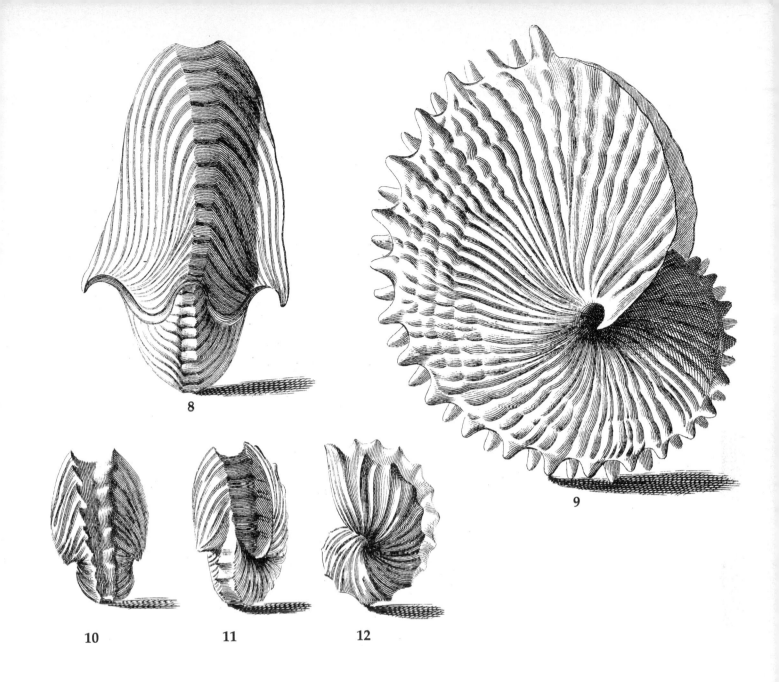

1, 2: Cypraea mauritania *Linné, the humpbacked cowrie, 2 to 4 inches, Indo-Pacific.*

3: Cypraea asellus *Linné, the little donkey cowrie, ½ to 1 inch, Indo-Pacific.*

4, 5: Trivia quadripunctata *Gray, the four-spotted trivia shell, ¼-inch, Caribbean. Trivias resemble cowries in that the body whorl grows over the other whorls, covering the spiral shape.*

6, 7: Ovula ovum *Linné, the egg cowrie, 2 to 4 inches, Indo-Pacific. Many island tribes in the Pacific decorate the tall prows of their seagoing canoes with dozens of white egg cowries in the belief that the shells serve as eyes, enabling the craft to "see."*

8: Argonauta argo *Linné, the common paper nautilus, 5 to 10 inches, warm seas worldwide.*

9: Argonauta nodosa *Lightfoot, the knobbed paper nautilus, 5 to 10 inches, Indo-Pacific.*

10–12: Argonauta hians *Lightfoot, the brown paper nautilus, 2 to 3 inches, warm seas worldwide. The delicate shell of the paper nautilus is not a shell at all in the proper sense of the word, but a cradle which the octopuslike female clasps with two of her eight arms, and in which she lays her eggs.*

1: Perotrochus teramachii *Kuroda*, *Teramachi's slit shell*, 6 inches, Japanese waters. Only twelve species of slit shells, named for the deep notch in the aperture of the shell, are known to have survived from the abundance of previous ages. They were known only from fossil remains until 1855, and were considered extinct. All the species live in deep water—the specimen shown here, quite rare, was taken by fishermen dredging in the depths off Japan.

2: Voluta ebraea *Linné, the Hebrew volute, 7 inches, southern Caribbean.* Similar to the music volute but lacking the musical characters, this shell has numerous wavy lines of russet and brown. It is fairly common down to Brazil, and has been found off West Africa.

2

4

3

3: Mitra mitra *Linné, the episcopal miter, 6 inches, Indo-Pacific.* This brilliant shell, lavishly ornamented with reddish orange on a pure white background, is one of the most widely distributed of the miter shells and one of the most popular with collectors. Most of the more than 625 miter species come from the Indo-Pacific area.

4: *A dozen specimens of textile cones,* Conus textile *Linné,* ranging in size from 2 to 3½ inches, at one time called tent cones because the handsome shell is covered with wavy, tent-shaped lines of dark chestnut on russet. They are also called cloth-of-gold cones. One of the most widely distributed of the family, C. textile has caused many a collector's heart to palpitate prematurely because of its close similarity in appearance to the much rarer glory-of-the-sea cone, C. gloriamaris. It has also, unfortunately, stopped hearts entirely, for it is the largest of the venomous cones, and is quite capable of killing humans with its poison barb.

The chambered nautilus, Nautilus pompilius *Linné,*
7 to 8 inches, although 10-inch specimens are known,
lives in the Indo-Pacific. The shell is invariably
brown-striped and has a pearly luster; the inside is
mother-of-pearl in shades ranging from pink to
aquamarine. The animal bears little resemblance to
its cephalopod relatives; it has almost one hundred
slender tentacles in rows around its mouth and eyes,
each of which can be withdrawn into a little sheath
at the first sign of danger. The nautilus fills the
abandoned chambers in its shell with a gas, an
arrangement that enables it to move vertically in the
water by emerging from the living chamber, thereby
diminishing its specific gravity by increasing its
volume, or by going back in, which reverses the
process.

1: Tibia insulaechorab *Roeding, the Arabian tibia, 6 to 8 inches, Indian Ocean. Six species, collectively known as the shinbone strombs, make up the* Tibia *genus. They are closely related to the common pink conch of Florida and the West Indies.* T. insulaechorab *is the most common, although it occasionally produces a rare specimen with a yellow aperture; all species, however, are collector's items.*

2: Phyllonotus regius *Swainson, the regal murex, 5 inches, eastern Pacific, Gulf of California to Peru. Collected from mud flats at low tide, this is considered the handsomest of the Central American murices.*

3: Pitar dione *Linné, the royal comb Venus, 1 to 2 inches, from the Caribbean to Panama. To see this unusual shell is to understand why specimens with all spines intact are rare. The extravagant growths extending from the posterior region of the valves indicate that this is a tropical species. In all, there are more than four hundred species of Venus clams found all over the world, including the plain-Jane edible quahog, as well as more ornate types. A species very similar to the royal comb Venus,* P. lupinarius *Lesson, the Pacific comb Venus, is commonly found to depths of one hundred feet from the Gulf of California to Peru.*

4: Cellana radiata *Born, 1½ inches, Indo-Pacific.*

5: Harpa costata *Linné, the imperial harp, 2 to 4 inches, Indian Ocean off the island of Mauritius. A main distinguishing feature of this rare shell is the set of more than forty ribs set close together. Captain William Bligh, of H.M.S. Bounty fame, brought back a specimen in 1810, and the shell has been a favorite with collectors ever since. It has always sold for high prices at shell auctions, and now that collecting restrictions have been imposed by the local Mauritian government, available specimens have become scarcer and even more expensive.*

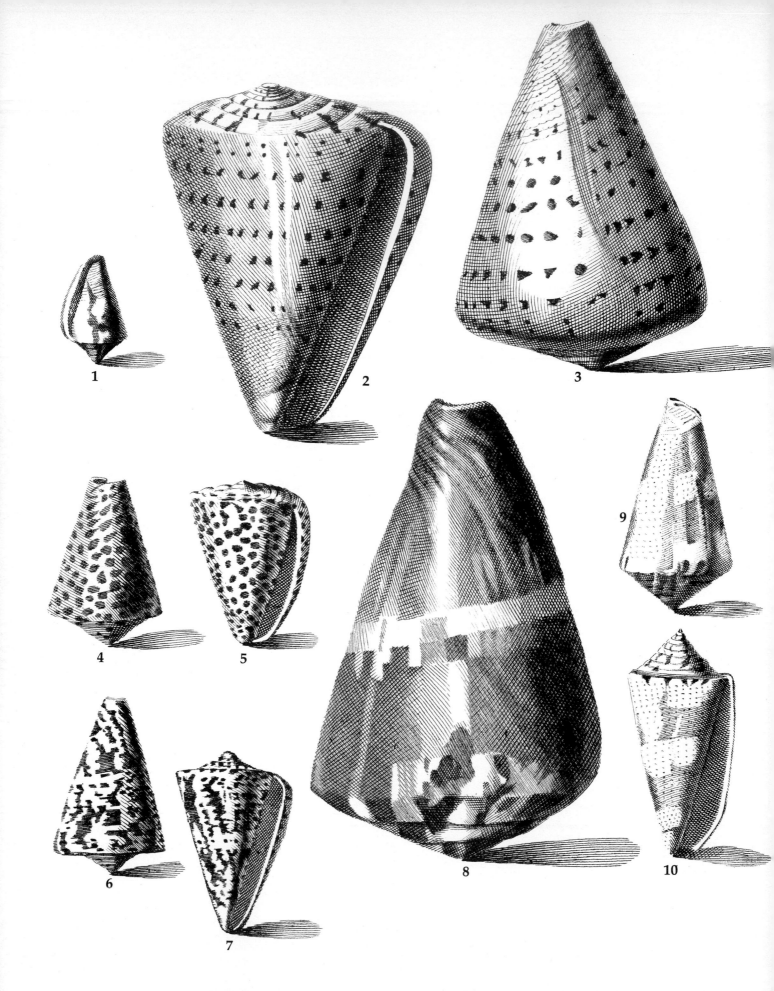

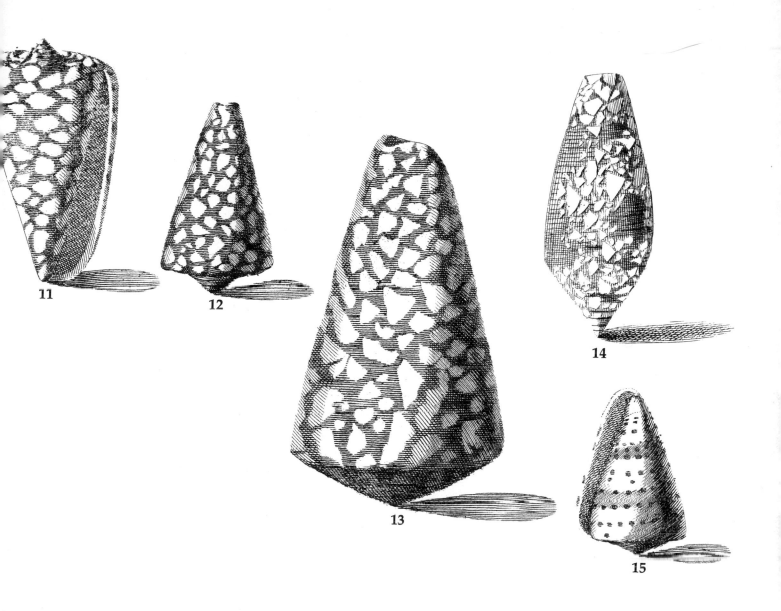

1: Conus coronatus *Gmelin,* the crown cone, 1 inch, Indo-Pacific.

2, 3: Conus betulinus *Linné,* the birch cone, 4 to 6 inches, Indo-Pacific.

4, 5: Conus spurius *Gmelin,* the alphabet cone, 3 inches, Caribbean.

6, 7: Conus litteratus *Linné,* the lettered cone, 3 to 5 inches, Indo-Pacific.

8: Conus vexillum *Gmelin,* the vexillum cone, 4 inches, Indo-Pacific.

9, 10: Conus magus *Linné,* the poisonous magus cone, 3 inches, Indo-Pacific. *The poison of* Conus magus *causes sustained muscle contractions or* spastic paralysis, and medical researchers are working to develop from it a drug to restore mobility to injured or diseased muscles.

11–13: Conus marmoreus *Linné,* the marbled cone, 3 to 4 inches, Indo-Pacific. *The marble cone, strikingly beautiful but another of the poisonous species, is readily identified by its white to pinkish angular spots on a dark background; it is the shell that Rembrandt rendered in reverse in his famous etching.*

14: Conus aulicus *Linné,* the princely cone, 5 inches, Indo-Pacific. *Closely related to the textile cone, the aulicus cone is relatively rare and is probably also poisonous to man.*

15: Conus glaucus *Linné,* the gray cone, 2 inches, southwest Pacific.

1

2

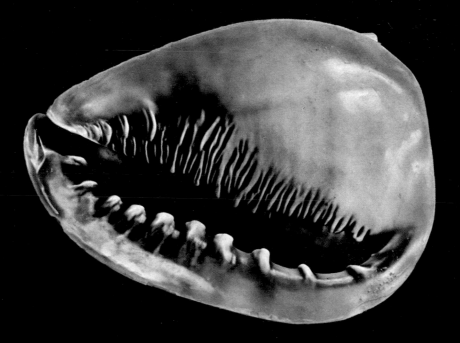

1: Architectonica perspectiva *Linné,*
the perspective sundial, 2½ inches,
South Pacific. There are some forty
species of sundials, all from tropical
seas, and all among the most beautiful
of sea shells. They have such an
enormous navel that the inner parts
of the helicoidal turns can be seen
clearly. Legend has it that gazing at
the umbilicus of the Atlantic sundial,
A. nobilis Roeding, inspired
Leonardo da Vinci to design his
famous spiral staircase at the Chateau
of Blois. Interestingly, the various
species of Architectonica *are also*
known as staircase shells.

2: Cassis madagascariensis
Lamarck, the queen or emperor
helmet shell, 8 to 12 inches,
southeastern United States to the
West Indies. Helmet shells were so
called, it is said, because they
resemble the head armor worn by
medieval knights. The scientific name
of this species was the result of a
mistaken belief that the shell came
from Madagascar. The queen is the
largest of the three large helmet
shells, also called conchs, that are
fairly common in the West Indies. The
others are C. tuberosa *Linné, the*
king helmet or conch, preferred for
cameo work because of the dark inner
layers of its shell, and C. flammaea,
the dwarf flame conch.

3: Strombus listeri *Gray, Lister's*
conch, 4 inches, Indian Ocean. Once
considered extremely rare—the first
specimen was brought back to
England in 1620, but the second didn't
make it until 1869—this shell was
rediscovered in recent years. Now
fishermen in Thailand and Burma
harvest more than five hundred
specimens a year.

4: Strombus gallus *Linné, the*
rooster-tail conch, 5 inches, from
Florida to Brazil. This is a
comparatively rare shell and one of
the smaller conchs. It is named for its
wide, flaring lip.

3

4

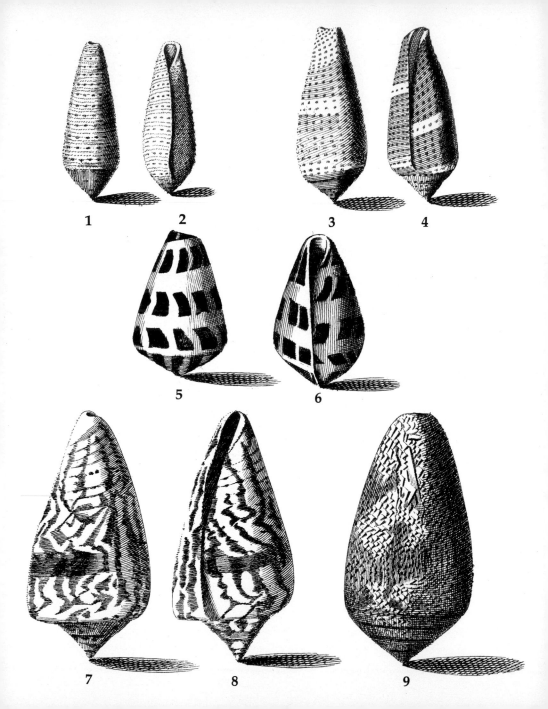

1, 2: Conus nussatella *Linné, the nusatella cone, 2 to 3 inches, Indo-Pacific.*

3, 4: Conus granulatus *Linné, the glory-of-the-Atlantic cone, 2 to 3 inches, western Atlantic. Considered rare in the nineteenth century, this brilliant scarlet cone commanded a higher price than any other shell at an 1853 Rotterdam auction.*

5, 6: Conus ebraeus *Linné, the Hebrew cone, 1 to 2 inches, is one of the most common of the family, widely distributed across six thousand miles of the Indo-Pacific.*

7, 8: Conus spectrum *Linné, the spectrum cone, 2 to 3 inches, western Pacific.*

9: Conus textile *Linné, the cloth-of-gold cone, 4 inches, Red Sea and western Pacific south to Australia. Named for the famed cloth its color pattern resembles, it is one of the most venomous of cones, with a sting capable of killing a good-sized octopus.*

10, 11: Lambis chiragra *Linné, the chiragra spider conch, 5 to 9 inches, southwest Pacific. This is a juvenile specimen, with the basic adult shape but lacking the characteristic spiny projections.*

12, 13: Conus striatus *Linné, the striated cone, 2 to 4 inches, Indo-Pacific. Fishing with poisoned harpoon, this shell pulls its swiftly dying prey close, then swallows it—or as much of it as will fit.*

14, 15: Conus bullatus *Linné, the bubble cone, 3 inches, central Indo-Pacific. Extremely rare, and unique among cones for its porcelaneous surface.*

16: Conus geographus *Linné, the geography cone, 3 to 5 inches, Indo-Pacific. Deadliest of the cones in terms of human victims, and noted for its ability to ingest fish larger than itself.*

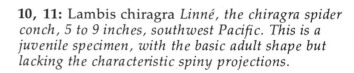

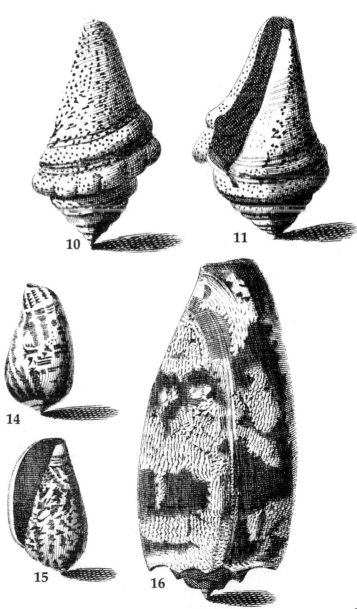

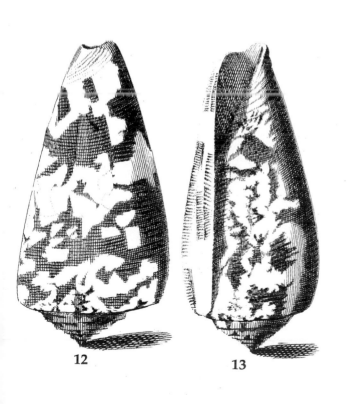

10   11

12   13

14

15   16

1: Cypraea tigris *Linné, the tiger cowrie, 3 to 5 inches, Indo-Pacific. These shells are among the most widely distributed cowries. Some Hawaiian specimens grow to giant size.*

2: Turbo marmoratus *Linné, the green turban shell, 5 to 8 inches, Indo-Pacific. This is a highly polished specimen of a handsome shell that at one time, before plastics, was very important to the pearl button industry.*

3: Telescopium telescopium *Linné, the telescope shell, 3 to 5 inches, Indo-Pacific. Shown here are a natural shell and one cut away to display the inside whorls. Observing that perfect inner spiral, it isn't difficult to understand how a gastropod shell inspired Archimedes to invent the helical screw.*

4: Trochus niloticus *Linné, the commercial top shell, 3 to 5 inches, Indo-Pacific. The shells shown here are, from the left, a natural specimen, a polished shell, and a shell polished and cut. This large, heavy species with a thick nacreous layer was fished so extensively for the button trade that it almost became extinct; plastics came along just in time to save it.*

5: Strombus gallus *Linné, the roostertail conch, 6 inches, Bermuda to Caribbean.*

6: Strombus bulla *Linné, the bubble conch, 2 inches, Indo-Pacific.*

7: Strombus aurisdianae *Linné, the Diana conch, 3 inches, Indo-Pacific.*

5

6

7

1: *Assorted spindle shells of worldwide distribution. The spindles (Fusinus) are all tropical and carnivorous. The shell is usually heavy, with a long siphonal canal, and gracefully shaped. Fusus acus, the needle spindle, is the most graceful of all, reducing slimness to its ultimate in a shell. The giant of the genus, F. proboscidiferus of Australia, ranges up to* 12 *inches, with occasional specimens as long as 2 feet.*

2: Murex pecten *Lightfoot, the Venus comb murex, 4 to 6 inches, Indo-Pacific. The murex shells are known for their bizarre ornamentation, but how a snail, using only its fleshy mantle, could construct such a delicate edifice as this is difficult to comprehend.*

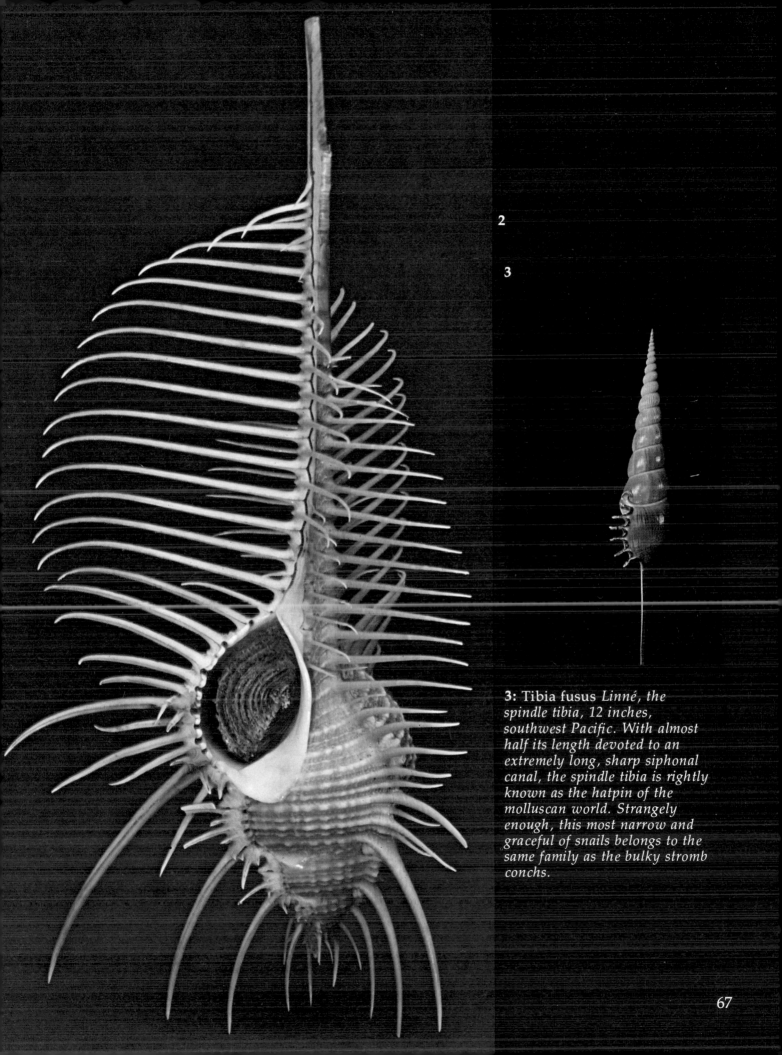

3: Tibia fusus *Linné*, the spindle tibia, 12 inches, southwest Pacific. With almost half its length devoted to an extremely long, sharp siphonal canal, the spindle tibia is rightly known as the hatpin of the molluscan world. Strangely enough, this most narrow and graceful of snails belongs to the same family as the bulky stromb conchs.

1–3: Melongena melongena *Linné, the Caribbean crown conch, 4 to 5 inches, West Indies.* Melongena *conchs, related to the* Busycon *whelks, are limited to three species, the one in the West Indies, one in Florida and Alabama, and one on the Pacific coast of Yucatan in Central America. They range in size from 4 to 8 inches, and are highly variable in shape, size, and color, as well as in the type and number of rows of spines; some are spineless, some are single-spined, and some are multispined. In addition, some have high spires and others are dwarf-spired.*

4–7: Voluta musica *Linné, the music volute, 3 inches, West Indies to Brazil. This is one of a family of beautiful and striking shells much desired by collectors and often referred to as the aristocrats of the molluscan world. It gained its name from its unusual markings, which bear a strong resemblance to the five lines of the musical staff and even include notelike spots. One of the first shells named by Linné in 1758, it appeared in so many variations that some two dozen additional names were applied to it over the next century, leading to considerable confusion.*

68

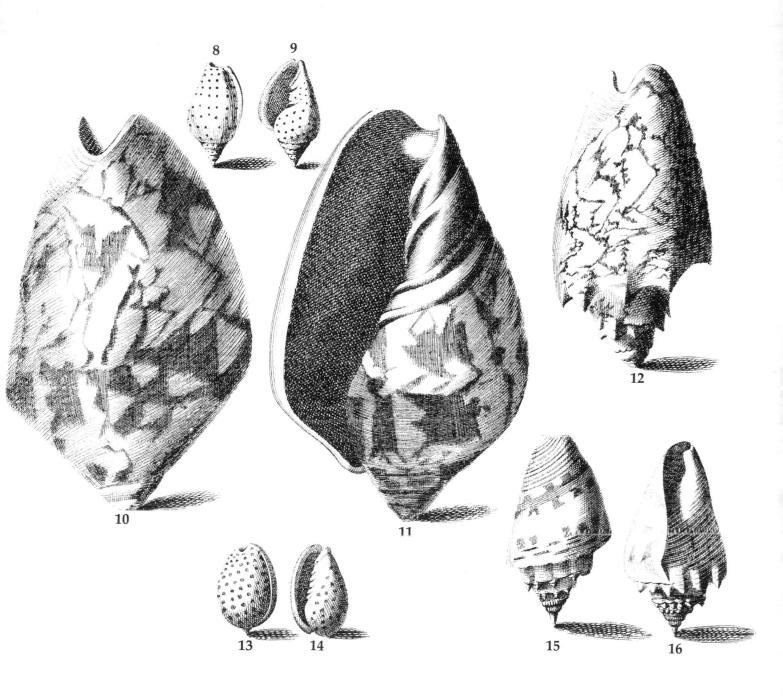

8, 9: Glabella faba *Linné, 1 inch, West Africa.*

10, 11: Voluta nobilis *Lightfoot, the noble volute, 8 inches, western Pacific. A majority of the world's two hundred or so species of volutes live in depths from ten to one hundred feet, but a few have been dredged from two miles down. Many are quite small, others reach the monster size of 20 inches. About three-quarters of the known species inhabit the waters of Australia, but the entire Indo-Pacific is rich in volutes. One of the rarest is the noble volute.*

12: Voluta vespertilio *Linné, the bat volute, 3 inches, Indo-Pacific. This small but sturdy shell displays great variation in color, surface markings, and degree of spinal development, and occasionally, perhaps in one of ten thousand tries, turns out a left-handed specimen.*

13, 14: Persicula persicula *Linné, the peach marginella, 1 inch, West Africa.*

15, 16: Aporrhais pespelicani *Linné, the pelican's foot shell, 2 inches, North Atlantic and Mediterranean.*

1

2

3

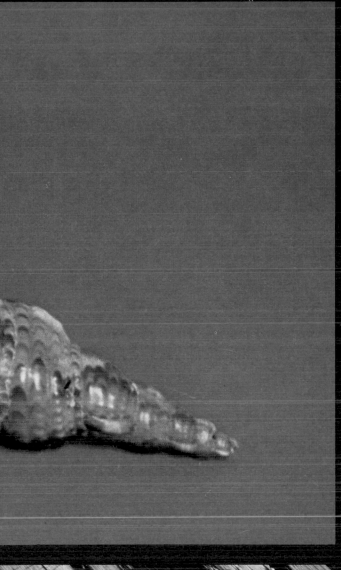

1: Charonia tritonis *Linné, Triton's trumpet, 14 inches, Indo-Pacific. The tritons are among the largest gastropods, and are usually tropical. Trumpet tritons are found in the Caribbean and the Mediterranean as well as in the Pacific.*

2: Voluta imperialis *Lightfoot, the imperial volute, 7 inches, Philippines. This shell is found on sandy bottoms from the shallows to de   f sixty feet, primarily in the waters of the Philippine Archipelago. In some areas it is called the Chinese emperor's crown. A handsome species in an aristocratic family, it is much in demand by collectors and, happily, is not rare, although perfect specimens with all their spines intact are hard to come by.*

3: Cassis tuberosa *Linné, the king helmet shell, 5 to 8 inches, western Atlantic. This edible snail ranges from southern Florida to the West Indies and south to Brazil. Because of its popularity with cameo-cutters, it is sometimes called the sardonyx helmet.*

4: Lambis chiragra *Linné, the spider conch, 5 to 9 inches, Indo-Pacific. The spider conchs are unusual in several ways. Most gastropods continue growing throughout their lives but not spider conchs; they stop growing after developing the fingerlike spines around the margin of the shell upon reaching sexual maturity. In some species, the shells of males and females are different, a condition rare among mollusks.*

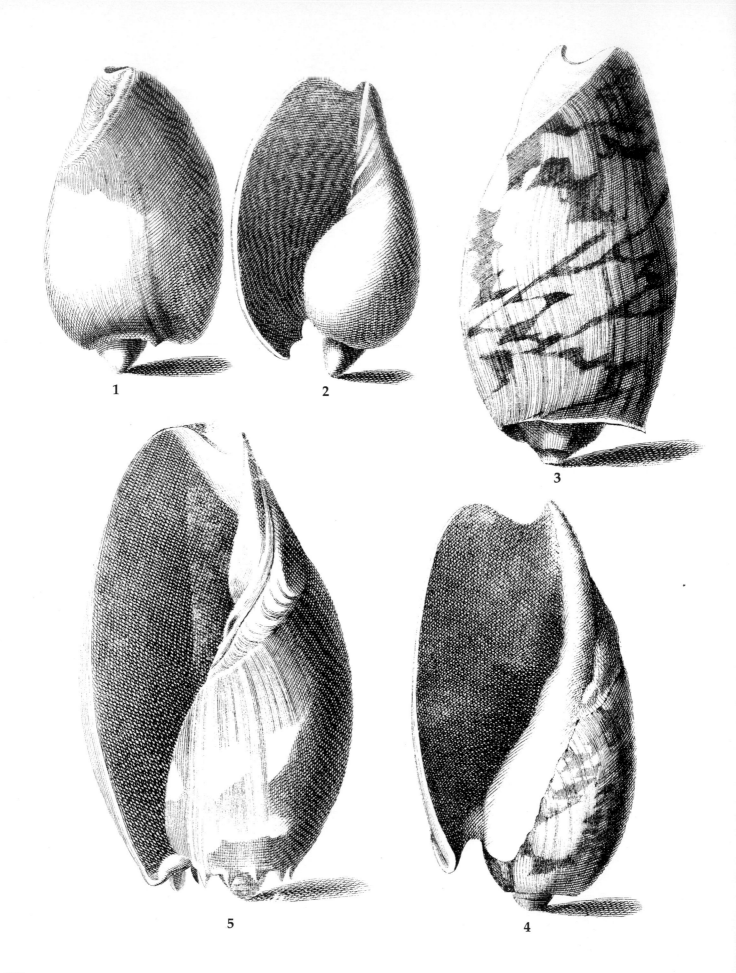

1 2

3

5 4

6

7

8

9

10

11

1, 2: Cymbium olla *Linné, 4 to 6 inches, the jug volute, eastern Atlantic. The* Cymbium *genus of the Volutidae family contains eight species of large volutes inhabiting mud bottoms to depths of two hundred feet off the coast of West Africa, from Spanish Morocco south to Angola. They are unique in the family in that they hatch their eggs inside the female's oviduct, and the young grow a thin shell before leaving the maternal shelter. These shells look so much like melon shells that, in many collections, all specimens of both types are identified under one name or the other. Like the melon, or bailer, shells, they have been used extensively in primitive cultures as tools and receptacles for liquids.*

3, 4: Cymbium cymbium *Linné, the elephant snout volute, 10 to 14 inches, eastern Atlantic. Its name stems from the fact that the shell has an unusual, depressed, snoutlike area where its spire should be. Natives used these big showy volutes for bailing out*

their boats and canoes by grasping the rounded part of the shell and, with a backhand motion, scraping the lip along the bottom of the craft.

5: Melo aethiopica *Linné, the Ethiopian volute, 6 to 14 inches, Indo-Pacific. This is one of the so-called bailer shells, and can hold up to a gallon of water in its melon-shaped shell.*

6–11: Harpa harpa *Linné, the common harp shell, 2 to 4 inches, Indo-Pacific. The harp shells are a small but beautiful group, with fewer than a dozen known species, all native to tropical waters; they are fairly common in the Indo-Pacific, but do not occur in the Caribbean or Mediterranean Seas. The most abundant species is the common harp shell. Few shells are as gaudily showy as the harps, which are distinguished by numerous axial ribs stretching from the spire to base like pleats in a dress, or, as the common name suggests, like the strings of a harp.*

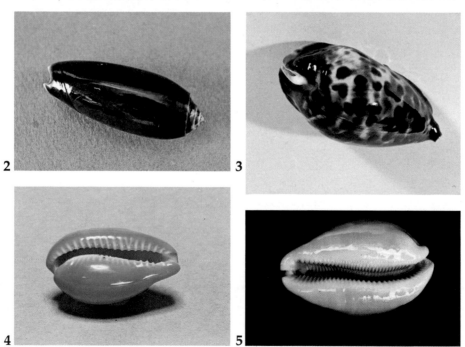

1: Persicula accola *Roth and Coan*, ½ inch, western Panama. *A penny in the center of the picture graphically illustrates the tiny size of these pretty shells, members of the Marginellidae family.*

2: Oliva vidua *Roeding, 2 inches, Indo-Pacific. Olive shells rival the cowries in the beauty of their gleaming, highly polished shells. They need no artificial polishing, for the mantle, enveloping the shell, lays new layers on the outside and constantly rubs the shell to keep it free of encrustations. These oval shells all have a similar form, with great color variations even among members of the same species, making identification particularly difficult. In most cases, accurate classification depends upon knowing the geographic location where the shell was taken.*

3: Cypraea friendii *Gray, Friend's cowrie, 3 inches, western Australia.*

4: Cypraea pyrum *Gmelin, the pear cowrie, 2 inches, Mediterranean Sea and the coast of northeast Africa.*

5: Cypraea aurantium *Gmelin, the golden cowrie, 3 to 4 inches, Indo-Pacific. This shell, one of the most valuable and popular of the cowries, has been found in the Philippine, Marshall, Solomon, and Fiji islands. In the past, before aqualung divers opened new areas to discovery, most golden cowries were taken from the treacherous coral reefs of the Fiji Islands. Until only recently, the golden cowrie was a symbol of royalty in Melanesia, and could be worn only by tribal chieftains.*

6: *A sampling of marginella shells. Most margin shells are small, below an inch in length, largely pear-shaped, and very colorful. Wide and lacelike, the mantle covers the snail when it crawls, polishing the shell and rendering it porcelaneous. The animals live in sand in shallow water, mostly in warmer seas. Closia bullata, the bubble margin shell, from South America, grows to more than 3 inches—a giant among pygmies. Some of the most interesting species inhabit the coasts of northwest Africa; one of these, Persicula cingulata, is so elegantly patterned that coastal tribesmen consider them sea jewels, collect them by the thousands, and string them as necklaces. In the United States, Atlantic and Gulf Coast Indians made a type of shell money from marginella shells.*

1, 2: Murex tribulus *Linné, 3 to 5 inches, Indo-Pacific.*

3: Murex pecten *Lightfoot, the Venus comb murex, 4 to 7 inches, Indo-Pacific. Murex shells are found all over the world, but are most common in tropical waters. The name murex comes from Latin and means "purple fish," a particularly fitting cognomen for a group of creatures containing the snails that gave the peoples of the Mediterranean the famous Royal Tyrian Purple dye of antiquity. Of the more than two hundred fifty known species of murex shells, the one most eagerly sought by collectors is the Venus comb murex, a strikingly beautiful shell whether you see in its shape a Roman comb or the picked-clean skeleton of a fish.*

4, 5: Strombus gibberulus *Linné, the humpbacked conch, 2 inches, Indian Ocean. Small, smooth, and roundish.*

6, 7: Strombus aurisdianae *Linné, Diana's ear conch, 2 to 3 inches, Indo-Pacific.*

8: Strombus ureus *Linné, the little bear conch, 1 to 2 inches, southwest Pacific.*

9, 10: Strombus raninus *Gmelin, the hawk-wing conch, 2 to 4 inches, Caribbean, named for its markings and the shape of its flaring mouth.*

11, 12: Strombus canarium *Linné, the dog conch, 1 to 3 inches, southwest Pacific. This shell and the Diana's ear conch belong to a group with a high shoulder on the lip, and sometimes a projecting spike.*

13: Strombus gallus *Linné, the rooster-tail conch, 5 inches, Caribbean. A major characteristic of the true strombs, or conchs, of which there are more than fifty species living in warm seas throughout the world, is a wide, flaring outer lip.*

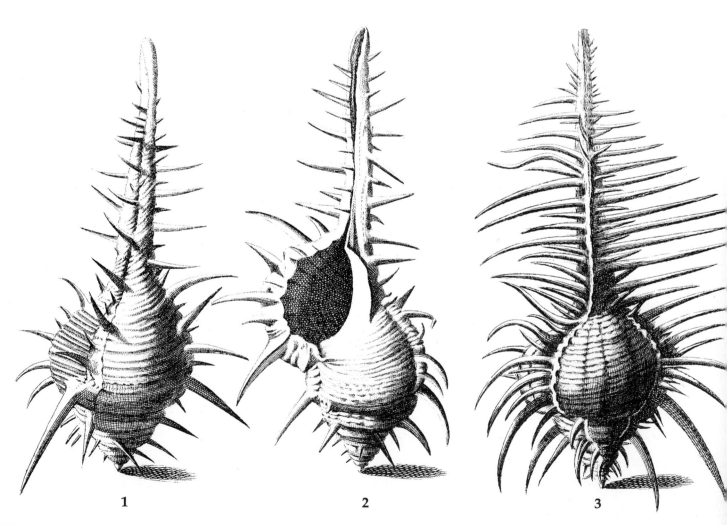

1   2   3

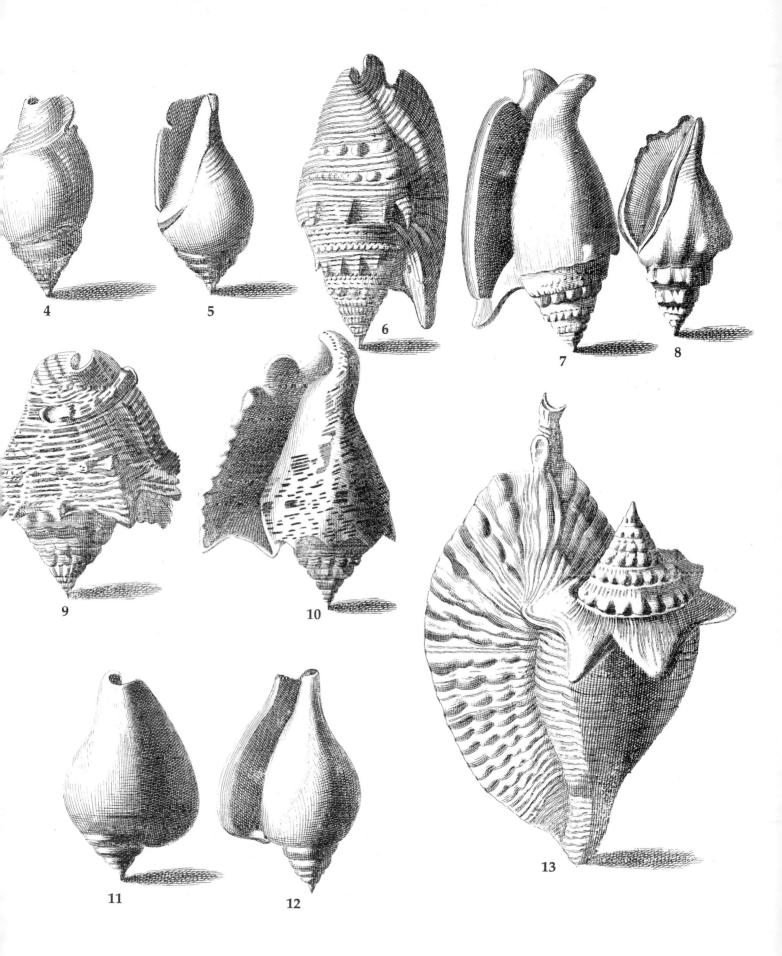

4   5   6   7   8

9   10

11   12   13

1

1: Chicoreus palmarosae *Lamarck, rose-branch murex, 5 inches, Indo-Pacific. Some of the most beautiful specimens of this spectacular shell with pink-tipped fronds come from Ceylonese waters.*

2

2: Voluta nobilis *Solander, the noble volute, 4 to 6 inches, southwest Pacific. This is a young specimen of a heavy, uncommon shell found in the waters around the Malay Peninsula. The volutes, exquisite in form, color, and pattern, are ranked by collectors among the aristocracy of shells. There are about two hundred species, most of them rare. The shells are generally vase-shaped, with a tapering spire that is usually capped by a hemispherical protoconch, the animal's embryonic shell. They are among the most mobile of gastropods, crawling about with comparative rapidity.*

3

4

3: Muricanthus nigritus *Philippi, the black murex, 4 to 6 inches, western Mexico and the Gulf of California.*

4: Murex cabritii *Bernardi, Cabrit's murex, 2 to 4 inches, southern Florida and the Caribbean. In this pinkish-buff shell the number and length of the slender spines can vary considerably, and may be entirely lacking in some individuals.*

5: Phyllonotus regius *Swainson, the regal murex, 5 inches, Gulf of California to Peru.*

5

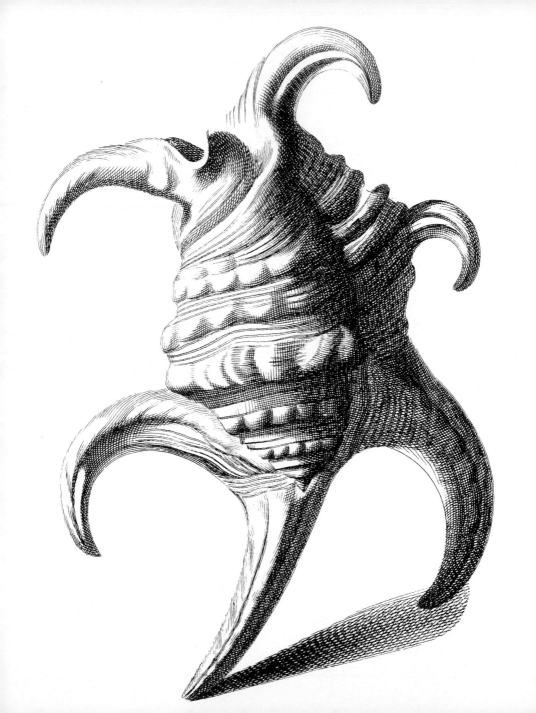

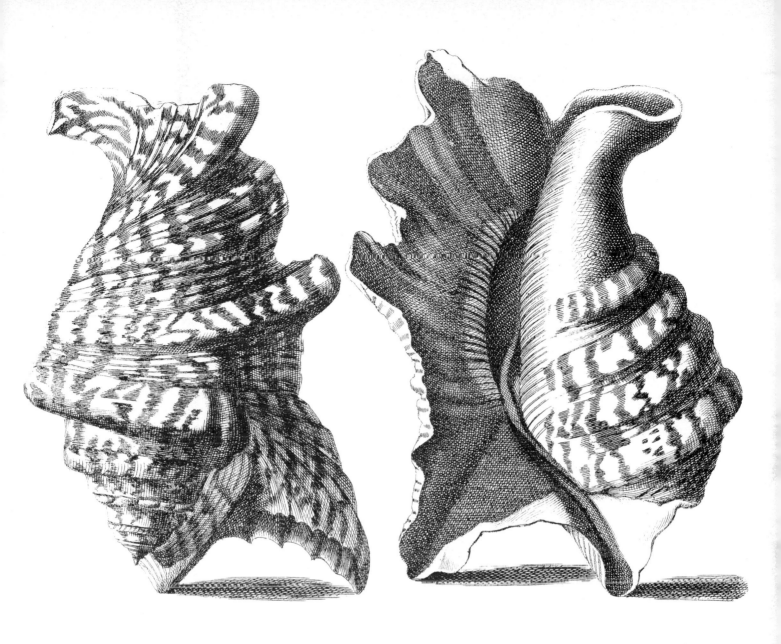

Lambis chiragra *Linné, the chiragra spider
conch, 5 to 9 inches, southwest Pacific. Undoubtedly
the strangest members of the Strombidae family are
the spider conchs, of which there are only nine
known species. Their soft parts are much like those of
other strombs, and they also have the unusual round
eyes mounted on the ends of tentacles. Even their
shells are similar, except for one thing—in the spider
conchs, the lip of the shell, rather than flaring out
into a wing, sends out six or eight long, curved
fingers that look, to most people, like huge spider
legs. Juveniles lack these spines, and in some species
the males are much smaller than the females and
have very short spines. Despite their frightening
appearance, spider conchs are no more dangerous
than sheep, since all the species are strictly
herbivorous.*

1, 2: Strombus dentatus *Linné, the toothed conch, 2 inches, East Indies.*

3: Lambis lambis *Linné, the common spider conch, 4 to 6 inches, the most common of the Indo-Pacific spider conchs.*

4, 5: Strombus marginatus *Linné, the marginate conch, 2 inches, from the Bay of Bengal.*

6, 7: Strombus fragilis *Roeding, the fragile conch, 1 to 2 inches, East Indies.*

8 and following pages: Strombus gigas *Linné, the queen or pink conch of Florida and the West Indies, up to a foot long, and for many years the shell most likely to be brought home by tourists. Unknown in the Old World, its discovery excited collectors in Europe, and great quantities have been shipped there for making porcelain, cameos, and ornaments. Overcollecting has reduced the species, and the state of Florida now controls the numbers that can be taken there. So important is the pink conch to the economy of the Bahamas that it appears on both postage stamps and coins.*

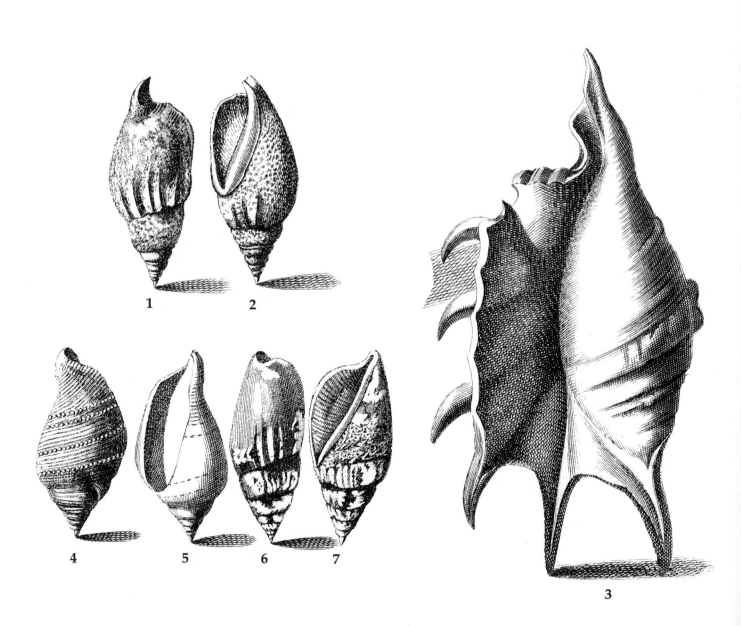

1   2

4   5   6   7

3

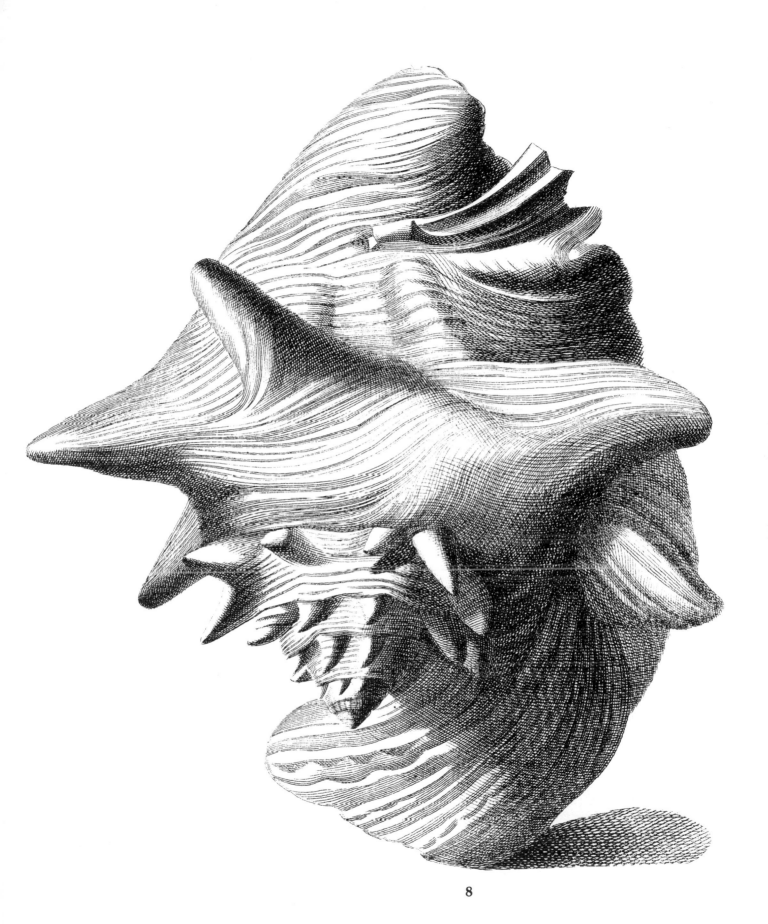

8

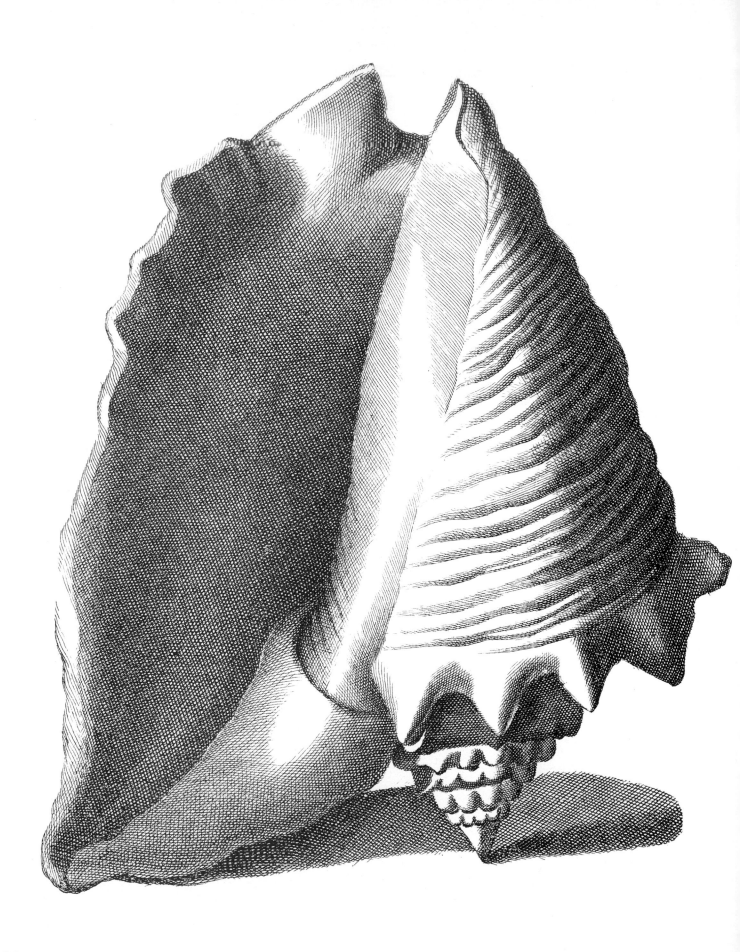

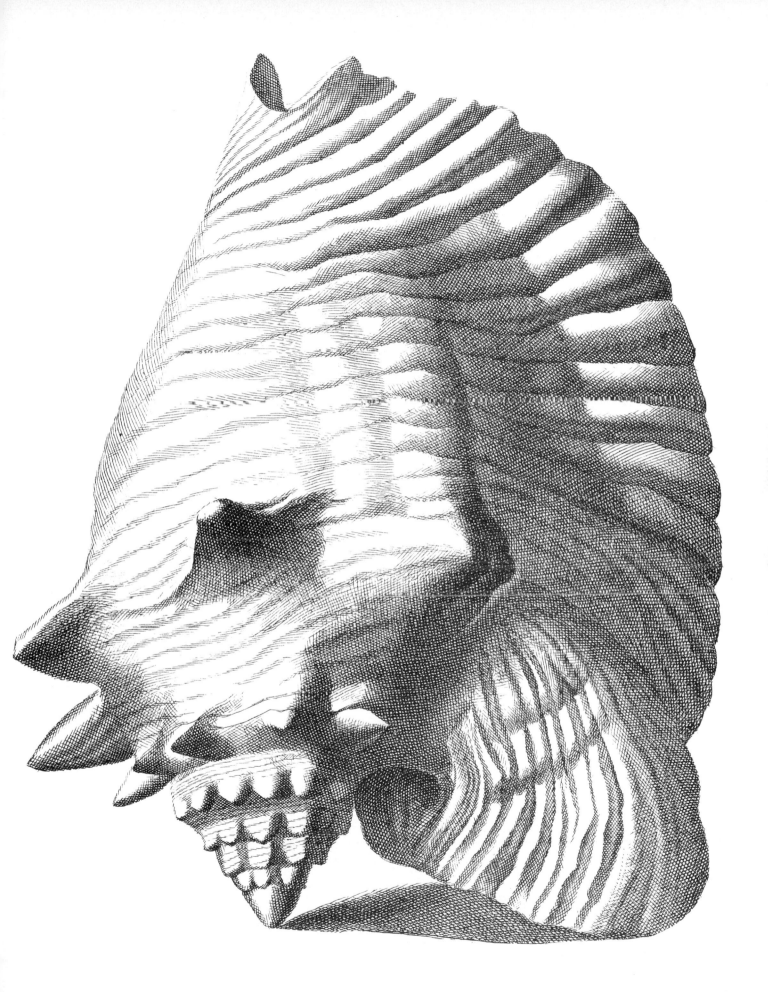

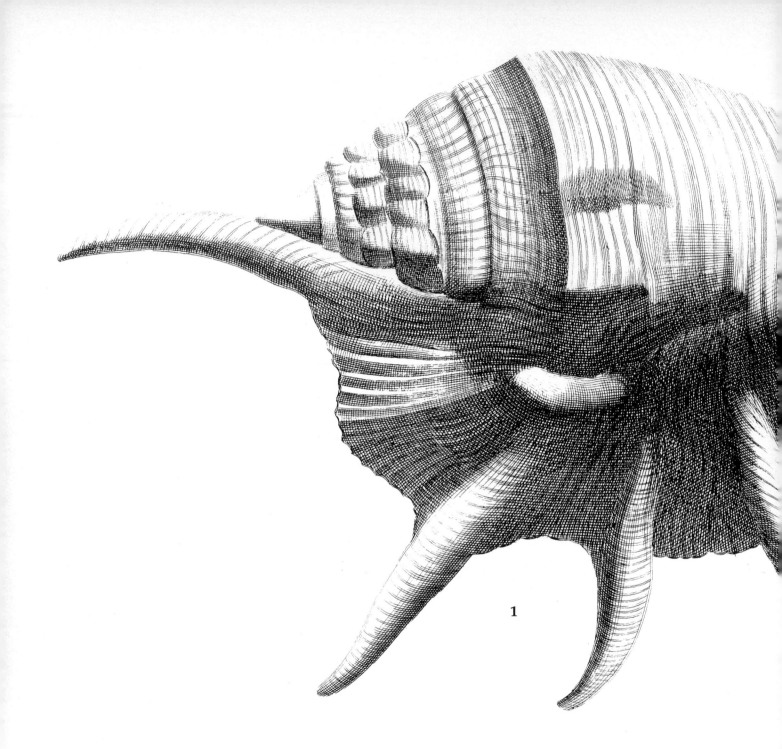

1: Lambis truncata *Lightfoot, the giant spider conch, 10 to 14 inches, Indian Ocean. This is not only the largest member of its family, but also one of the most common, which makes it easier for collectors everywhere to add a spectacular shell to their collections.*

2: *A young scorpion spider conch,* Lambis scorpius *Linné, 5 to 6 inches, western Pacific. This shell was involved in a conchological mystery. A century and a half ago a similar shell was described and named* L. robusta, *the false scorpio conch. Since no other*

specimens showed up over the next hundred years or so, it was assumed that the false scorpio had been confused with the common scorpio. After the Second World War, however, several more false scorpios were found among the reefs of Tahiti, proving that the false scorpio wasn't a real scorpio but a false one.

3, 4: Lambis lambis *Linné, the common spider conch, Indo-Pacific. Contrary to a popularly held belief, the spiny projections on the shells of spider conchs have nothing to do with the animal's method of locomotion. Like most other conchs, they have lost*

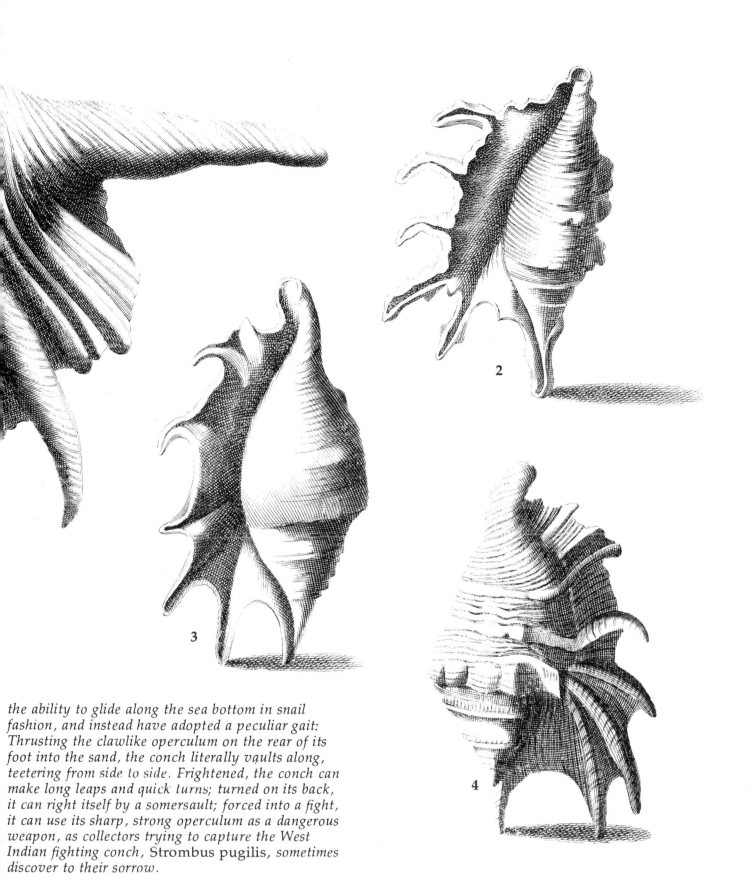

the ability to glide along the sea bottom in snail fashion, and instead have adopted a peculiar gait: Thrusting the clawlike operculum on the rear of its foot into the sand, the conch literally vaults along, teetering from side to side. Frightened, the conch can make long leaps and quick turns; turned on its back, it can right itself by a somersault; forced into a fight, it can use its sharp, strong operculum as a dangerous weapon, as collectors trying to capture the West Indian fighting conch, Strombus pugilis, sometimes discover to their sorrow.

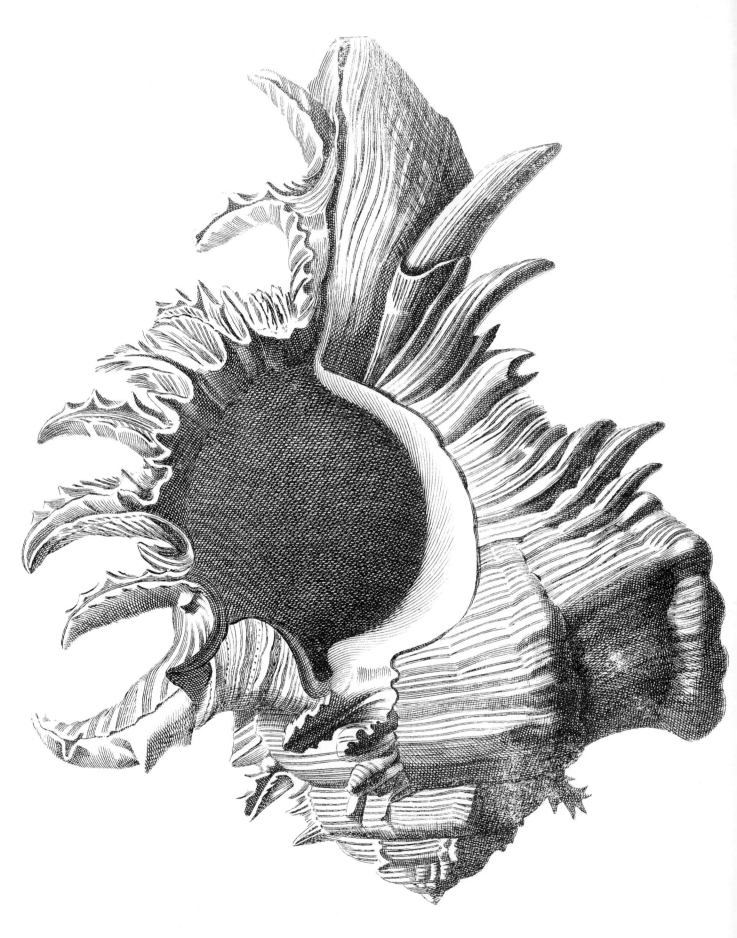

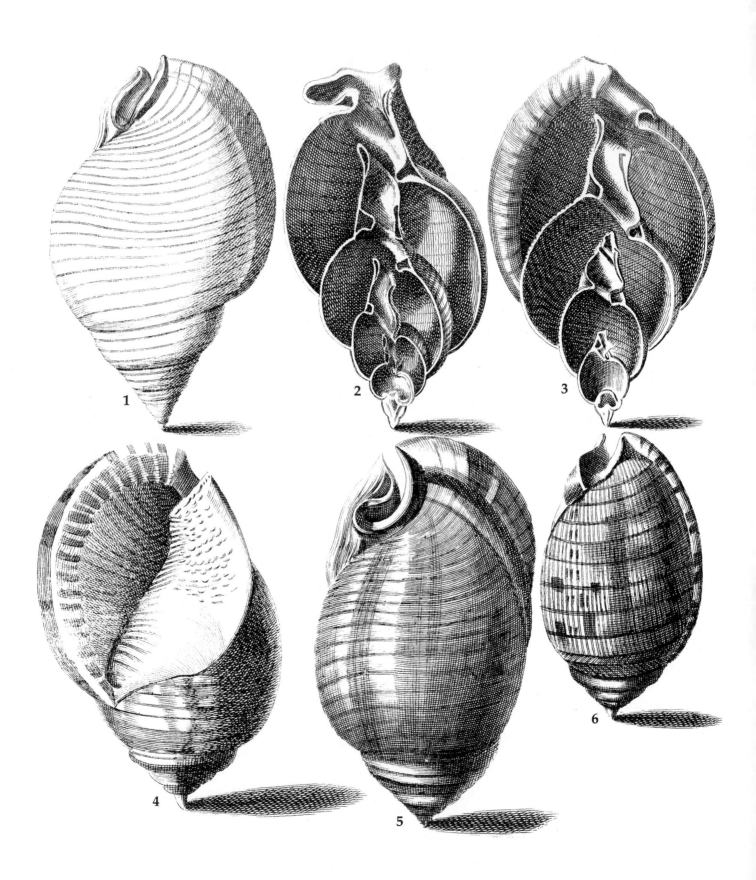

Preceding pages: *Two views of Chicoreus ramosus Linné, the ramose murex, 4 to 10 inches, Indo-Pacific.*

1–3: Phalium granulatum *Born, the Scotch bonnet, 3 inches, western Atlantic.*

4, 5: Phalium granulatum undulatum *Gmelin, the wavy bonnet, 3 to 4 inches, Mediterranean.*

6: Cypraecassis testiculus *Linné, the reticulated cowrie helmet, 3 inches, Caribbean.*

7–12: Casmaria erinaceus *Linné, the vibex helmet, 1 to 2 inches, Indo-Pacific. These shells can show an extremely wide variation in color, shape, and markings.*

13, 14: Tonna dolium *Linné, the spotted tun, 2 to 3 inches, Indo-Pacific.*

15–17: Phalium areola *Linné, the areola bonnet, 2 inches, Indo-Pacific. Also known as the checkerboard helmet in Australian waters.*

1–3: Cassis cornuta *Linné, the horned helmet shell, 8 to 12 inches, Indo-Pacific. Like so many shells in this tropical region, the horned helmet was first observed and named by the great Dutch naturalist George Eberhard Rumphius in the seventeenth century. Linné adopted many of his names when he performed his prodigious taxonomical efforts in the middle of the next century. One of the primitive trumpet shells, the helmet was used in Borneo to call the cows home.*

4: Cypraecassis rufa *Linné, the bull mouth helmet shell, 4 to 6 inches, Indo-Pacific. Also known as the* red helmet, *this shell, especially the somewhat smaller and thicker shells of male specimens, was the most common of the four large shells used in the making of cameos some years ago. Color layers in the male shell range from a light "whitish" orange to a dark brownish orange.*

5, 6: Phalium glaucum *Linné, the gray bonnet, 3 to 4 inches, Indo-Pacific.*

7, 8: Phalium plicatum *Linné, the braided bonnet, 3 to 4 inches, Indo-Pacific.*

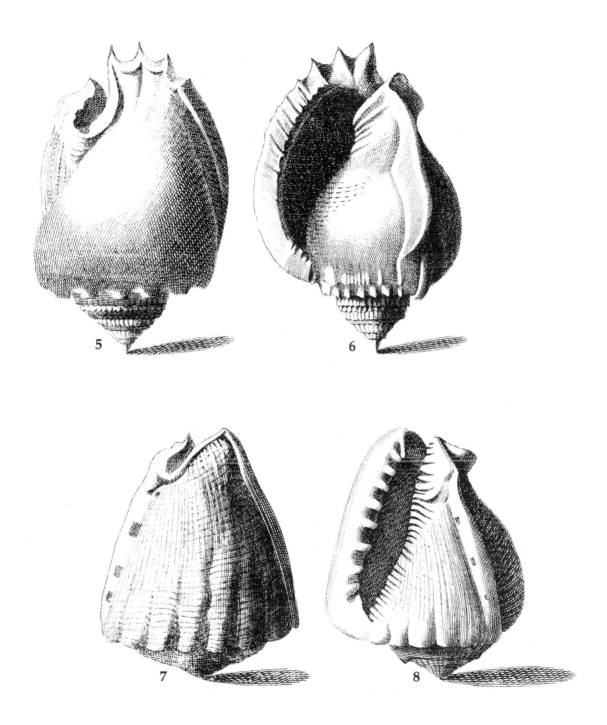

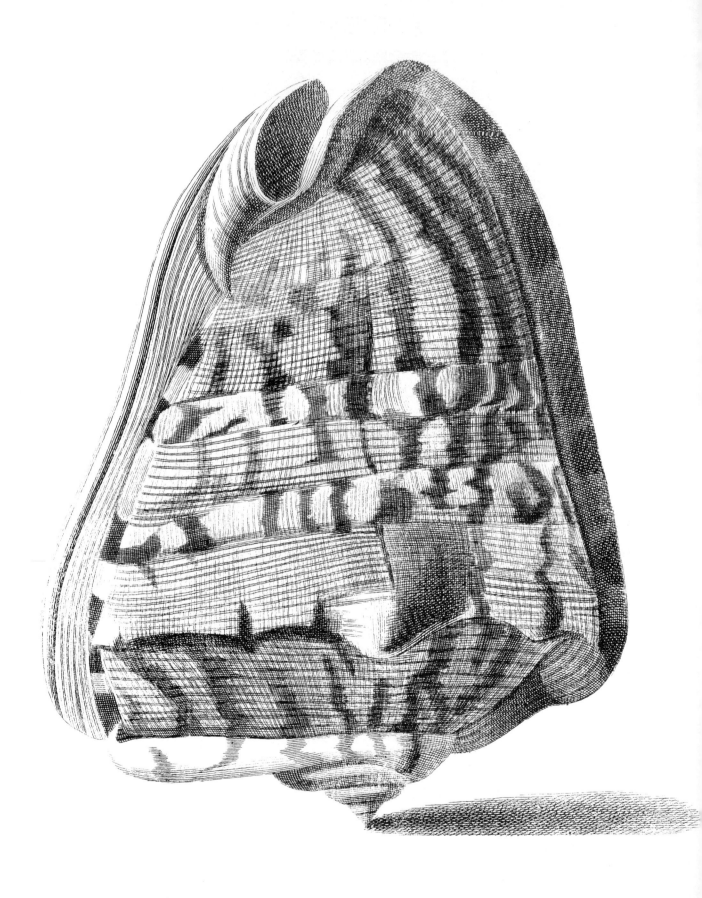

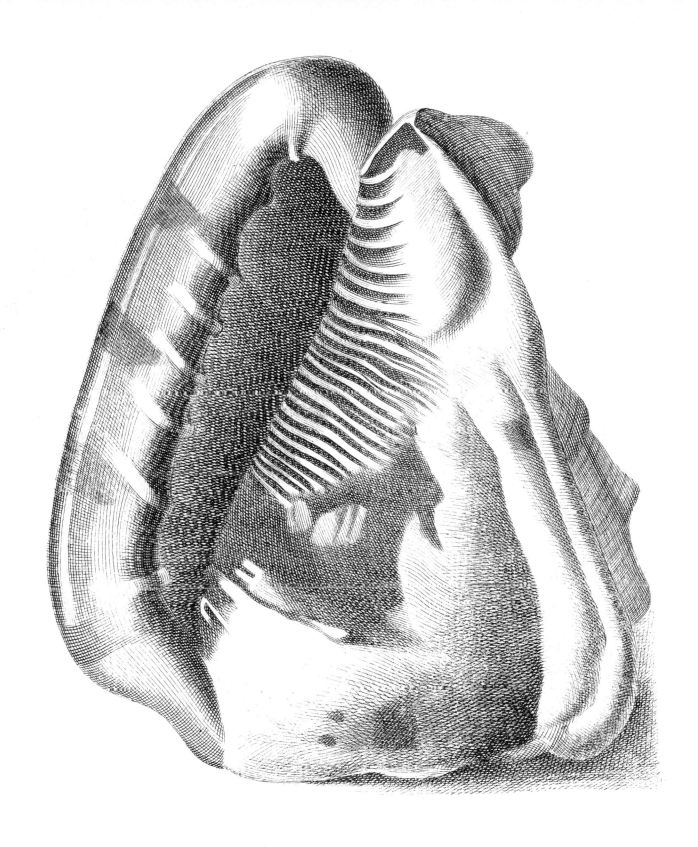

Cassis tuberosa *Linné, the king helmet shell, 5 to 7 inches, southeastern United States, the Caribbean, and parts of South America. Also called the king conch, it is the best-known of the three large helmet shells that are fairly common in the West Indies; the others are the dwarf flame conch, C.* flammaea, *and the queen conch, C.* madagascariensis. *The queen is the largest, but the king is preferred for cameo work because of the very dark colors it displays beneath its outer layers. Being edible, the king contributes to the culinary arts, too.*

1   2   3

1, 2: Buccinum undatum *Linné,* the common northern whelk, 2 to 4 inches, northern Atlantic. Also known as the wavy whelk, it is a common shell of moderately deep waters, and is equally at home in temperate and polar regions. It is a popular food in England and northern Europe. The egg case of the waved whelk resembles a coarse sponge, and sailors of long ago, using them as a substitute for soap, called them "sea wash balls."

3: Achatina fulica *Bowdich,* the giant African land snail, 5 to 6 inches.

colonies just under the surface of the sand, and
when exposed by wave action quickly anchor a
slender foot in the sand and pull themselves out
of sight—in one instant, the beach seems littered
with pretty, jewellike shells, but in the next it is
empty. When this little clam dies its valves often
remain hinged together; following violent storms
many are cast ashore, where they lie open like
butterflies with wings expanded. Sandpipers and
other shore birds feast on coquinas, and so do
people who know how to make the delicious
soup called coquina chowder. The shells are also
valuable, especially in such places as Florida
and Bermuda, where coquina stone, consisting
largely of compacted Donax shells, is used in
construction.

5: Aplustrum amplustre *Linné,* the banded
bubble shell, 1 to 1½ inches, Indo-Pacific.

6: Spondylus americanus *Hermann,* the
Atlantic thorny oyster, 3 to 5 inches. The
beating of the waves and the grinding action of
sand have worn away the bizarre spines of this
beachworn specimen.

1–3: Fasciolaria tulipa *Linné, the true tulip shell, 4 to 6 inches, western Atlantic. This is one of the most handsome of American shells. It is a shallow water species found from North Carolina south to the West Indies, and occasionally reaches 10 inches in length. A rare deep-red specimen is a collector's delight.*

4, 8: Pleuroploca trapezium *Linné, the trapezoid-shaped shell, 7 inches, western Indo-Pacific. This shell is an Asiatic relative of P. gigantea Kiner, the Florida horse conch, at a maximum of 2 feet the largest gastropod in our waters.*

5: Turbinella pyrum *Linné, the sacred chank shell, 7 inches, Indian Ocean. So dense in construction that it feels almost as heavy as lead, this shell has for centuries been held sacred to Vishna in the Hindu religion; sinistral specimens are particularly revered.*

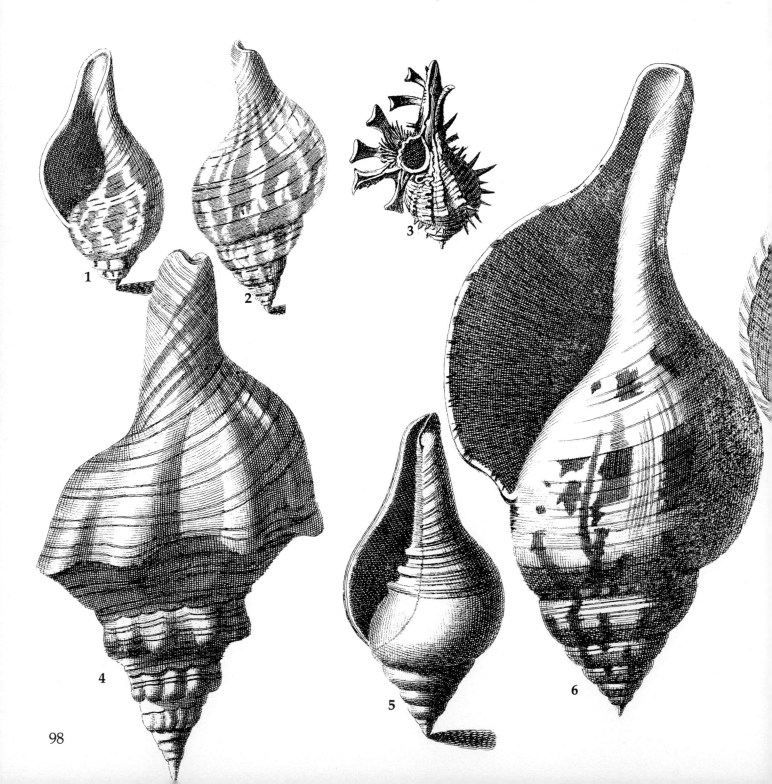

6: Homalocantha scorpio *Linné, the scorpion murex, 1 to 2 inches, Indo-Pacific. This small, delicately sculptured shell is usually dark brown or black in color, but occasionally an albino specimen is found.*

7, 10: Neptunea antiqua *Linné, the antique Neptune shell, 5 to 7 inches, North Atlantic.*

9: Distorsio anus *Linné, the distorted triton, 2 to 3 inches, Indo-Pacific. This shell belongs to a group of smaller tritons marked by strong distortions of the whorls and aperture, and extreme development of the apertural "teeth."*

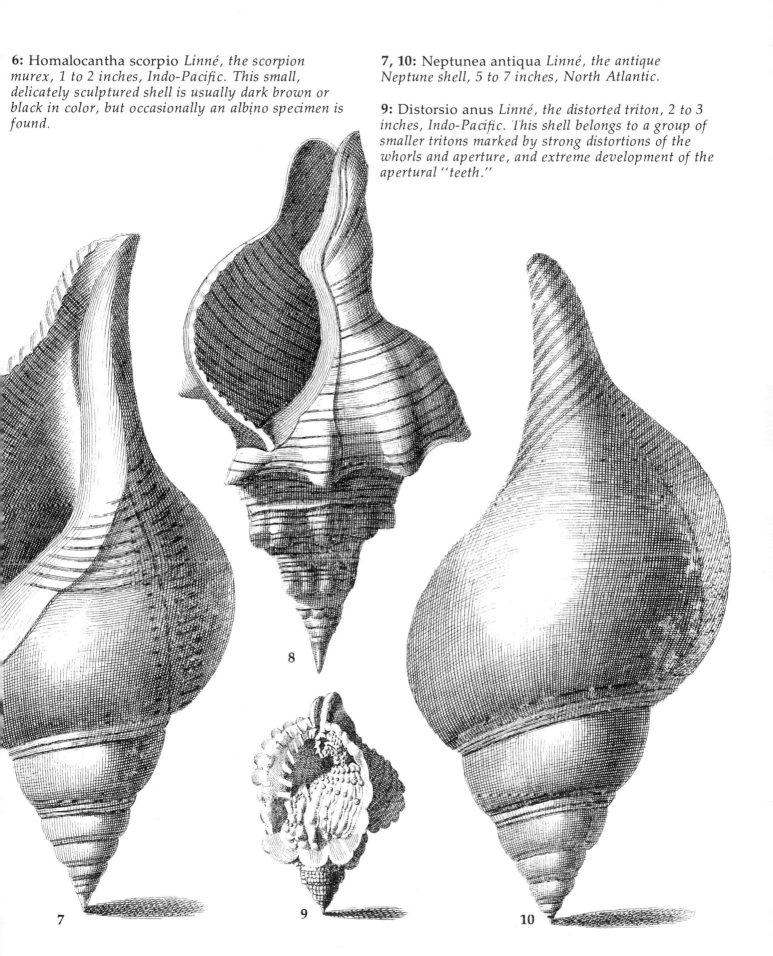

7

8

9

10

1: Guildfordia yoka *Jousseaume, 3 to 5 inches, Japan. This is one of the Guildfordia star shells that Japanese fishermen dredge from the waters around Honshu Island.*

2: Tugurium solaris *Linné, the sunburst shell, 3 to 5 inches, South Pacific. These unusual members of the carrier family produce their own ornamentation instead of cementing dead shells, stone, and bits of coral to their shells.*

3: Patella miniata *Born, 1 to 2 inches, South Africa. The Patellidae, known as the Old World limpets, number about four hundred species and are found in large numbers along rocky cliffs in all seas. Although they are capable of moving about for short distances in search of food, they always return to the same*

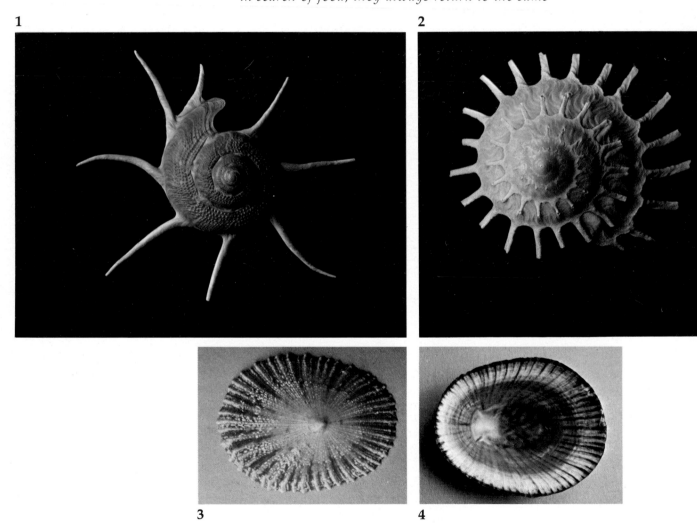

1

2

3

4

pot. There they remain for such long periods that he sharp edge of the shell carves its imprint into the tone. Limpets cling so tenaciously to their rocky bodes with their strong foot that they are almost mpossible to move without a sharp-edged instrument o pry them loose. Wrote the poet Wordsworth:

Should the strongest arm endeavor
The limpet from its rock to sever,
'Tis seen its loved support to clasp
With such tenacity to grasp,
No wonder that such strength should dwell
In such a small and simple shell.

5: Cellana nigrolineata *Reeve*, 1½ inches, Japan.

6: Phalium glaucum *Linné, the gray bonnet hell, 3 to 4 inches, Indo-Pacific.*

6 left: Harpa costata *Linné, the imperial harp, 2 to inches, Indo-Pacific.*

6 right: Harpa ventricosa *Lamarck, 3 to 4 inches, Indo-Pacific. There are only twelve species of harp hell, but most are fairly common throughout the Indo-Pacific. They are noted for extraordinarily rich color and markings, and for their deeply sculptured ibs which stretch from spire to base like the strings of a harp. Harp shells have no operculum for a imple reason: The shell is so much smaller than the animal that the head, tentacles, and foot still rotrude when the creature is inside as far as it can o. The protruding parts, incidentally, are all as olorful as the shell.*

7: Turbo petholatus *Linné, the tapestry burban, 2 inches, Indo-Pacific.*

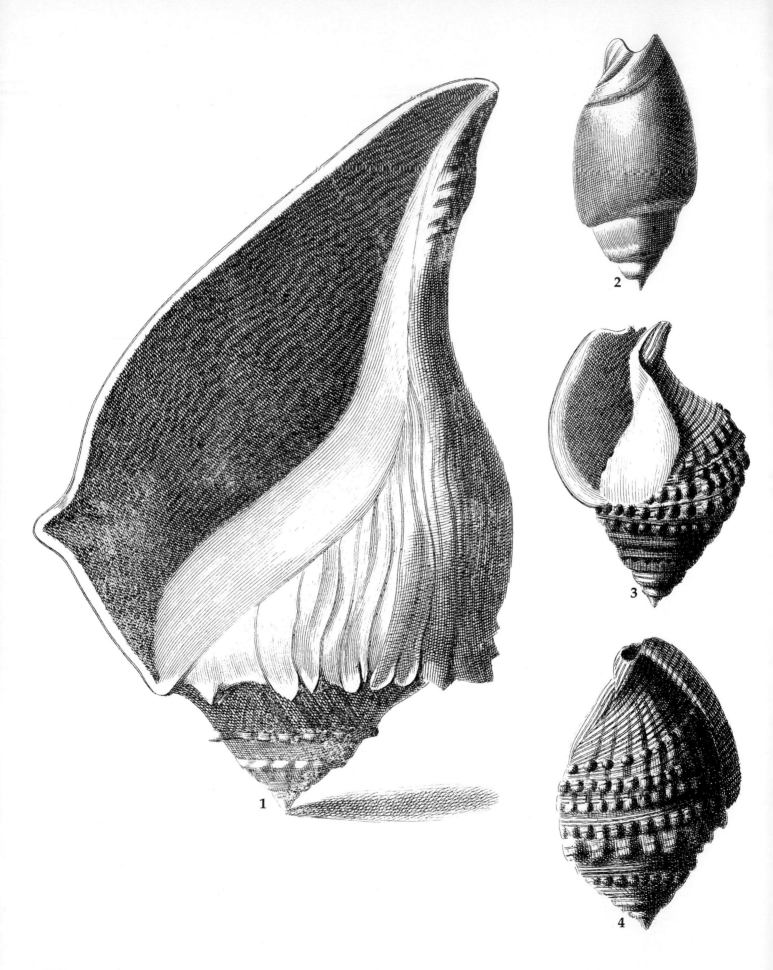

1

2

3

4

1: Busycon carica *Gmelin,* the knobbed whelk, 5 to 8 inches, Cape Cod to central Florida. Low knobs on the shoulder of the shell give it its name.

2: Ancilla glabrata *Linné,* the smooth ancilla, 2 to 3 inches, lower Caribbean; one of the olive shells.

3, 4: Galeodea echinophora *Linné,* the spiny bonnet, 2 to 3 inches, Mediterranean.

5, 6: Busycotypus canaliculatum *Linné,* the channeled whelk, 5 to 8 inches, eastern United States. It is most easily recognized by its deep, widely channeled suture, the continuous spiral line on gastropod shells where the whorls meet, and its thick, heavy periostracum. American Indians made an attractive bead from the twisted core of the channeled whelk.

Opposite left: Chlamys senatoria *Gmelin, the noble scallop, 4 inches, Indo-Pacific.*

Opposite right: Lyropecten nodosus *Linné, the lion's paw, 5 to 6 inches, North Carolina to the Gulf of Mexico and the West Indies.*

Above: Cardium costatum *Linné, the costate or ribbed cockle, 4 to 5 inches, West Africa. Beautifully sculptured, the costate cockle has wide raised ribs and deep grooves so arranged that, when the valves are closed, the ribs of one valve fit into the grooves of the other. On the end of each rib grows a short spine that is hollowed out on the inside.*

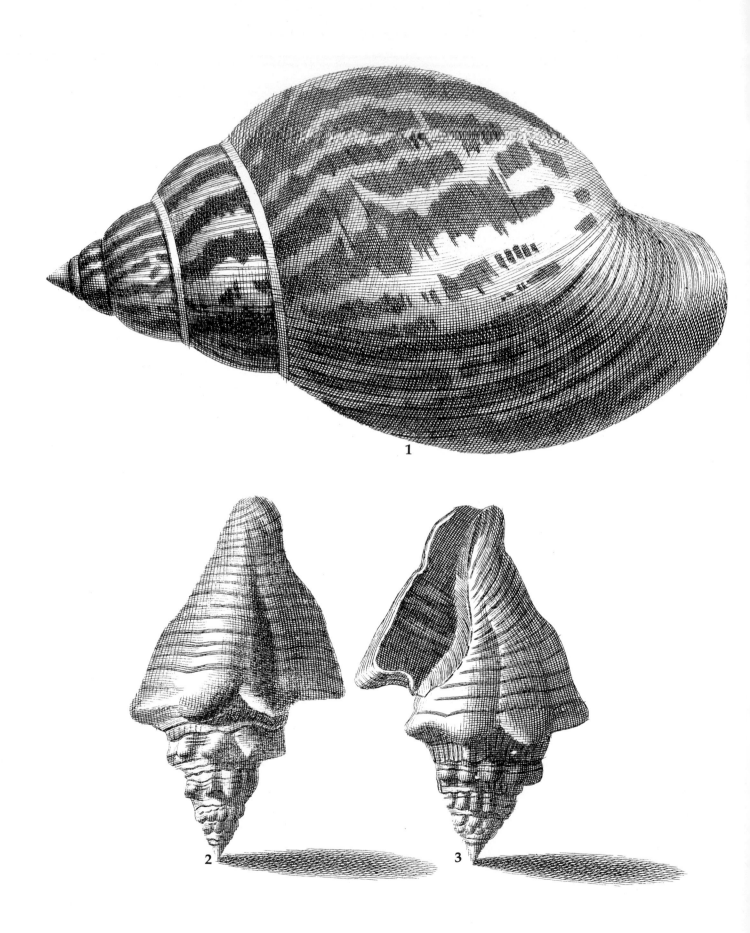

1: Achatina fulica *Bowdich, the giant African land snail, 5 to 6 inches.*

2, 3: Strombus gigas *Linné, the pink conch, 12 inches, Florida and the West Indies. This is a juvenile specimen of this popular shell (see page 82).*

4, 5: Charonia tritonis *Linné, Triton's trumpet, 14 inches, Indo-Pacific. These large shells have been used for thousands of years in many parts of the world as horns, blown in religious ceremonies as well as in calling warriors to battle. Sometimes the tip was* cut off; sometimes a hole was drilled in one of the early whorls and a mouthpiece of metal or bamboo inserted. Polynesian islanders made an inch-round hole near the apex of the shell, inserted into it the end of a three-foot-long bamboo cane, bound and cemented the two together with fine braid and resinous gum from the breadfruit tree. According to early travelers, trumpeters standing on platforms in large war canoes blasted out sounds far noisier and more terrifying than those of drums. Species related to the Pacific triton summoned slaves to work on the sugar plantations of the West Indies, and announced the arrival of fishermen sailing into Corfu Harbor.

1

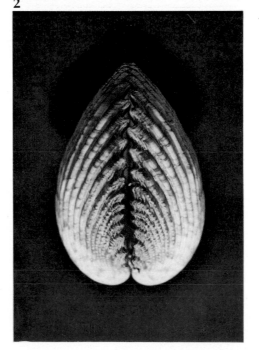

2

1: Spondylus americanus
Hermann, the Atlantic thorny
oyster, 3 to 5 inches, western
Atlantic. Thorny oysters are also
called chrysanthemum shells
because their spines, some long,
some short, some curved, and some
straight, resemble the petals of that
flower in the process of unfolding.
They are more closely related to
scallops than to oysters, and live
cemented to hard objects on the
bottom of warm seas. The Atlantic
version is one of the most sought-
after shells, but perfect specimens
are very rare. Its peculiar hinge
teeth are said to have been the
inspiration for the first mechanical
door hinge. In years past, poorly
informed American tourists often
paid fancy prices at Parisian

souvenir stands to buy this
attractive but common shell native
to American waters.

2: Trachycardium magnum
Linné, the large cockle, 2 to 3
inches, Bermuda to Brazil.

3: Pinna carnea *Gmelin, the flesh*
pen shell, 9 to 12 inches, from
Florida to the Caribbean. This
large, fragile shell, also known as
the amber pen, is rare in Florida.
Like others of its family, it lies on
the bottom with its narrow end
buried in sand, keeping itself in
place by a strong byssus attached
to buried rocks or other hard
objects. It is related to the common
pen shell of the Mediterranean, P.
nobilis Linné, the noble pen,

3

famed in ancient times for the
"cloth of gold" spun from its
byssus. Several Lopha frons
oysters are attached to this
specimen.

4: Chlamys livida *Lamarck, 2 to 3
inches, Indo-Pacific.*

4

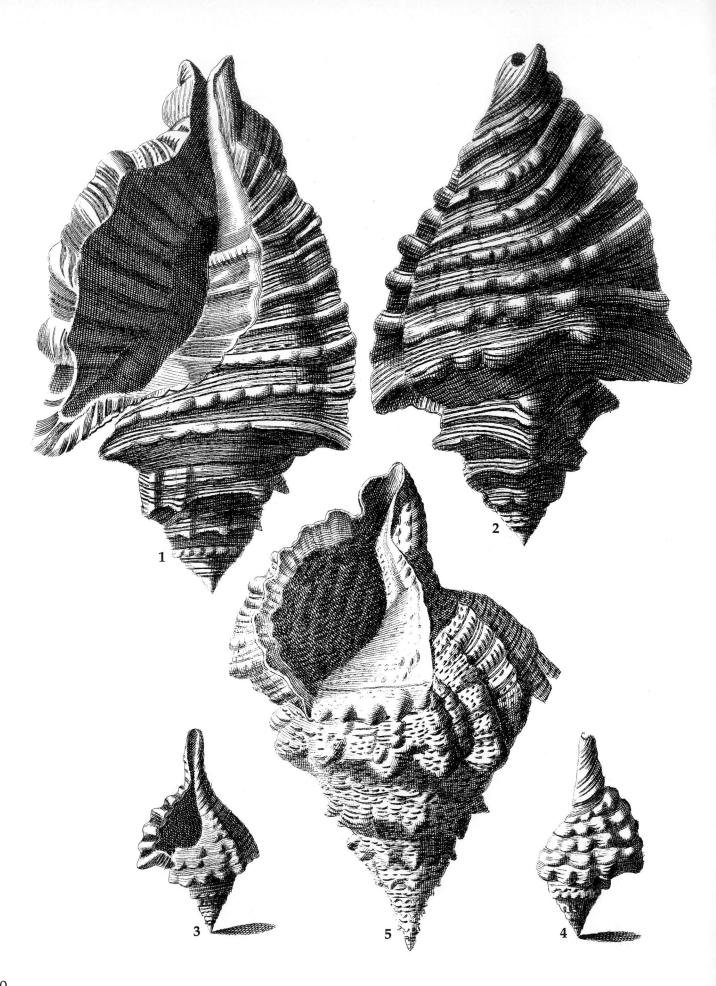

1, 2: Cymatium femorale *Linné, the angular triton, 5 to 8 inches, from southeast Florida and Bermuda through the Caribbean to Brazil. This beautiful triton shell, orange or golden-brown to reddish-brown in color, is most easily recognized by its roughly triangular shape and the wide, heavily corded shoulder of the body whorl. Its thin but rough periostracum flakes off when dry. These uncommon shells live on sandy bottoms, often in eelgrass, in depths from three to thirty feet.*

3, 4: *A juvenile specimen of the angular triton.*

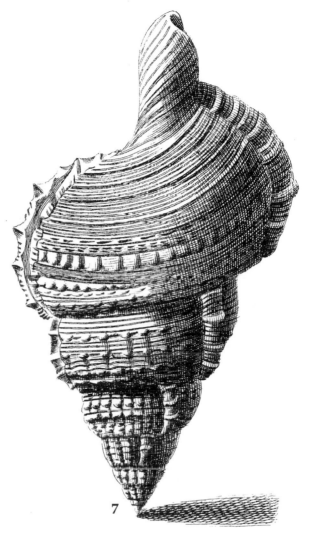

7

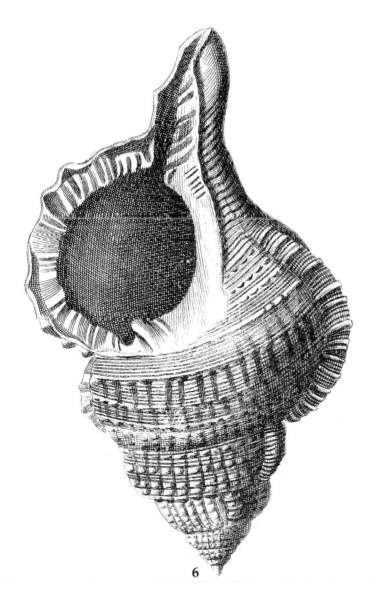

6

5: Charonia lampas *Linné, a Mediterranean triton shell that grows to a length of 8 to 10 inches. In the famous painting,* Neptune and Amphitrite, *by Jan Gossaert (ca. 1478–ca. 1533), Flemish master of the nude and classical mythology, Amphitrite wears a scallop shell in her hair while Neptune sports a* C. lampas *as a sort of shelly codpiece.*

6, 7: Ranella olearum *Lamarck, 4 to 8 inches, Africa.*

Opposite: *Simple pivoting stands show off to best advantage dozens of shells on a dealer's shelves.*

Below: *The large family of miter shells, the Mitridae, contains some 625 species, most of them—and certainly the largest and most colorful—from the Indo-Pacific region. Carnivores, they live in sand, under rocks, and on coral reefs, and rarely appear until dark. They come in a variety of shapes, with smaller members resembling cones, olives, and conchs, but generally they are spindle-shaped with an acutely pointed spire, reminiscent of the official headdress of a bishop in the Western Church, hence the name "miter."*

1, 2: Mitra cardinalis *Gmelin, the cardinal miter, 2 to 3 inches, Indo-Pacific.*

3, 4: Mitra mitra *Linné, the episcopal miter, 3 to 6 inches, Indo-Pacific.*

5, 6: Mitra papalis *Linné, the papal miter, 3 to 4 inches, Indo-Pacific.*

7: Mitra stictica *Link, the pontifical miter, 2 inches, Indo-Pacific.*

8, 9: Mitra papilio *Link, the butterfly miter, 2 inches, Indo-Pacific.*

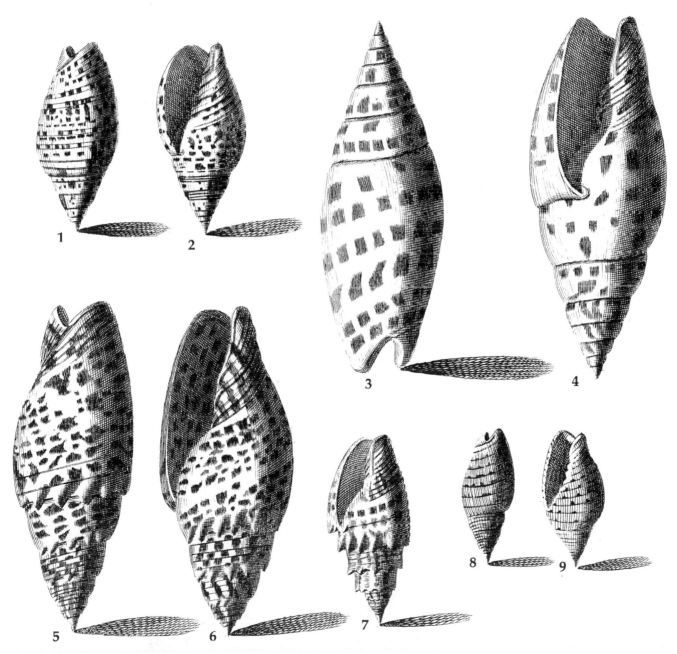

1, 2: Trochus niloticus *Linné, the commercial top shell, 5 inches, Indo-Pacific. Also called the great top shell, this species is the largest and heaviest of the family. Top shells are usually low and broadly conical in shape, much like a child's toy top. Under a limy outer layer that is usually colorfully ornamented, the shell is made of mother of pearl, and takes a lustrous polish when the outer layer is ground away. Consequently, they have been much used in the manufacture of mother-of-pearl buttons and ornaments. The commercial top also was a favorite in the collections of a century ago, especially when its outer layer—chalky white marked with red and green—was polished off, leaving an exquisite five-inch top of iridescent silver.*

3, 4: Terebra maculata *Linné, the marlinspike shell,* 10 inches, Indo-Pacific. The long, drill-like *Terebridae, also known as auger shells, comprise a family of perhaps three hundred species distributed in all warm seas, but especially in the shallow tropical waters of the Indo-Pacific. Like cones, some members possess a poison gland, but they are not known to be dangerous to man. The few small, drab species living in North American waters cannot compare with their highly colored relatives to the south. T. maculata, known also as the spotted auger, is representative of the gaudy tropical types—heavy and solid, with many closely wound flat whorls, and two bands of colored spots, one chestnut, the other purple or slate-blue, on a creamy ground color, and separated by a line of dark brown or black. The most sharply pointed of all shells, the augers were used by South Sea islanders first as food, and then as tools to carve their dugout canoes.*

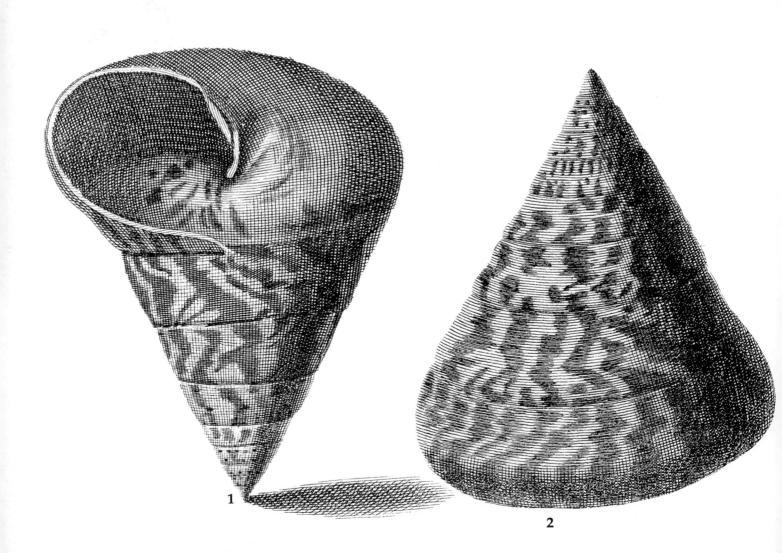

1

2

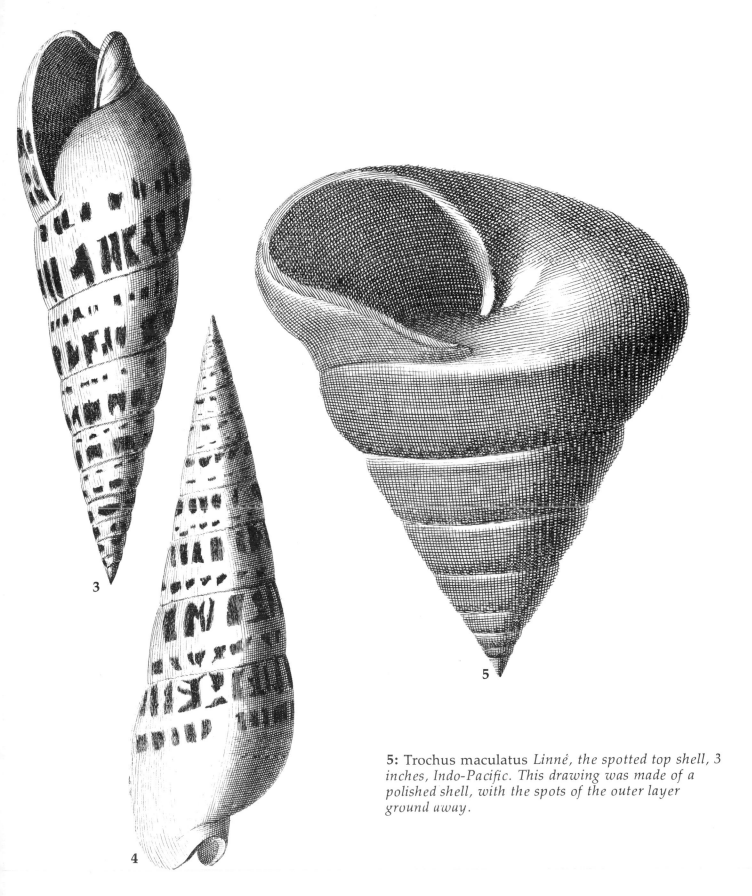

5: Trochus maculatus *Linné, the spotted top shell, 3 inches, Indo-Pacific. This drawing was made of a polished shell, with the spots of the outer layer ground away.*

1, 2: Clanculus pharonium *Linné, the strawberry top shell, 1 inch, Indian Ocean.*

3, 4, 17: Turbo argyrostomus *Linné, the silver-mouthed turban shell, 2 to 3 inches, Indo-Pacific.*

5, 6: Calliostoma ziziphinum *Linné, the lotus top shell, 1 inch, Mediterranean.*

7–10: Neritopsis radula *Linné, the rasp nerite, 1 to 2 inches, Indo-Pacific.*

11, 12: Turbo setosus *Gmelin, the setose (bristly) turban, 3 inches, Indo-Pacific.*

13, 14, 18, 19: Turbo petholatus *Linné, the tapestry turban, 3 inches, Indo-Pacific. U.S. servicemen stationed in the Pacific during the Second World War learned from the islanders how to make rings and other jewelry from the shiny blue green "cat's-eye" operculum of the tapestry turban, also sometimes called the cat's-eye turban.*

15, 16: Gibbula magus *Linné, the magic gibbula, 1 inch, Mediterranean.*

20, 21: Turbo marmoratus *Linné, the green turban shell, 8 to 10 inches, East Indies to Australia. This big shell with its thick layer of mother-of-pearl nacre under a green outer layer is highly esteemed for carving in the Orient, as well as for making buttons and ornaments. Mounted in silver, the shell made an exquisite monarch's drinking cup; in India, its thick operculum, 3 to 4 inches in diameter, is called the "Disk of the Moon" and is used as a paperweight.*

20

21

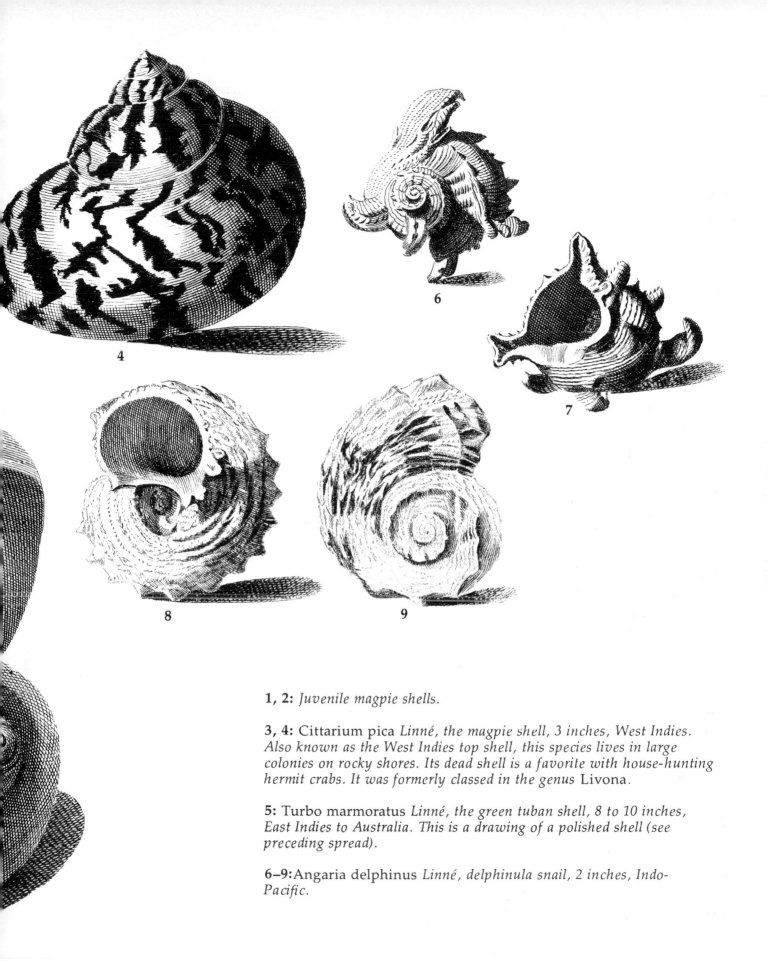

1, 2: *Juvenile magpie shells.*

3, 4: Cittarium pica *Linné, the magpie shell, 3 inches, West Indies. Also known as the West Indies top shell, this species lives in large colonies on rocky shores. Its dead shell is a favorite with house-hunting hermit crabs. It was formerly classed in the genus* Livona.

5: Turbo marmoratus *Linné, the green tuban shell, 8 to 10 inches, East Indies to Australia. This is a drawing of a polished shell (see preceding spread).*

6–9: Angaria delphinus *Linné, delphinula snail, 2 inches, Indo-Pacific.*

Shells and Man

Our remotest ancestors had the closest of associations with the molluscan world, and there was, at least in the beginning, nothing profound about the relationship. It has been truly said that man's initial appreciation of a shell was proportional to the size and flavor of the shell's occupant. Huge mounds of discarded shells along coasts and watercourses all over the world, some of them more than a mile long, half a mile wide, and twenty-five-feet deep, attest to the appetite of our prehistoric forebears as well as to the importance of mollusks in their diet. Even after developing the weapons that made them reasonably proficient hunters, primitive peoples filled out their menus in the old food-gathering ways, and those living near water often found that oysters, clams, mussels, and various gastropods were easier to catch and more plentiful than rabbits, deer, and other game.

Early people, with only their own ten fingers to do their bidding, must also have learned quickly the value of shells as utensils and tools. They probably first used large univalve shells as containers for water and other liquids; even today, in coastal areas of Greece, people store olive oil in the capacious shells of *Tonna galea*, the helmet tun; and the aptly named baler shell, *Melo amphora*, has been standard equipment in dugouts and canoes for millenia in those areas where it occurs. Other shells were pressed into service as scrapers, knives, choppers, borers, hoe blades, and arrowheads, especially on

sandy coasts and low coral islands where stone was unavailable. Then came a technological breakthrough—instead of using a certain shell for a tool, primitive man shaped it into something he wanted: an awl, perhaps, or a fishhook. From that point it was a relatively small step to piercing the most colorful shells gathered from the beach, stringing them on a thong, and creating necklaces, bracelets, belts, and other decorative devices to delight the primitive eye and satisfy the inner hunger for personal beautification and adornment.

We don't know exactly when all this happened; what we see as relatively small steps from eating an animal to using its shell as a body ornament may well have taken tens of thousands of years. And it needn't have happened in the order presented here, since even the earliest humans may have been so fascinated by the colorful shells they had just emptied at supper that they found a way to attach them to neck, wrist, ankle, hair, ears, nose, or lips then and there.

What we do know, from archaeological diggings in the Mediterranean areas of Europe and the Middle East, is that our ancestors of more than thirty thousand years ago were piercing polished seashells and stringing them with seeds, bones, and animal teeth to make necklaces and bracelets. Many of the shells were dinner discards, but other, rarer types were present in abundance enough to suggest that if early man did not travel far in seeking ornamental shells, he had a lively trade going with tribes in other areas. A case in point: in 1895, archeologists digging in a cave in the Dordogne district in the southwest of France unearthed the remains of a Cro-Magnon man, together with a red helmet shell and several cowries, all of which came from the Indian Ocean. This was not an isolated case; cowries and other rare shells from tropical seas have been found elsewhere in Mediterranean prehistoric digs.

As the centuries slipped by, shells became more and more an important part of human life. Kitchen middens and grave sites from the Neolithic, or New Stone Age, in Liguria have given up Triton's trumpets, *Charonia nodifera*, with their tops knocked off, substantial evidence that they had been used as horns, perhaps for religious purposes, perhaps to call the people to arms in time of danger, or perhaps simply to frighten away evil spirits. Primitive peoples throughout history and from all over the world have blown such horns, wherever shells of a suitable size and shape can be found, although sometimes for very prosaic reasons—in Borneo, for example, to call domesticated water buffalo. Trumpet shells, conchs, helmet shells, and frog shells were the most commonly used, and were converted into horns by being perforated at or near the apex, or sometimes in the side of one of the upper whorls. Sometimes, too, in more advanced cultures, the apex would be ground off and a mouthpiece of metal or bamboo added. Depending upon the size of the shell, the type, and the abilities of the blower, the sound that comes out can squeak, or can boom loud enough to be heard for miles.

In Polynesia, large shell trumpets decorated with human hair and bones were used to call men to battle. Peruvian Indians also decorated their conch trumpets with locks of human hair. Hopi Indians in southern Arizona used conch horns, while the Chickasaws of Florida, according to De Soto, the

Trumpet shell

Spanish explorer, made their horns out of helmet shells and large whelks, as well as conchs. Down in Mexico, diggings reveal that the Aztecs blew both the West Indian chank, *Turbinella angulata*, and the Caribbean horse conch, *Pleuroploca gigantea*, and laced jingling "tinklers" of tented olive shells, *Oliva porphyria*, to their arms and ankles when they danced. Since the olives, which were intricately carved with faces, are Pacific shells, the evidence suggests that the Aztecs maintained trade relations with both coasts. Shell horns have also been blown in Papua and New Guinea, in Japan and along coastal Asia, in India, in Fiji, New Hebrides, Tonga, and the Society Islands, but apparently not in Australia.

Lest we come to the conclusion that the American Indian and Pacific island cultures exhaust the list of primitive peoples utilizing shells as horns, let us not forget the early Minoan culture of Crete, where musical trumpet shells were used in religious ceremonies, and the mythology of Greece, the land to which our own culture traces many of its origins. In those legends of antiquity, Triton, half man and half dolphin, is the son of Poseidon, god of the sea, and also Poseidon's chief trumpeter. He is often depicted blowing a large conch shell to gather the various water and river spirits into attendance for his father, and is supposed to have signaled the end of the Deluge with a blast on his horn.

On the other hand some of the less-developed areas of the world, particularly the islands of the Pacific, have authored large volumes of fascinating shell lore, which, fortunately, are still fresh enough for us to read. For water carriers, the natives of northern Australia and New Guinea knock a thumbhole into the body whorl of full-grown false trumpet shells, *Syrinx aruanus*, which weigh almost five pounds and have a capacity of about three quarts. Bailer shells, besides the use for which they were named, are cut into ladles, spoons, and other utensils and tools. Large auger shells, such as the marlinspike, *Terebra maculata*, have served as nature's own boring devices on some surprisingly tough substances.

Most Melanesian and Polynesian tribes carved mother-of-pearl shells into fishhooks, sizing them for the different types of fish they hoped to catch, and sometimes adding feathers, as we do on fishing lures. When the quarry was octopus, they replaced the feathers with a good-sized cowrie shell, first toasting it in an open fire to give it a reddish tint, which the cephalopod apparently found irresistible. The Maoris, aborigines of New Zealand, made similar hooks but used pieces of the iridescent *paua*, the iris abalone, instead of pearl oyster shell. Bivalve shells liberally lined with mother-of-pearl were converted into breastplates by many islanders, and are still worn by some, especially in the British Solomon Islands. In Victorian times, natives made iridescent shells into eyeglass cases for the trading ships, and even today native craftsmen carve designs in the backs of large pearl oysters and sell them to the tourist trade.

The natives of New Caledonia wore large white tun shells as helmets, keeping them in place with chin straps of fur from the flying fox. Young Solomon Islands warriors could not put on their forehead the "killer's badge," a cowrie decorated with a long feather, until they had slain their first enemy in battle. In some island cultures, the tribal chieftain would not go to war without a headpiece, carved from the shell of the giant clam, which was vested with supernatural powers in an ancient ceremony. If the war was won, the clamshell got the credit. If the war was lost, the chief took the blame; his head and his ineffectual talisman were both buried deep in the ground. Melanesian tribes believed they had no chance of winning a battle unless they festooned the prows of their war canoes with egg-shaped seashells, the white *Ovula ovum*.

A shell rattle made and used in dances by Nootka Indians on Vancouver Island, British Columbia.

For centuries, Fiji Islanders considered the golden cowrie, *Cypraea aurantium,* a symbol of royalty, and believed that the soul took up residence in the shell after death; therefore, only chiefs could own and wear the golden cowrie. Some Solomon Islanders of exalted rank wore crowns of small sea snails, strung in strands, and white chest plaques carved from the valve of the great clam. Forehead disks, called *kapkap,* were cut from large pearl shells and overlaid with intricately carved filigree-work in tortoiseshell. At least one Solomons tribe made elegant ceremonial drinking cups for the aristocracy from large green turban shells, *Turbo marmaratus,* embellishing them with precious stones and silver mounts.

Many islanders cut cone shells into rings and strung them together like beads in necklaces; larger disks they wore as amulets. On India's Coromandel Coast, the wrists and ankles of girls were encircled from infancy with bands cut from the whorls of the sacred chank, *Turbinella pyrum.* In the days when human sacrifice was more common in some primitive cultures than we would like to believe, a charm called *pakuisia,* carved from the giant clam's shell, was hung from the neck of the victim, usually a child, as an essential part of the ritual to appease the gods.

In New Zealand and elsewhere in the South Pacific, the men of many tribes used sharp-edged shells to shave their beards. Throughout the Indo-

Pacific area, small univalves took the place of dice in games of chance, gamblers rolled, and won or lost on the position of the shells at rest, apertures up or apertures down. Early in their history, the Japanese began including a strip of dried abalone meat, now wrapped in flowery paper, with every gift as a token of good luck. And as insurance for the future, the prospective bride in some South Sea cultures made a headband composed of thousands of tiny rice shells—not for herself, but for the groom-to-be to wear as a way of announcing to all the other eligible young ladies of the tribe that this particular fish had been hooked and would soon be landed.

The Golden Fleece of Greek mythology, sought by Jason and the Argonauts through many adventures, had been worn by a magical ram that had the power of speech and flight. At the instigation of Hermes, the ram saved Phrixus and his sister, Helle, from their jealous stepmother by flying them from Boeotia to Colchis. During the flight across the strait between Europe and Asia, Helle fell off the ram and was drowned; the stretch of water was named Hellespont in her honor. Phrixus, safely reaching Colchis, sacrificed the ram, and hung its pure golden fleece in a sacred grove guarded by a sleepless dragon. The ram became the constellation Aries, Phrixus married a daughter of King Aeëtes, and the scene was set for Jason's dramatic quest.

Like many of the legends of antiquity, the story of Jason may have some basis in fact. Not that anyone believes in flying rams wearing coats of golden wool, but some modern historians have suggested that the coveted Golden Fleece may have been the fabulous cloth of gold, one of the most remarkable products obtained from the molluscan world. The cloth was woven from the byssus of the noble pen shell, *Pinna nobilis*, of the Mediterranean (the byssus is a brushlike cluster of strong threads that some bivalves secrete to moor themselves to

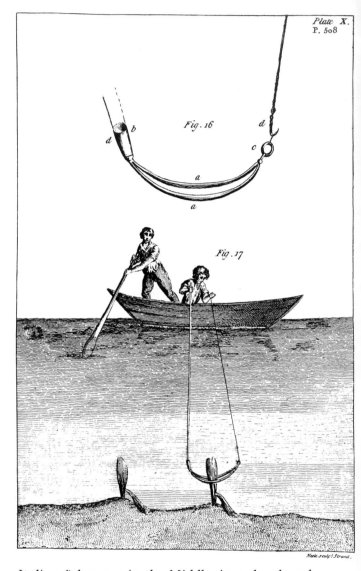

Italian fishermen in the Middle Ages developed ingenious long-handled tongs to take the pen shell, Pinna nobilis, *and its valuable byssus from the bed of the Mediterranean.*

the sea bottom and underwater rocks). The noble pen, a brittle shell that grows to a length of two feet, lives partially buried in mud or sand, sometimes among rocks; it is not a pretty shell, but its byssal threads are long, fine filaments of a striking bronze-gold color and a high metallic sheen.

After washing, drying, combing, carding, and spinning, these threads, sometimes called sea silk, were woven into a textile that looked as if it were composed of gossamer gold, and was so soft and fine that a shoulder cape made from it could be passed through a lady's finger ring. Because of the difficulties encountered in finding and harvesting pen shells with the byssus still attached—in medieval times fishermen probed for them on the sea floor with barely manageable twenty-foot-long tongs—and because it took a pound of byssus to produce three ounces of finished threads, fabrics made of *Pinna* silk were the most expensive of textiles, and truly the cloth of kings. According to Procopius, Byzantine historian of the sixth century A.D., a reigning emperor sent a robe of the precious stuff as a gift to the satrap of Armenia. Cloth-of-gold collars bedeck and bedizen the necks of kings and lords in illuminated manuscripts from the fourteenth and fifteenth centuries. In 1745, a pair of sea-silk stockings was presented to Pope Benedict XV, so wondrously fine that the gift arrived enclosed in a silver snuff box. Queen Victoria also owned a pair, and, it is said, she found them delightfully soft and warm.

Cloth of gold was woven of *Pinna* silk from ancient times until this century. The art in later years was kept alive in the coastal areas of Sicily and Calabria, where the threads, mixed about one-third with conventional silk, were knitted into gloves, caps, stockings, and even coats. The industry died out for economic reasons after World War I, but a determined *turista* with a fat enough wallet and the patience to search can still find, in some out-of-the-way fishing village in southern Italy, a scarf or gloves made of the same golden fabric that legends were made of, thousands of years ago.

> Who hath not heard how Tyrian shells
> Enclose the blue, that dye of dyes,
> Whereof one drop worked miracles,
> And colored like Astarte's eyes
> Raw silk the merchant sells?
>   Robert Browning

The phrase "born to the purple" is usually said of a child of royal, noble, or very wealthy family, or of someone of the highest and most privileged rank in an organization. It dates back at least to the tenth century A.D., when it was added to the title of the Byzantine emperor, Constantine VII, who reigned from 913 to 959. Originally it was rendered as "born (or cradled) *in* the purple," and was applied to any child born of the imperial family in the palace at Constantinople, where there apparently was a special lying-in room called the *porphyra*, which in Greek means purple. There is some difference of opinion among scholars as to whether *porphyra* really referred to a room or to something else, the writers of old having used it in a disconcerting variety of ways. Some spoke of a house "anciently appointed" for the empresses during childbirth. Some spoke of a palace in Constantinople called "the purple palace," others of the "palace of porphyry" (a dark, purplish red rock quarried extensively in ancient·Egypt). Some referred to an apartment in the palace with walls of porphyry, and others to a special chamber draped with purple hangings. And still others alluded to the purple blankets in which the imperial children were wrapped at birth.

Whichever way we turn, the symbolism is readily apparent: The royal child is brought into the world in a purple room or a purple palace and is immediately wrapped in a purple robe—in other words, born in

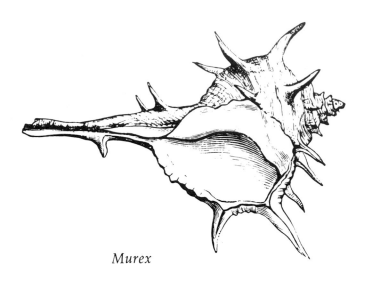

Murex

the purple, the color of royalty. But why purple? Why not green or pink or yellow?

That brings us back to shells. Sometime around 1500 B.C., the Egyptians and Cretans discovered that several small, unimpressive-looking sea snails produced a thick, creamy liquid that changed color when exposed to direct sunlight. The colors it changed to included yellow, green, blue, and, finally, purplish red—all in the space of about ten minutes. They used the fluid as a dye, but, unfortunately, it was not permanent. Then the citizens of Tyre, one of the city-states of ancient Phoenicia, developed a system for making the dye colorfast. They kept the process secret, sharing it only with their sister city, Sidon, and in a short time the two enterprising city-states built up a profitable monopoly that lasted for centuries. So famous did the dye become that it was known throughout the ancient world as Tyrian purple. And so expensive was cloth dyed with it that the name often was given a new dimension—*royal* Tyrian purple—because few people other than royalty could afford it.

Since royalty abounded in those days, however, there was a great demand for cloth dyed with Tyrian

purple, which wasn't the purple we are familiar with, but, depending upon the type of shell and the processing, was a variety of shades ranging from violet to dull crimson and magenta. The snails most often used were *Murex brandaris, Murex trunculus,* and *Thais haemastoma*, and they were used in astronomical numbers, for each tiny creature exuded only a drop or two of the liquid; it has been estimated that the juice from ten thousand snails would be needed to dye a man's necktie. Huge mounds containing shells in incalculable numbers can still be seen near Tyre and Sidon, the present-day cities of Sur and Saida in Lebanon. Similar mounds have been unearthed at more than thirty other locations in the Mediterranean, among them Sicily, Utica, Carthage, Malta, and Cadiz. These locations, colonized by the Phoenicians, served as subsidiary dye factories and trade stations. Thus, as historians reconstruct the picture, the Tyrian dye industry was responsible for much of the early exploration and colonization of the Mediterranean, for as the Phoenicians exhausted the supply of murex shells off their own shores, they had to search out new sources somewhere else.

Our knowledge of the Phoenician dye-making process comes largely from Pliny the Elder, the Roman naturalist. The snails, being carnivorous, were caught in lobster pots baited with ripe cockles. Small shells were crushed in stone mortars, larger ones were cracked open so that the soft parts, especially the mantle, where the dye-producing gland was located, could be removed. The animals were steeped in salt water for several days. Then came a lengthy simmering process in lead or tin vats lasting up to ten days, during which workmen skimmed off the fragments of boiled flesh as they rose to the surface. The dye was tested periodically, and when it was judged to be done it was strained to remove any leftover impurities. At this juncture, the liquid was a pale green and contained no hint of red

126

or purple. But skeins of wool, cotton, linen, and silk dipped in it and allowed to dry in the sun—and sometimes treated in a weak lye solution when the color came out muddy—turned into one of the many shades in the family of reds. The most coveted was rich crimson, which Pliny, covering both ends of a poetic spectrum, compared to deep-red roses or congealed blood. Paler shades, he tells us, were obtained by diluting the dye with an equal amount of human urine.

Considering the millions of snails that had to be caught to keep the industry going, and the lengthy process involved, it isn't surprising that woolen robes dyed with Tyrian purple were, as Pliny complained, almost as costly as pearls. According to one estimate, it took some three hundred pounds of liquid dye to treat fifty pounds of wool, which resulted in a price, during the reign of Augustus, of one thousand dinarii for a single pound of dyed wool. In these days of galloping inflation, that equates to something like five hundred dollars a pound—but it's peanuts compared to the price of the dye itself, which eventually reached the equivalent of *ten thousand dollars a pound!* At those prices, it must have cost Antony and Cleopatra a pretty penny to outfit her royal barge with a full set of sails dyed Tyrian purple—and some say the *entire fleet* was so provided—for the battle of Actium.

Once stained, however, the cloth was permanently colored, something that could not be said about many of the dyes in use at the time. Plutarch relates that Alexander the Great, after conquering Persia, found in the royal treasury more than five thousand pounds of purple-dyed cloth that had been part of the treasure amassed by Darius the Great; although the cloth had lain in storage for almost two hundred years, its color was still fresh and unfaded.

As the centuries rolled by, Tyre and Sidon grew immensely rich through their monopoly, and they paid homage to the lowly snail that had made it all possible by imprinting its image on their coins. They had become antiquity's greatest traders and sailors, piercing the deserts with great caravans and sending their galleys to every corner of the Mediterranean and beyond, carrying bales of beautifully woven and dyed materials throughout the known world. Kings and queens, satraps and governors, merchant princes and high priests all dressed themselves and their idols in robes of purple, draped their palaces and temples in purple, and mummified their royal dead in wrappings of royal purple. Even in republican Rome, senators and consuls wore togas bordered with bands of purple to set them apart from the common crowd.

Finally, after more than a thousand years, the huge, flourishing purple dye industry was brought crashing down by the whim of one man. The man was Emperor Nero, and his method of destruction was simple: He declared that only he, the emperor, could wear purple. Since Rome controlled most of the world, including Tyre and Sidon, that left the two cities with just one major customer, hardly enough to sustain a business, no matter how many robes he wore.

The secret of making royal Tyrian purple dye was supposed to have been lost with the collapse of the industry, but somebody remembered or somebody rediscovered it. Even before the fall of Rome, purple was being used extensively for bishops' robes and altar coverings in the expanding Christian church, and later, as we have noted, in the household of the Byzantine emperors. A similar process was also in use in other areas of the world, and there is the fascinating possibility that the fine hand of the Phoenicians was involved.

We know that mariners from Tyre and Sidon, searching for murex shells and trade, covered the Black Sea and the Mediterranean. There is also evidence that they passed through the Strait of

Gibraltar and dared the Atlantic, sailing north to the British Isles and south down the western coast of Africa. Some historians believe they completed the circumnavigation of Africa, rounding the Cape of Good Hope and eventually reaching the East Indies. There is even the possibility that one or more of their vessels, caught in the grip of fierce Atlantic storms, were blown to the shores of the New World two thousand years or so before Columbus.

In their visits to the British Isles, the Phoenicians obtained a "black purple" dye, similar to the Tyrian purple but less brilliant. It was derived from the dog whelk, *Nucella lapillus*, and mounds containing enormous numbers of *Nucella* shells have been found in Ireland. These mounds, so similar to those in the Mediterranean, suggest subsidiary dye factories and trading stations. At any rate, the early Britons used the *Nucella* exudation to color their garments and, sometimes, themselves—Roman invaders of later centuries reported being attacked by howling "blue Britons."

The Venerable Bede, writing in the eighth century, mentions the art of making purple dye, and in the Middle Ages the stuff was used in the painting of illuminated manuscripts, and, in diluted form, for staining parchments and vellum, the better to set off the gold and silver lettering with which they were decorated. The Irish were still using it in 1684 to dye fine linen, but elsewhere the process went into decline and disuse, probably because of its costliness, and only a few families held and passed on the secret. In more recent years, until the advent of synthetics, the juice of the dog whelk was used primarily for marking laundry—a fate from which, thankfully, the royal Tyrian murex was spared.

Half a world away from Tyre and Sidon, the Indians living in the regions now known as Mexico, Central America, and Peru had been producing a deep purple dye from wide-mouth rock shells, *Purpura patula*, for centuries before the official coming of the white man. Pre-Columbian purple-dyed textiles have been found in Mexico and Peru, and ancient paintings from Mexico show chieftains in capes and breechcloths dyed purple, and their women in purple skirts. Did the Indians learn the art of producing mollusk dye from some roving band of Phoenicians? There isn't much evidence to go on, but some ethnologists think so.

Whatever the historical truth, the Indians made one important improvement over the Phoenician system: They learned that it wasn't necessary to crush the animals to extract the dye. Instead, they picked the snails from the rocks at low tide and blew on them. This made the animal retreat into its shell and exude a thick liquid, which was caught in a calabash bowl. The Indians returned the snails to their places in the rocks and continued on their "milking" rounds, leaving the snails alive and well to manufacture more of the precious liquid. During the gathering trip the women of the tribe soaked agave threads in the dye and let them dry in the sun, a process that sent them through the familiar color change—from yellow to green to blue to rich magenta.

In the seventeenth century, reported one early traveler, the Indians of Costa Rica had developed a tidy business, producing purple-dyed cloth for export to the wealthy grandees of Spain. The industry eventually spread to the West Indies, where hand-dyed cotton skirts, called *de caracollio*, while not in the same league as robes of Tyrian purple, strained tourist budgets. The advance of synthetic dyes has made life much easier for the *Purpura*, but it is said that the Tehuantepec Indians of southern Mexico still keep them working in the old way.

About twelve miles west of the Euphrates River in

southern Iraq, a number of wind-scoured mounds rise out of the barren desert. One of these mounds, called Tell el-Obeid, is the site of a prehistoric village, built when much of the surrounding area was a swamp and the Euphrates still flowed nearby. The people who lived here were not highly civilized. Their huts were constructed for the most part of reed matting and light wooden poles plastered with mud and clay. Wooden doors swung on stone hinges, floors were made of beaten mud, fireplaces of crude bricks. They were a primitive agricultural people, and made hoes and adzes of chipped stone, sickles of hard-baked clay. They had mastered the art of pottery-making, and turned out pieces finely painted with geometric designs as well as ordinary cooking ware. They wore roughly woven garments, made on looms that employed stone weights, and for personal decoration they wore necklaces of shells and beads, the latter cut from shells or chipped from quartz, obsidian, and carnelian.

These long-gone people hold a special fascination for us because they had come to this area from the east, possibly as conquerors from Iran or India, as early as the fifth millenium B.C., and were living there at the time of the great Deluge, described in the Bible and other ancient writings. We are reasonably sure of this because archaeologists discovered the pottery, necklaces, and other artifacts under an eight-foot-thick bed of clay that, tests showed, had been deposited by water. They are interesting also because from their primitive drowned village there rose the great Sumerian city of Ur, which by 3500 B.C. had grown into a flourishing commercial center in the southern reaches of Mesopotamia, often called "the cradle of civilization."

In the fifteen hundred years that elapsed between the settling of the prehistoric village on Tell el-Obeid and the ascendancy of the metropolis of Ur, the Sumerians had come a long way. Their knowledge of agriculture had expanded greatly, they had invented cuneiform writing and the potter's wheel, and they were able to build great temples and palaces from brick and stone, graced by terraced "hanging" gardens. They were also highly skilled at working with precious metals and jewels, which makes all the more surprising their continued fascination with shells, which they combined with gold, silver, lapis lazuli, and other gemstones in their finest works of art. Wooden chests, game boards, and harps were ornamented with inlays of lapis lazuli, shells, and mother-of-pearl, often separated by bands of gold. Animal heads cast from gold or copper had eyes of white shell inlaid with bits of blue lapis; the manes of lions and the fleece of rams were composed of stylized curls carved from white shells.

These items, and more like them, were taken from the royal tomb of Queen Shub-ad, who reigned with King A-bar-gi about 3000 B.C. (The king apparently died first, and evidence suggests that his "death pit" had been plundered by the very workmen who were burying his wife in an adjacent tomb.) Among the exquisite gold and silver cups, bowls, and lamps placed around her burial couch were two fashioned in the shape of cockleshells. There also were a number of real cockleshells filled with a green paint identified by the archaeologists as a cosmetic—eye shadow for the lady to use in the shadowy world of the other side.

The Egyptians also used shells for ornament, but only in jewelry: polished silver pectorals (medallions to be worn over the chest) shaped like the giant scallop, *Pecten magellanicus*, and pectorals of pearl oyster valves filed smooth; stylized golden cowries strung into necklaces with beads of pale amethyst; real cowries interspersed with other shells and beads; and bracelets of tiny matched snail shells or rectangles of highly polished mother-of-pearl.

"We wanted to restore some of the admiring awe man has experienced throughout history for the work of these strange sea creatures," wrote Marguerite Stix in the introduction to The Shell— Five Hundred Million Years of Inspired Design, which she co-authored with her husband, Hugh Stix. In the process of accomplishing that, Mrs. Stix fashioned some awe-inspiring works of her own. Starting with flawless specimens of natural shells, she added settings and embellishments of gold, silver, and rare gems to create exquisite, shimmering, one-of-a-kind baubles that sell for hundreds and thousands of dollars in the most exclusive shops. "A shell," said Mrs. Stix, "is a beautiful piece of sculpture. There is nothing more exciting."

The Minoans made far more extensive use of shells, probably because they were an island people. The "Men of the Isles," as the Egyptians called them, built a temple to the Great Mother of the Gods, symbol of earth's fertility, and carpeted the floor with seashells in honor of the other deities who ruled the seas. They decorated clay drinking

A famous use of the scallop in art, The Birth of Venus, by Botticelli. Also known as "Venus on the Half Shell," it was painted in 1478.

cups with raised cockleshells, and wine jars with octopuses. On the walls of the palace of King Minos they painted pictures of priestesses, wasp-waisted and bare-breasted, blowing conch horns, and they adorned their burial chambers with conchs rendered in alabaster.

When the Minoan civilization went into decline about 1400 B.C., the cultural center of the Aegean passed to the mainland and Greece. Archaeologists digging in the ruins of Olynthus, an ancient town at the northern end of the Aegean, uncovered a beautifully preserved two-handled burial urn dating from about 370 B.C. Its colors still bright, the urn tells a story that is a recurring theme in Greek art, the birth of Aphrodite, goddess of love and beauty. Fully grown, she rises from a white scallop shell, a miracle witnessed by Poseidon, god of the sea, and Hermes, messenger of the gods. Hovering on outstretched wings in the background is Eros—the fact that in ancient mythology Eros was considered Aphrodite's son apparently disturbing the artist not one whit.

The origin of the legend of Aphrodite—or Venus, as the Romans knew her—is lost in the mists of time. Many of her attributes suggest that she was Asiatic before becoming Greek—she is identified with Ishtar of Assyria and Astarte of Phoenicia. Homer, in the Iliad, calls her the daughter of Zeus and Dione, but other Greek poets speak of her rising naked from the ocean foam in an open scallop shell—the Greek *aphros* means "foam." Greek artists seized the theme eagerly, repeating it in wall paintings, pottery, and figurines, including the small terra-cotta statuettes sold as votive offerings in shops near the goddess's shrines in Athens, Corinth, and other cities.

Other shells seized the Greek imagination. The shape of the turret shell gave Archimedes, mathematician, inventor, and ancient physicist, his idea for the revolutionary helical screw. Another genius, unnamed, found inspiration for the capital of the Ionic column in the growing circle of the interior structure of the chambered nautilus, a perfect logarithmic spiral, with each turn of the shell about three times as broad as the preceding turn.

The Romans, assimilating the Greek pantheon by merely changing the names of the players, showed Venus and her scallop in similar ways, especially in mosaics and murals, some of which have been unearthed in Pompeii. They became particularly enamored of the scallop, the symmetry of which appealed to their engineering genius, and adopted it as a symbolic motif in many architectural applications, such as deeply etched scalloped niches in buildings, altars, and tombs. It was also used in the design of humble domestic utensils, trays, fruit dishes, perfume bottles, and cosmetic jars. The earliest known architectural use of the scallop, a grotto beside a spring at Baniyas in Syria, dedicated to the rustic god Pan, dates from 87 B.C. The idea caught on, and many other shrines using the scallop niche motif were erected in Pompeii and neighboring Herculaneum. In the eastern half of the empire, the shell niche was used on every conceivable type of monument and was especially popular with designers of marble sarcophagi. In fact, the scallop enjoyed an unusual significance in Roman funerary customs, frequently appearing as a medallion behind the portrait busts of the dead, on the stone cists containing the ashes of cremation, and on lead coffins.

Meanwhile, half a world away, the great Indian civilizations of the Americas were using shells in their art in ways strikingly similar to those of the Mediterranean lands. In the Taltal region of Chile, archaeologists opening graves found the lance points and arrowheads expected of a primitive hunting people of 3000 B.C., but also the unexpected—scallop shells that had been worked by some ancient craftsman into drinking vessels or

POSTE AERIENNE RF
NOUVELLE-CALEDONIE ET DEPENDANCES
LAMBIS CHIRAGRA LINNE (PTEROCERES)
50F

ISRAEL
MALEA POMUM
2.00

ISRAEL
CYPRAEA ISABELLA
2.00

GRENADA 75 CENTS
WEST INDIAN FIGHTING CONCH Strombus pugilis

GRENADA 25 CENTS
PURPLE SEA SNAIL Janthina janthina

1'
Chicoreus ramosus
KENYA

長崎鳳凰螺
TIBIA FUSUS (LINNÉ)
1.00
中華民國郵票

GRENADA $1
NOBLE WENTLETRAP Epitonium scalare pernobilis

GRENADA 2 CENTS
YELLOW COCKLE Trachycardium muricatum

50c
Janthina globosa
KENYA

60c
Cassis rufa
KENYA

琉球郵便 RYUKYUS
3c
ライン Lambis

POSTES 10F
Tympanotonus radula
REPUBLIQUE TOGOLAISE

POSTES 20F
Tonna galea
REPUBLIQUE TOGOLAISE

CÔTE FRANÇAISE DES SOMALIS
RF POSTES
25F
STROMBUS TRICORNIS (HUMPHREY)

CÔTE FRANÇAISE DES SOMALIS
POSTES
10c
TRIDACNA SQUAMOSA (LAMARCK)

CÔTE FRANÇAISE DES SOMALIS
POSTES RF
30F
TROCHUS DENTATUS (FORSKAL)

On May 1, 1840, the world's first postage stamp, the famous Penny Black bearing the likeness of young Queen Victoria in profile, went on sale in Great Britian. Only nineteen years later, in 1859, the government of the Bahamas issued its first stamp, also featuring the queen, with another first—a queen conch shell in the lower right-hand corner. Since then, at least fifty countries have issued stamps depicting various members of the mollusk family, either as the main element in the design or in a supporting role. The record for number of appearances? *Turbinella pyrum*, the sacred chank of the Hindus, has appeared on 345 major Indian issues. A visit to shell-stamp producing countries would make a fascinating journey, for in addition to those shown here, the itinerary would include such stops as Japan, the Maldive Islands, the Philippines, the Cook Islands, the Comoros, Cuba, the Netherlands, Fiji, Morocco—even landlocked Switzerland.

lamps. Peruvian vases from 900 B.C. were made to resemble the thorny oyster. Shells were used as containers for perfumes and ointments, not only in their natural state but in reproductions of gold, silver, and pottery. In one legend, Quetzalcoatl, the god-hero of the Mayans, Toltecs, and Aztecs, emerged full-grown from the shell of a gastropod; in others, Peruvian and Toltec fertility goddesses were born in this same Aphroditelike manner, the miracle recorded in painted vases and earthenware figurines. Quetzalcoatl lived in a palace built of shells, says the legend, most of his temples were lavishly decorated with shells, and he was often depicted sitting on a shell pedestal.

The Mayans, whose civilization, the highest in Central America, reached its peak between 300 and 900 A.D., have been likened to the Greeks and Egyptians for their proficiency in mathematics, astronomy, art, and architecture. They decorated their public buildings with shells, used them at burial ceremonies for important personages, used them as cult symbols, and also as receptacles to hold jade and cinnabar, the most precious symbolic objects in their religion. They even used shells in their study of mathematics: Unlike so many early peoples, the Mayans mastered the concept of zero, and represented it in their glyphs by a type of cowrie. Another unusual use was reported by Bishop Diego Landa in 1566 in his *Relacion de las Cosas de Yucatan*, wherein he describes the custom of young girls wearing scallop shells as a pubic covering until they are married.

In the great pueblos and caves of southwestern United States, archaeologists have found many thousands of marine shells from Pacific waters and the Gulf of Mexico. Ancient trade items, they were used primarily for ornamentation, and to a lesser extent for ceremonial purposes. Medicine men made rattles from bivalve shells, boring and stringing them like coins. Tiny snails were strung in necklaces up to forty feet long. One bracelet contained two hundred perfectly matched olive shells set with turquoise; other bracelets, made from the outer rim of clamshells, were worn by the dozens. Cones and olives became bells, rattles, and pendants, sometimes painted or intricately carved with birds, snakes, and other creatures. Mosaics were made of pieces of abalone shells and polished stones; wooden combs and other objects had inlays of shell. An artistic peak was reached at the end of the fourteenth century with such objects as a pink scallop shell, inlaid with turquoise and shaped into the familiar thunderbird motif in such a way that the radiating ribs of the shell simulated the bird's feathers. Indians elsewhere in North America used shells for personal adornment as well as for ceremonial and utilitarian purposes, but rarely did their artistry approach that of the desert dwellers of the Southwest.

Shell bracket under an arch in the Cathedral of St. James of Compostela, 1078.

In Europe, the early Christians continued to use shells as decorative motifs in much the manner as the Romans and Greeks before them. Shells appeared on the coins of seaside cities, on coffins and sarcophagi, and in the shape and form of the mosaic alcoves and dazzling gold canopies discovered in Rome and Ravenna. With the spread of Christianity during the Middle Ages, the scallop of antiquity was depicted in cathedral stained glass windows all over Europe, but more so in the south than in the north, where the ties to the ancient cultures were tenuous at best. For similar reasons, perhaps, shells appear infrequently in the medieval art of Europe, with the notable exception of works devoted to St. James, patron of Spain, whose symbol was the scallop.

The Renaissance took shells and other natural objects from the exclusive province of religion, stripped them of their symbolic trappings, and allowed them to be used in art for what they were—natural objects. Once more the shell appeared as a common decorative and architectural device. The symmetrical scallop, known as "the Venus shell," was especially favored, and was borrowed so frequently as a canopy above Madonna paintings and as a niche for statues that such usage became almost a convention. Bramante's Tempietto in Rome, the forerunner of St. Peter's, is decorated both inside and out with scallop-shaped niches. Verrocchio used the shell often both in paintings and in sculptures. Correggio used them in his frescoes at Parma. They are found in the works of Michelangelo, Filippino Lippi, Raffaelino del Garbo, and countless others.

Not to be forgotten is the famous story of Leonardo da Vinci's design for a spiral staircase, inspired by his study of the snail's interior whorls, which was built into the Château of Blois, where he spent his declining years. Da Vinci's stair has long been credited with being the first of its kind, but it

The Triton Fountain in Rome's Piazza Barberini, one of the most spectacular of Bernini's creations.

is apparently predated by a Mayan tower with an inner circular stairway found at Chichen Itza in Mexico; the Mayan builders called it *caracol*, their word for snail, and the conquistadores put the word into Spanish as meaning spiral stair.

If the scallop was the favorite shell of the Renaissance, then Venus was the favorite subject, which isn't surprising, since renewed interest in the themes from ancient mythology offered a respectable excuse to indulge in the newly discovered fascination with the nude human form. Of all the renderings, the most famous is probably Botticelli's *The Birth of Venus*, now at the Uffizi Gallery in Florence, which shows the goddess,

Above: *To bear public witness to the fact that he was a knight of the order of St. James, patron of Spain, showing the scallop in his family coat of arms wasn't enough for a wealthy Spanish grandee and city official of Salamanca in the early sixteenth century. He built a palace of golden-brown sandstone and studded the exterior wall with some five hundred scallop shells carved of stone. The building still stands, splendidly baroque, and for the convenience of tourists is listed in guidebooks as the* Casa de las Conchas.

Ralph Bigot   Ralph FitzNichol   Martin Chamberlain

Geoffrey de Langley   Oted de Grunson   William Dacre   Robert de Scales

Roger Prychard   William Tracy   Walter de Everyley   Nicholas de Odaingselles

John de Uffard   Simon Crombe   John Danyell   Wat de Malecastre

modestly trying to cover her nakedness with her long golden tresses, preparing to step ashore from a large scallop shell. Titian's *Venus Anadyomene*, somewhat more buxom than Botticelli's and considerably less inhibited, rises directly from the sea, while a scallop shell floats symbolically nearby.

In England, France, and Holland, painters often used shells as decorative elements in portraits, especially when the subject was a naturalist. In Holland, in response to the growing passion for collecting shells and other curiosities from the new lands and displaying them in "cabinets," there developed a new school of artists who specialized in painting collectors in the midst of their collections. Curiously, Rembrandt never depicted shells in his paintings. The single shell among his hundreds of etchings, a marble cone, *Conus marmoreus*, became famous because it was backward—Rembrandt had carefully etched his signature in reverse on the metal etching plate, but drew the shell as he saw it, so that the resultant print was a mirror image, coiling to the left instead of to the right.

By Rembrandt's time, the sixteenth century, shells were disappearing from paintings, as were the formal backgrounds in which for the most part they had been used. But they survived—and thrived—in architecture, sculpture, and the art of gold- and silversmiths. Giovanni Lorenzo Bernini, the great sculptor and architect who had such a strong influence on his peers and followers that he is considered more responsible for the appearance of modern Rome than any other person, created innumerable memorials, buildings, statues, and fountains. What more natural application for the shell motif than in a fountain? And Rome is full of fountains. Bernini's most famous, the Triton Fountain in the Piazza Barberini, shows a merman rising from the sea on two deep scallop valves, blowing spumes of water from a raised trumpet shell.

A fourteenth-century painting by Simone Martini of St. James of Compostela, equipped with pilgrim staff and scallop shell.

Some architectural applications of shells became famous as curiosities. A wealthy city official in Salamanca, proud of his membership in the order of St. James, patron of Spain, built a palace of golden brown sandstone and had the exterior walls studded with hundreds of carved sandstone scallop shells, the scallop being the saint's emblem. The building still stands in its baroque splendor, and is listed in guidebooks as the *Casa de las Conchas*.

With the seventeenth century, the metalsmiths came into their own, creating spectacular pieces in gold and silver, many of which were marked by a lavish use of shells, either in their natural state or worked in precious metals. Chambered nautilus shells, stripped of their outer layers of calcium to reveal the mother-of-pearl underneath, were dressed ornately in gold and silver, mounted on fantastic bases, and used as chalices and cups. Often they were engraved with scenes from far-off lands and embellished with castings of fanciful creatures. Perhaps the most famous example of the metalsmith's art is housed today in New York's Metropolitan Museum of Art. One of the few surviving works of Benvenuto Cellini, the incomparable Renaissance sculptor and designer, the exquisitely rendered piece is thought to be a salt cup, probably ordered as a wedding present for a lady of the nobility. It cannot really be described adequately—a scallop of gold with a gold-and-enamel mermaid serving as a handle, the shell balanced on the wings of a basilisk, itself crouched on the back of a turtle, both creatures also meticulously worked in gold and enamel. In the accepted symbolism of the age, the turtle represented prudence and chastity; the basilisk, eternity and divine vigilance; and the mermaid or siren, a seductive woman.

During the next several centuries, shells gained popularity in a variety of directions. Tableware, snuffboxes, bonbon dishes, wall basins and cisterns all bore the shape of shells. Plaster ceilings took the shape of scallop shells; shell motifs shaped paneling and fireplaces. Thomas Sheraton, the famous cabinetmaker, found many uses for the shell motif and signed his pieces with a shell in marquetry, an idea that led to the creation of a marvelous assortment of marquetry inlays in trays, tea boxes, and tabletops. Thomas Chippendale carved shells into the legs of his tables and chairs, mirror frames, headboards, and secretaries. Pavilion furniture consisted of an entire set of chairs and tables in the form of shells, with each chair seat carved and painted to represent a scallop.

People in England and on the Continent who had both time and the money to spend built fantastic grottoes, pavilions, and fountains out of shells. Called follies, some of them took the form of artificial caves made of rocks, crystals, shrubs, and moss, as well as shells. Others were airy rooms, with the entire interior, both walls and ceiling, decorated with classical architectural elements made of shells. One of the most gracious and famous was the shell pavilion at Goodwood Park in Sussex, England, which the Duchess of Richmond and her two daughters spent seven years, from 1739 to 1746, decorating. Another was the grotto at Oatland's Park, where the Duke of York hosted a lavish supper for the Emperor of Russia and the other victors of the Napoleonic Wars; in addition to pink and white shells, mirrors, and crystal sconces, the grotto had a truly extraordinary feature—one of the corridors leading to it was lined in its entirety with the teeth of horses killed on the field of Waterloo.

Mother-of-pearl became very popular about this time, and thin sections of it were used as inlays in all sorts of objects, from papier-mâché boxes and trays to sewing tables, chairs, tableware, and sword handles. Shells of all sorts became so fashionable, in fact, that importing them developed into a profitable trade. In 1830, for example, a young British businessman named Marcus Samuel established a modest company to trade with the Orient. His shop was located in what was then called Sailors' Town, near the Tower of London, a district devoted to providing the needs of seamen and ships. Intrigued by the colorful shells and shell bric-a-brac brought home by sailors, Samuel bought the shells, mounted them in boxes, and offered them for sale. When they sold well, he and his brother, Samuel Samuel, went into the business in a bigger way, sending manufactured goods to the East and bringing back cargoes of exotic wares, especially the polished seashells that became so dear to the hearts of Victorian ladies. Their

*The seashell creations of Helen Coolidge Woodring, a professional artist of Wilmington, Delaware, have raised an old Victorian craft to new levels artistry. Mrs. Woodring's works follow a variety of themes and styles—African primitive, Pennsylvania Dutch, Art Nouveau, mermaids, elegant crewelwork designs incorporating various animals, and even Rorschach blot patterns, satire, and humor. "The White Unicorn," her interpretation of the famous French tapestry, hangs in Wilmington's distinguished duPont Hotel collection, and she is represented by her shell works in many other American collections, and in London and Paris, as well. Shown here are **(opposite)** a parrot created primarily of blue mussel shells, and **(above)** a geometric pattern called "Kaleidoscope."*

company later grew into a large shipping concern called, appropriately enough, the Shell Transport and Trading Company. Marcus Samuel died in 1874, and his sons, Marcus and Samuel, now running the company, decided to get into a new business. They took on the world monopoly held by John Rockefeller and the great Standard Oil Company by contracting to sell kerosene to fuel the lamps of the Orient. To do this they needed a different kind of ship, and when their first tanker was launched in 1892, they christened it *Murex*, after the famous purple-dye shell of antiquity. Since that time, every tanker carrying the golden scallop trademark of the Royal Dutch/Shell Group of oil companies has been named after a member of the mollusk family.

The Victorian taste for trinkets and clutter included at least one shell on every mantel, shell-

Joan Miró's Composition with Shell, *1931.*

decorated boxes, mirrors, and picture frames, shell paperweights, shell crucifixes and shrines, and miniature shell gardens—shadowboxes or bouquets resplendent with flowers painstakingly put together of natural-color shells. A variation on the theme were "sailor's valentines," hinged wooden boxes filled with small, colorful shells in intricate designs, often with an endearing message spelled out— "Remember Me" or "The Giver Loves You." The tradition was that lonely sailors fashioned these touching souvenirs during their off-watch hours to prove they thought of no one but their wives or sweethearts on the long voyage. The truth, however, offers a different picture. Because there were so many prodigal jack-tars who wasted their time in cards and other vices and therefore faced the icy prospect of going home empty-handed, a lively local business blossomed in Barbados, last port of call for most vessels returning to New England, Great Britain, and the Netherlands. For a fitting fee local craftsmen were happy to provide elaborate samples of their shell handiwork—including endearing messages composed to order. But the secret eventually leaked out—the valentines were always made of shells from the West Indies, the shells were laid on beds of crushed Barbados newspapers, and sometimes the valentines even carried labels, such as "Native Manufacturers in Fancy Work," which careless sailors forgot to remove.

Today we are experiencing a revival of interest in shell crafts—honestly performed—and with the aid of modern adhesives and waterproofing substances the art has soared to new inspirational levels. Modern designers are also reviving one of the oldest of arts, blending gems, precious metals, and shells to make breathtakingly beautiful pendants, bracelets, necklaces, and other articles of jewelry. The ancient art of cameo-carving rose to new heights during the Renaissance, and flourished until economic pressures caused a decline. Even in the great Italian centers of cameo manufacture, Florence and Torre del Greco, few young aspirants could be found with time and patience enough to learn this painstaking and demanding craft. There is hope, however, for a revival in this great art form, with Asia possibly leading the way.

The shell is making a comeback in modern painting, too. Joan Miró, for example, chose a scallop shell as the focal point in a pattern of fascinating shapes, calling his 1931 work *Composition with Shell*. And in the years since, no less-noted an artist than Salvador Dali has used shells, often startlingly lifelike, in a number of paintings, as well as in a huge mural for the Spanish exhibition at the Brussels Fair in 1958.

Many writers have tried to explain the phenomenon of the shell's hold on the imagination of man since the earliest days, but the idea may have been expressed best in a lecture by the distinguished American architect, Frank Lloyd Wright: "Here in these shells we see the housing of the life of the sea. It is the housing of a lower order of life, but it is a housing with exactly what we

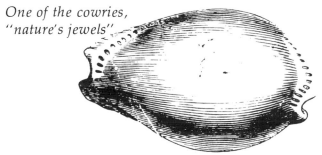

One of the cowries, "nature's jewels"

lack—inspired form. In this collection of houses of hundreds of small beings, who themselves built these houses, we see a quality which we call invention. The beauty of their variations is never finished. It is not a question of principle of design. This multitudinous expression indicates what design can mean. Certainly Divinity is here in these shells in their humble form of life."

Cowrie shells have been called the jewels of the molluscan world, and it's easy to see why: They have a pleasing egglike shape, a glossy enamel shine imparted by nature, and among the family of more than one hundred and eighty species there are many that wear striking designs and beautiful colors. Which makes it all the more difficult to understand why *Cypraea moneta* won its name and fame as the money cowrie, for it is small, not very attractively colored, and so abundant as to be otherwise worthless. Yet this was the shell chosen by early peoples to serve as a form of currency. In fact, it may well have been the very first "money," judging by evidence unearthed at prehistoric burial sites in Egypt, in China, in Russia near the Caspian Sea, in Germany, and in the Scandinavian countries bordering the Baltic Sea. What makes this evidence all the more interesting is the fact that money cowries and *Cypraea annulus*, the gold-ring cowrie, which also served as shell money in some areas, are tropical water snails, occurring primarily in the South Pacific and Indian Oceans, many miles from the burial grounds of northern Europe.

The reasons for the popularity of money cowries as a medium of exchange may well have been the very elements that would have rendered them unmemorable as collector's items—their small size was a convenience, their abundance meant a constant and continuing supply of new money, and their wide distribution gave them instant recognition. They also had the advantage of being easy to string on thongs with little fuss and bother, unlike most other forms of shell money, which had to be cut, shaped, and drilled. They were so widely used, in fact, that when the first metal coins were introduced early in the seventh century B.C. almost simultaneously in Lydia, the wealthy empire of Croesus, and in China, those of the latter were shaped like cowries. A short time later, Greek coins bearing a likeness of the cowrie appeared.

145

The name cowrie, from the Hindi *kauri*, dates from the seventeenth century. The early Greek name meant "little pig," a reference to the shell's smooth, rounded back. Following suit, the Romans called them *porci* or *porculi*, from which was derived the Portuguese *porcelana*. When Portuguese traders brought the first chinaware to Europe from the Orient in 1518, they called it porcelana because its hard, glossy surface was like the shell of the cowrie. The French *porcelaine*, which is the direct antecedent of our word porcelain, served the same double duty. Europe eventually produced beautiful porcelains of its own, but only after a long, difficult struggle, for the composition of chinaware was kept secret for many years. Many people thought it was composed of ground cowrie shells, and one Edward Barosa, who lived in the sixteenth century, claimed that it was made "from marine shells and eggshells buried in the earth for eighty or a hundred years."

The minting of metal coins had little effect on cowrie usage in most areas of the world. Alexander the Great found them being used extensively as currency in India in the fourth century B.C., and Marco Polo saw them serving as money in China in the thirteenth century A.D. As late as 1845, in fact, the official exchange rate for one Indian rupee was sixty-five hundred cowries. Earlier in that century, a European living in Cuttack, on India's northeast coast, paid in cowries to have his bungalow built— 16 million of them! Even more fantastic is the story of the church built in India at a cost of four thousand pounds sterling, but paid for with 160 million cowries.

No one knows when the cowrie was first introduced into Africa as a medium of exchange, but it must have been early, because the eastern coast of the continent is lapped by the waters of the Indian Ocean, the home, along with the tropical Pacific, of *Cypraea moneta*. For hundreds of years, in trade for ivory, cowrie shells by the hundreds of tons were shipped from Ceylon, the Maldive and Laccadive Islands, and other ports in the Indian Ocean, where they occurred in untold millions, to Zanzibar and East Africa. From there, they were traded inland, where tribal leaders counted their wealth in cowrie shells and used them to decorate their canoes, their weapons, their wives, and themselves.

The farther a people lived from the source of the money cowrie, the more they valued it. For this reason, shipmasters of the seventeenth and eighteenth centuries amassed fortunes by trading cheap goods for *Cypraea moneta* and *annulus* in the Pacific islands, and then exchanging the shells for gold, ivory, slaves, and other valuable products on the Atlantic coast of Africa, where neither of the money cowries occurred. Before inflation reared its ugly head, two nice cowries would buy a nice wife. Later, the price leaped to twenty-five hundred, and then out of sight—up to sixty thousand shells for a young, pretty, healthy bride, with twenty thousand the going rate for your everyday wench.

Early in the 1700s, a European traveler watched Arab slave traders weigh out twelve thousand pounds of cowries to pay a black chieftain for six hundred slaves captured during a raid on a neighboring tribe—twenty pounds of shells per slave. Twenty-five hundred shells bought a cow; five hundred a goat; twenty-five a chicken; a fine elephant tusk cost a thousand. Over the course of the next century, as cowries were dumped on the African market in unprecedented numbers, tribal chiefs became cowrie millionaires and prices soared—between twenty and one hundred thousand shells for a single slave, depending upon age, sex, and condition, and between one hundred thousand and a quarter of a million for an elephant tusk.

Cowrie currency—commonly threaded forty shells to a string—was legal tender in many areas well into the nineteenth century, and is said to be acceptable still in some remote areas of Africa and Australia. In the early 1800s, the British still collected revenue from their African holdings in cowries and put the shells right back into circulation on the marketplace. In 1848, when you might expect more modern forms of money to have put the cowries out of business, sixty tons of shells were imported from the East Indies into Liverpool, and the following year the amount quintupled to three hundred tons, all destined for trade on the Guinea coast. The traffic went on at least as late as 1873, for in that year the four-masted bark *Glendowra*, bound for Liverpool from Manila with six hundred bags of money cowries in her cargo, went aground in fog on the Cumberland coast of England and was pounded into pieces by storm-driven surf. For years afterward, delighted shell collectors picking over the Cumberland beaches thought the species had moved north.

Money cowries saw only limited use in the United States. Some have been found in Alabama diggings, but experts believe these were brought over on early Spanish ships in anticipation of trade, a practice that was soon discontinued when the traders learned that the shells held no great charm for East and Gulf Coast Indians. It was a different story out West, however. The Hudson's Bay Company brought money cowries into the Great Lakes area of Canada and north-central United States and traded them to the Crees and other tribes for furs. Not long after, the tribes of the western plains became cowrie addicts when they discovered that from a short distance away the shells were almost indistinguishable from elk's teeth, which were highly prized but were becoming increasingly difficult to obtain.

In the islands of the Indo-Pacific, where money cowries are almost as common as pebbles, other types of money were made from shells. On the volcanic island of Malaita, most populous of the Solomons, women made pierced beads from colorful jewel-box shells (*Chama*) and strung them into bridal belts. Elsewhere in the Melanesian Islands, brides were once purchased with doughnut-shaped disks, two or three inches thick and up to nine inches in diameter, carved from the valves of the giant clam, *Tridacna gigas*. The number of disks in the asking price was determined by the beauty, rank, and connections of the bride-to-be, and many a hot-blooded young man borrowed so many disks from relatives and friends that he was still carving new ones to pay everybody back when the young beauty he had gone into hock for was toothless, wrinkled, and gray.

The Indians of North America used a variety of objects for money. In the upper reaches of the Missouri River, one hundred elk teeth would buy a pack horse; out on the Great Plains and down in pueblo country, the same horse could be had for a dozen perfect tail feathers from the golden eagle. Other mediums of exchange included beads of bone and copper, as well as woodpecker scalps, but the most widely used was shells.

Among the tribes of the Pacific northwest, including coastal Canada and Alaska, the polished white tusk or tooth shell, *Dentalium pretiosum*, was used as money. This tubular univalve shell, shaped like a miniature elephant's tusk, was ideal for stringing into necklaces because it was open at both ends. Gathering it was difficult, however, which accounted in large part for its value. In one common collecting method, the Indian squaw paddled the canoe while her mate dragged a primitive, long-handled rake across the sand or mud of the bottom, hoping to raise a batch of the shells. After removing the animal inside, the squaws sorted the shells and strung them on fine thread made of deer sinew, sometimes artistically adding pieces of iridescent abalone shell and tufts of colorfully dyed goat hair. The size and condition of a shell determined its value, the larger ones, about two and a half inches long, being the most desirable. They were often used as ornaments, and a warrior dressing to the teeth for some ceremonial occasion might wear an especially fine specimen in a hole pierced in his nose.

Used as money, called *hai-qua* or *haik-wa*, the shells were strung in fathom lengths—six feet, or about the distance from fingertips to fingertips of a man's outspread arms. The standard of exchange was established by a strand of twenty-five of the largest and finest shells, which had a value of about fifty dollars in gold. The smaller the shells, the more on a fathom strand and the lower in value the strand—yet at one time a string of forty perfect shells was enough to buy a slave. The smallest shells and defective specimens, strung in varying lengths called *kop-kop*, were used for "making change." The Indians usually wore their store of shell wealth as necklaces, since they had neither pockets in their clothes nor safety deposit boxes, but some carried them in "purses" made of animal horn.

The trade routes brought tusk shells inland, where the Sioux, Cheyenne, Blackfoot, Pawnee, Arapaho, and other plains tribes adopted the custom of using them for personal ornamentation, often decorating themselves from head to toe. The beginning of the end for these shells as a form of currency coincided with the arrival of trappers from the Hudson's Bay Company offering colorful and warm woolen blankets in exchange for furs. The decline was hurried along in the mid-1800s by unscrupulous traders who, playing on the average Indian's ignorance of the value of gold, bought up his metal with great quantities of a much more common tusk shell brought in by the shipload from Europe, depreciating the local shell coinage in the process.

In California, abalone shells were cut into pieces and used as money, and were considered extremely valuable. Along the coasts of the Gulf of Mexico and the southeastern United States, several types of shell money were developed. Indians from Maryland down to the Carolinas, for example, used strings of *roanoke* (also *roenoke* or *roanoak*), which were composed of pieces of cockleshell with holes drilled through for stringing. Since the shell bits were neither uniform nor finished, cockleshell roanoke was not very valuable; nor was the roanoke made from *Marginella* shells, highly polished little snails ranging in size up to an inch. To catch them, the Indians baited lines with oysters, did something else for a while or took a nap, and came back later to haul up the line with its cargo of oysters now covered with carnivorous margin shells. With their tips filed off to facilitate stringing, the colorful little shells made attractive necklaces, but because they were so easily caught they had practically no value to the coastal Indians—so they took them on trading trips and increased their value considerably in bartering with the inland tribes.

The shell money with which most of us are familiar is wampum, the currency used up and down the eastern seaboard of North America and inland along the trade routes. Wampum was made by coastal tribes from New England to Virginia from the shell of a clam which they called *quahog*, which science calls *Mercenaria mercenaria*, and which ordinary people know by a fistful of names—hard clam, hard-shelled clam, round clam, cherrystone clam, little-neck clam, and quahog. The fully grown quahog has a thick, grayish white shell four inches or so in diameter; inside, the shell is white, with a broad band of purple or blue, about a half inch deep, around its lip, much like the border on a Roman senator's toga. The most valuable wampum was made from this colored band; the less valuable, since there was more of it, was made from the white part of the shell, and also from the columella, the axial column and thickest part of various whelk shells.

What is wampum? To us, it is merely shell beads strung and laced together in belts that the Indians used as money. To the Indians, however, it was more than that. In fact, the Indians of Columbus's day and for some time after would not have known what the word wampum meant. They called the disks and cylinders that they cut from the white of the quahog and the whelk *wamp-unp-eeg*, which meant "strings of white beads." The purple beads were called *su-kahn-hog*. These names were too much for the early explorers and colonists to handle. They simplified matters for themselves by lumping all shell money under one shortened name— *wampum* in New England and *peeg*, or *peak*, in Virginia. Some sources maintain that *wampum* referred to the purple disks and *peeg* to the white, no matter where you were. The question soon became academic as *wampum* became the accepted term for all forms of eastern shell money.

Wampum beads, usually about an eighth of an inch in diameter and a quarter to a half inch long, were not easy to make. In one system, the Indian craftsman worked pieces of shell on a grindstone or rubbed them down between two rubbing stones until he had a polished cylinder. In later years, to bore a hole through the bead, he might use a pump drill. This device consisted of a long piece of wood with a triangular metal tip, and a crossbar attached to it by thongs. When the crossbar was pulled down, the thongs stretched out, and when it was released they sprang back, twisting around the drill handle. Rapid up-and-down pressure on the crossbar spun the drill so efficiently that a similar device is still used by jewelers today. A more primitive and time-consuming method, using a sliver of flint or a nail stuck in the end of a cane, was described thusly by an early observer named Lawson: "they roll it continually on their thighs with their right hand,

holding the bit of shell with their left; so, in time they drill a hole quite through it, which is very tedious work."

With the hole drilled through, the beads were strung on a thread made of animal sinew or twisted from filaments of slippery elm, then pulled back and forth between two grooved stones until they were circular, uniform in size, and as smooth as china. This was an important step, for although there were different sizes of wampum, each bead on the same strand had to be exactly the same size. The test came when an Indian pulled a string across his nose; one bead smaller or larger than its fellows was grounds for refusing to accept the whole string. It has been noted that, by attaining this level of perfection even though working without machines, the Indians invented the world's first completely uniform currency, long before the development of uniform metal coins with milled edges.

The art of making shell beads and wampum went far back into the roots of Indian culture. Beads of various sizes and carved gorgets and medallions, also made from the quahog shell, were first used as ornaments. Formed into belts, the wampum originally was used to provide credentials to Indian ambassadors, to record treaties and other important transactions between Indian nations, and to record notable historical events. For these purposes, the beads were dyed various colors and shades, and were strung in complex and often beautiful patterns that could be read by specially trained Indian interpreters. A number of old treaty belts have been preserved, including the famous one that the Delaware tribes of Pennsylvania gave to William Penn as a record of his land treaty with them. Another famous piece of wampum, the war belt on which Pontiac recorded the emblems of the forty-seven tribes and villages that joined in his war of extermination against the white man, was the largest known, six feet long and four inches wide.

The Indians used wampum in other ways, burying it with their dead, paying ransom with it, giving it as a present, and paying the price of blood with it—six strings were the value put on a man's life. Using it as a form of money for everyday buying and selling, however, seems to have started with the arrival of white settlers, who standardized the length at a fathom and put a value of five shillings on it. In 1640, when Massachusetts fixed the value of wampum beads at four white or two purple for a penny, a fathom of the best wampum would buy a beaver pelt. In the early 1700s, wampum was even accepted as fare on the Brooklyn ferry.

In trading among themselves, the Indians measured their shell money in cubits—the distance from the elbow to the tip of the little finger. Whether someone was large or small made no difference; a cubit was the measure from elbow to fingertip. Thus the advantage lay with the big man in buying wampum and with the small man in selling it. Since the Indians were as clever in these matters as any people, it seems likely that they tried to outwit each other by employing a large or small agent on those occasions when their own cubit measure was too long or too short.

They were also as avaricious as any other people, if the remarks of observer Lawson, who held the Indian in low esteem, are to be believed. "This is the money," he wrote of wampum in 1714, "with which you may buy skins, furs, slaves, or anything the Indians have, it being their mammon that entices and persuades them to do anything, and part with everything they possess. . . . As for their wives, they are often sold and their daughters violated for it. With this they buy off murders, and whatsoever a man can do that is ill, this wampum will acquit him and make him, in their opinion, good and virtuous."

It should be noted that Lawson made these comments more than two centuries after the Indian had been introduced to the white man and his ways, and that for a good many of those two hundred years the white brothers, delighted to be in a land where seashells were the coin of the realm, had been trying to counterfeit them. They met with indifferent success at first, mostly because they could not match the patience, skill, and speed of the Indian craftsmen. Lawson, however, saw it another way: "An Englishman could not afford to make so much of this wampum for five or ten times the value. . . . The Indians are a people that never value their time, so that they can afford to make them and never need to fear the English will take the trade out of their hands."

But the English kept trying to do just that, as did the Dutch and others, and eventually the machines of the white settlers won the day—to the extent that Thomas Prince, the governor of Massachusetts, obtained through royal charter a monopoly on the manufacture of wampum in his colony. Eventually, the flood of counterfeit wampum resulted in its being outlawed as a form of currency. As late as 1844, however, two Scots in Bergen County, New Jersey, were still turning out spurious wampum for traders working the tribes of the Far West. But even out in the wilds its value was diminishing. "Below the Sioux," wrote the famous painter and chronicler of Indian life, George Catlin, in 1832, "and all along the whole of our Western frontier, the different tribes are found loaded and beautifully ornamented with it, which they can now afford to do, for they consider it of little value, as the fur traders have ingeniously introduced a spurious imitation of it, manufactured by steam or otherwise, and sold at so reduced a price as to cheapen and consequently destroy the value and meaning of the original wampum."

An epitaph of sorts for wampum was written by to a man named Wood in 1875: "As the white men have introduced tons of imitation wampum made of porcelain, which looks rather better than the real article, and is scarcely one-hundredth part of the value, the veritable wampum is so completely extinct among many of the tribes that, if one of the natives should wish to see a string of wampum, he must go to a museum."

Shells have been important to man as sacred symbols since prehistoric times, when primitive peoples wore them as amulets to ward off evil spirits and endowed them with supernatural powers over love, fertility, and even life after death. The shells most revered in early cultures were the cowries, which were widely regarded as sexual symbols, and have served as bridal gifts in primitive societies from the earliest days right up to recent times. The reason for the almost universal association of sex with the cowrie, anthropologists tell us, is traceable to a similarity in appearance between the underside of the live animal extruded from its shell and the female genitalia. The Romans called the cowrie *concha Venerea*, "the shell of Venus," and the mollusk's genetic name, *Cypraea*, was taken from Cyprus, the eastern Mediterranean island where the cult of the love goddess, Aphrodite in Greek and Venus in Roman mythology, originated.

Even a partial collection of cowrie contributions to mysticism through the ages and around the world makes an impressive list:

- Cowries were worn as breast and girdle female symbols by Cro-Magnon women, as evidenced by skeletons found in caves and prehistoric burial mounds in Germany, England, and Egypt.
- In Pompeii, women wore cowries to prevent sterility.
- In New Zealand, Maori women wore headbands of cowrie shells until their first child was delivered.
- In the Congo, young women wore a cowrie girdle to ensure both fertility and an easy delivery.
- In some South Pacific islands, an easy delivery was obtained by wearing a cowrie necklace during pregnancy.
- Even today in the Ryukyus and other parts of Asia, mothers-to-be clench cowries—preferably large ones, such as the tiger cowrie, *Cypraea tigris*—in each hand to help ease the pains of childbirth. The Japanese call this shell *koyasu-gai*, the "easy delivery shell."
- To guard their seeds against infertility, island farmers in the South Seas buried an egg cowrie at the end of each row of crops.
- The people of Togo and Dahomey used to put money cowries in graves so that their deceased relatives and friends could pay the ferryman for rowing them across the "great river," and would be able to buy food and pay their way on the other side.
- Ancient Egyptians put cowries over the eyes of their mummies to guarantee sight in the hereafter.
- Many Pacific islanders believed that "the sound of the sea" in a cowrie held close to the ear was really the voice of God.
- In the Congo, wooden fetishes looked down on ritual dances with eyes made of cowrie shells.
- Both the Algonquin Indians in Canada and cannibal tribes in Sierra Leone worshiped sacred cowries, taking them on hunting trips for luck and consulting them as oracles in time of war.
- In ancient China, the dead were buried with money cowries in their mouths as a surety that they would eat and live well in the next world. But even after death, status had to be maintained: The Son of Heaven, as the emperor was called, ranked at the top with a mouthful of nine shells; a feudal lord got stuffed with seven; an important official rated five; a minor official, three. Common folk had to be satisfied with a mouthful of rice, but this might be supplemented for the more affluent middle class by a cowrie tucked behind the last two molars.

While the cowrie was the most widely used sacred shell, others received their share of attention. Fiji Islanders believed that a left-handed whelk in the home was a prerequisite to family fruitfulness. Mexico's Aztecs depicted several of their gods and goddesses being born from conch shells. Many Polynesians believed that their god was present in the trumpet shells they blew during religious rites. Pueblo dwellers in New Mexico used jingling "bell straps" during the ritualistic corn dance held late every summer, the "bells" being large olive shells cut in half. In other ceremonies, the Indians of the Southwest used abalone shells as containers for sacred corn meal and the colored sands used in sand painting. Shinto priests in Japan used triton shells to call the faithful to service. And as late as the Middle Ages in Europe, snails emerging from their shells were used to symbolize the Resurrection.

One of the most revered shells of all time is the sacred Indian chank, *Turbinella pyrum*, a cream-colored, pear-shaped gastropod only five or six inches long but so densely constructed that it feels as heavy as lead. According to the ancient Hindu legend, an evil spirit stole the sacred writings during the time of the great flood and hid them in a chank shell. Vishnu, incarnation of the supreme being, took the form of a fish and dived into the sea, bringing both shell and scriptures back to dry land. Ever since, all Hindu representations of Vishnu show him carrying the chank shell in one hand, and the shell itself has exerted an uncommon influence over the lives of countless millions of Hindus.

At the beginning of their daily worship, Brahmans, members of the priestly caste, pray first to a chank shell held in the left hand, as Vishnu did, that their prayers may be heard. Every sepoy warrior once carried a talisman cut from the chank shell, and many wore necklaces of "buttons," called *krantha*, cut from the top of the shell. In the early Indian epics, the heroes urged on their warriors in battle by blowing loud blasts on their chank trumpets, each of which carried an exalted name, such as Sweet Voice, Lion's Roar, Jewel Blossom, and Eternal Victory.

Instead of bracelets of gold or silver, Hindu brides wear great numbers of beautifully lacquered and bejewelled armlets, anklets, bangles, and spangles cut from chank shells by craftsmen equally adept with either hand or foot saws, and sometimes both. When a woman dies, her chank ornaments are buried with her, a custom that may have started in prehistoric times: Neolithic and early Iron Age burial sites on the Tungabhadra River have given up bangles made from chank shells and cowries. Necklaces and amulets of chank shell are worn as charms against sickness and the evil eye, and lucky is the house with a whole chank shell buried in its foundations.

Like its close relative, the lamp conch of the West Indies, the chank, beautifully carved by Hindu artists, is used as an oil lamp in temples. Chanks also serve as storage containers for ceremonial oils, and as dispensers of medicine for the sick. Fortunate indeed is the person who finds a rare sinistral, or left-handed, specimen of a chank shell, for he is regarded as a special protégé of Vishnu, worthy of reverence from family and friends. These shells, highly venerated, are elaborately carved, inlaid with gold or even encased in it, set with precious stones, and treated as holy relics in the temples. Since left-handedness in a shell has so much religious significance in India, and since reversed chank shells are so relatively rare, clever entrepreneurs have racked up considerable success by importing quantities of Florida's normally left-handed lightning whelks, *Busycon contrarium*, and selling them as an affordable substitute.

Although it is not as ancient as the tradition of the sacred chank, the legend of how the scallop shell came to be the symbol of St. James, patron of Spain, and the emblem of pilgrims is fascinating. After the ascension of Jesus, one of the original twelve apostles, St. James the Greater, traveled to Spain to preach the gospel. His efforts were not notably successful, and after a few years he returned, with a few of the disciples he had gathered, to Jerusalem. There, in 44 A.D., he incurred the displeasure of Herod Agrippa and was beheaded, becoming the first of the apostles to suffer martyrdom. As it is recorded in the Acts of the Apostles: "Herod the king stretched forth his hand to vex certain of the church. And he killed James, the brother of John, with the sword."

So much for accepted facts. Now the legend, which originated in the eighth century, takes over, and with the help of some fabulous embroideries added in succeeding centuries, creates quite a vivid tapestry.

After the murder, seven of James's disciples rescued his remains and set sail for Spain in a ship that was piloted by an angel or a superhuman being. As they were cruising along the coast of Galicia, in the northwest corner of Spain, they passed a marriage procession on the shore. The bridegroom's horse, apparently frightened by the incorporeal helmsman on the vessel, bolted and galloped headlong into the sea. When the horse and rider surfaced and made it back to land, they were not only dry and unharmed, but were thickly encrusted with scallop shells—a miracle attributed to the presence of the saint's body.

Pulling into the port of Iria, now known as Padron, the travelers sought audience with Queen Lupa, pagan ruler of the region, and begged for a burial place for the apostle's body, this being the area where he had concentrated his missionary efforts. She referred them to the king, who promptly threw them into prison. Through some mysterious agency, perhaps the superhuman

being who had brought them to those inhospitable shores, they just as promptly escaped. The king chased them with his army, but came to a bad end with all his men when a bridge collapsed under their weight. The disciples now returned to Lupa, who offered them a pair of oxen to pull the cart in which they had placed the body of James—but treachery was afoot, for the oxen really were wild bulls. Nothing daunted, the disciples tamed the bulls with the sign of the cross, hitched them to the cart, and presented themselves once again to Queen Lupa— after dispatching a dragon along the way. Suitably impressed by all these wonders, the queen became a convert and turned her palace over to the disciples, who converted it, too, into a church. Here St. James was buried, with two of his faithful disciples eventually joining him, Athenasius on his right hand, and Theodore on his left.

During the next eight centuries, the palace-church disappeared, and the grave of St. James was lost. Then, early in the ninth century, a hermit named Pelayo had a dream in which the burial place of the saint was revealed to him. He related this vision to Theodemir, bishop of Iria, and at the location prescribed they found a small gravestone reading, "Here lies St. James, son of Zebedee and Salome, brother of John, whom Herod beheaded in Jerusalem." They also found the bones of the apostle and his two disciples. The date given for this discovery by an eleventh-century document was 808 A.D., and before too many more years had passed the news had spread throughout France and as far as Rome. King Alfonso II of the Asturias (791– 842) built a church over the crypt and called it Santiago de Compostela. Santiago is a sort of abbreviation of St. James in Spanish, and Compostela is a corruption of *campus stellae*, "field of the stars," and apparently refers to mysterious lights which played an important part in the vision of the hermit Pelayo.

The walled city of Compostela grew up around the shrine, which enjoyed only local fame until the eleventh century. This was a time when pilgrimages to holy places were popular ways of doing penance for sins committed and gaining indulgences. With the Holy Land occupied by infidels, Rome became the goal of most pilgrims. But then somebody "discovered" Santiago de Compostela, which was considerably closer to France, Germany, England, the Low Countries, and, of course, Portugal and Spain. Before long, the roads to Compostela—primarily the four old Roman roads across France to the Pyrenees—were packed with pilgrims. This large and growing siphoning-off of peripatetic penitents apparently did not sit too well with church authorities in Rome, for in 1049 the bishop of Santiago was excommunicated for giving excessive indulgences and using such pretentious phrases as "Apostolic See" in his title without authorization.

This did nothing to stem the tide of pilgrims following the "Way of St. James" from all over Europe over the next several centuries. In England alone, during one six-month period at the turn of the fifteenth century, one hundred and twenty-three shiploads of pious souls set sail from Bristol and other southern ports for Spain. Hundreds of other pilgrims crossed the Channel and made the overland trek down through France and across the Pyrenees along routes marked out in official travel guides.

How did the scallop shell become involved in all this? It is popularly believed that the first pilgrims to the shrine, going down to the beach to bathe after paying their respects and making their petitions, found the sands littered with shells of the beautiful Mediterranean scallop, now called the St. James scallop, *Pecten jacobaeus*, and decided to take a hatful home as a sign that they had completed the pilgrimage. This makes a pretty story, but one of doubtful authenticity, especially since the shrine is

some sixteen miles inland over hill and dale from the beach, and the beach is on the Atlantic coast of Spain, where the resident scallop is *Pecten maximus*. A far more likely explanation, according to reputable sources, is that fishermen shipped scallops by donkey cart over the hills to Santiago, where they were sold as food, and that some clever huckster began collecting the empty shells and hawking them to pilgrims as souvenirs of St. James—remember the miracle of the scallop-covered bridegroom rising from the sea?

The first concrete evidence that scallops had become the accepted badge of pilgrimage to Santiago occurs in a twelfth-century guidebook which states that shells to be attached to the cloaks of pilgrims were on sale in booths around the paved court north of the cathedral. The book also tells of an English knight miraculously cured of goiter by the touch of a pilgrim's scallop shell, and offers an explanation of the mystical meaning of the shell as a pilgrim badge.

From this point, the association of the scallop shell with St. James and his shrine at Compostela became so firmly entrenched that statues of the apostle always showed him with a scallop shell, usually attached to the pilgrim's hat he is wearing, and pilgrims took to having a representation of the shell embroidered on their cloaks on their way *to* the shrine. Variations on the legend of the bridegroom in the sea began to circulate, some of which converted the horseman to St. James himself. Another legend told of a great battle with the Moors in which St. James miraculously appeared, astride a white horse caparisoned in a rich housing decorated with scallop shells, and led the Christian host to victory.

As a result of all this emphasis on scallops, the selling of the shells at Santiago became so scandalously commercialized that several popes had to step in with corrective measures. Some say the

154

papacy gave the priests of Santiago de Compostela the power to excommunicate anyone who sold shells anywhere but at the shrine itself; others say that the new rules banned the sale of shells anywhere near the shrine or town; and still others maintain that by papal order the local church authorities exercised the right to confiscate all scallop shells and control all scallop shell sales. Whichever version is correct, it did not reduce the popularity of sales of the shell, which became so scarce locally that supplies had to be shipped in from other regions.

In 1493, Ferdinand and Isabella took time out from listening to Columbus's tales of the New World and founded the Knights of St. James, an order devoted to protecting and succoring the droves of pilgrims traveling to and from Compostela; their coat of arms bore a cross ending in a blood-red sword and a scallop shell. Many of those who made the pilgrimage put the scallop in their family arms upon returning home as a way of commemorating their feat—which in many ways it was, considering the tribulations and dangers of travel at the time.

One last point should be made regarding the pilgrim practice of attaching a scallop shell to cloak or hat. While the shell did announce to the world that the wearer had been to the shrine of St. James at Compostela, it was more than just a medieval bumper sticker. It apparently also served as a protective symbol, not only for the journey back but for all time: In many twelfth- and thirteenth-century churches there are sculptures and paintings of the Last Judgment that show the dead rising from their graves at the summons of the angel's trumpet, many of them holding aloft the pilgrim's shell as a "do-not-touch" sign to the waiting demons.

The overland Pilgrim's Way to Compostela followed the old Roman roads, marked by the solid lines. Dotted lines represent alternative routes.

Arms and crest of Sir Thomas Shank; from a manuscript ca. 1550.

The "little art and science" of heraldry, long associated with the aristocratic knightly caste, has roots that extend back to mankind's earliest days, when primitive tribes developed emblems, insignia, totems, and other devices to distinguish and identify themselves. These symbols were essentially picture words, and therefore rank among our first forms of visual communication. Peoples of all cultures and times used them, and it was from them that emerging civilizations developed their banners and seals and hereditary markings. The early Japanese, for example, devised a system of family emblems among the nobility that can be considered a form of heraldry; and Homer mentioned ancient Greek warriors carrying shields on which distinguishing symbols and devices were painted.

Heraldry as we know it, however—and it is more accurately called armory—was a feudal institution, developed by European knights during and following the Crusades of the twelfth and thirteenth centuries. Its rather sudden emergence is attested to in a reverse sort of way by the Bayeux Tapestry, attributed by tradition to Queen Matilda, wife of William the Conqueror, and her handmaidens. On an embroidered band of coarse linen, more than two hundred and thirty feet long by twenty inches wide, the so-called tapestry shows detailed—and fantastically accurate—scenes of the Norman invasion and conquest of England in the middle of the eleventh century. The type of armor that the knights wore and the various kinds of shields they carried are vividly illustrated, but nowhere on the tapestry does a coat of arms appear.

Why, then, did heraldry suddenly blossom? No one knows for sure, but it is generally assumed that the development of full suits of articulated armor brought a serious need for identification—with horsemen sheathed in metal from head to toe and hidden behind great shields, some distinguishing sign had to be added, not only to be able to tell friend from foe, but to enable the knight's foot soldiers to recognize him and follow him into battle. It was important to the heralds, too, who in time of war carried challenges, made a note of the men of rank present at a battle, and recorded the names of those lying dead after it.

Ready recognition was also a factor during the tournaments that characterized the times—those violent but chivalric games and contests by which the knights kept themselves and their steeds in combat condition. The step from training exercise to spectator sport was a short one, and gave the herald a new function not unlike that of today's sportscasters—to call out the insignia of the combatants, to announce their titles and won-and-lost jousting records, and to note their standing in the lists. To accomplish this, the heralds had to be able to identify contestants on sight, so keeping a record of armorial bearings and their owners followed naturally. Eventually, when full armor went out of style and the clash and clangor of tournaments were heard no more, the principal heralds were organized into a college of heraldry to serve as keepers and arbiters of the system—for instead of falling into disuse, the practice of creating personalized emblems on a shield was being picked up by all sorts of organizations, as well as by individuals who had never borne arms in battle: merchants, clergymen, scholars, craftsmen, and even, says one source, peasants.

There is a popular idea that every coat of arms tells a story, but this is much exaggerated. In the earliest days, when the emblems were simple and functional, a man might choose a lion for his standard as a symbol of his courage. Thus, the great seal of Richard I in 1189 displays a shield charged with a rampant lion; this, incidentally, was the first time an English sovereign's seal showed arms. Another man might choose a cross to show that he

had participated in the Crusades. And a surprising number of symbols were chosen simply and purely as pictorial puns, usually a play on a family name.

Some of these punning arms were so obscure as to be unintelligible in the language today, but others are obvious allusions: herrings for Herringaud, cocks for Cockfield, a roach for Roche, trumpets for Trumpington, scallop shells for one family named Shelley and whelk shells for another. (A very old book of heraldry depicts three creeping land snails for Shelley, with this explanation: "The bearing of snail doth signify that much deliberation must be shown in matters of great importance; for, albeit the snail goeth slowly, yet in time, by her constancy in her course, she ascendeth the top of the highest hill.")

The armorial bearings of Winch of Everton, 1669, Royal College of Arms of England.

Less obvious but translatable are crows (corbies) for Corbet; a portcullis (windy gate) for Wingate; swallows (hirondelles) for Arundel; and more scallop shells for Scales, which is close to the Anglo-Saxon word *skal* and the Dutch word *schelp*, both of which mean "shell." It is plain to see that the knights of medieval times did not consider the pun to be the lowest form of humor, and it would be interesting, therefore, to note their reaction to the biting comment of John Dennis, seventeenth-century playwright and critic: "A man who could make so vile a pun would not scruple to pick a pocket."

The use of shells in heraldry is not, however, limited to pictorial punning. While by no means as popular as lions, swords, bulls, and other heroic symbols, shells show up consistently—especially scallop shells, which are a principal part of the design in approximately four of every one hundred known English coats of arms. In round figures, this

Below: *Medieval knights carry armorial banners.*

Opposite: *Illumination in a copy of Froissart's Chronicles, including the arms of Philippe de Commynes, ca. 1450.*

works out to more than nine hundred English arms alone with scallops in them—names like Chamberlain, Langley, Bigot, FitzNichol, Spence-Colby, Tracy, Hopwood, and Danyell. Add to these the scallop-decorated arms from other lands—Conolly and Graham from Ireland, for example, and D'Amanzé, de Roton, and de Pompery from France—and you get some idea of the widespread acceptance of the shell as an important device in heraldry.

This popularity may be accounted for, at least in part, by the scallop's religious significance as the traditional badge of St. James, worn by knights returning from the Holy Wars and by pilgrims on their way home from the saint's shrine at Compostela, in Spain. Thomas Fuller, an English physician who died in 1734 at the ripe old age of eighty, is said to have penned these lines:

> The scallop shows a coat of arms,
> That, of the bearer's line,
> Some one in former days hath been
> To Santiago's shrine.

Coats of arms with scallop shells that clearly refer to the Crusades include that of the family Villiers,

which has shown five golden shells on a red cross since Sir Richard de Villiers took part in the crusade of Prince Edward. The Villiers arms returned to "the wars against the infidels" in the sixteenth century when Villiers de L'Isle-Adam, last Grand Master of the Knights of St. John of Rhodes, led the heroic defense of Rhodes against the forces of Suleiman the Magnificent. The arms of John Kendal, prior of the English Knights of St. John of Jerusalem in 1480 and commander of the mounted units pledged to protect pilgrims from the Turks, bore a cross and three scallop shells. Sir Walter Scott's lines describing Lord Dacre's "banner tall/ That streamed o'er Acre's conquered wall," refer to the exploits of the knight at the siege of Acre during the Third Crusade, exploits commemorated by three silver scallop shells on a field of red.

The scallop also shows up surprisingly often in St. George's Chapel in Windsor Castle, where each of more than seven hundred stall plates bears the arms of a Knight of the Garter, Britain's highest order, founded by King Edward III in 1348. The five silver scallops on a cross of black of Sir John de Grailly, one of the founding members of the order, are there, along with the arms of such other well-known names from English medieval history as Sir John Fastolfe, Thomas Lord Scales, Sir William Chamberlain, Thomas Lord Dacre of Gillesland, the Villiers, and the Russells, Dukes of Bedford.

The Order of the Garter is still very much in existence, and in recent years welcomed two new members whose names should be familiar to most of us, Sir Anthony Eden and Sir Winston Churchill—both with arms that prominently display scallop shells.

Shell collectors who are also stamp collectors have the best of two fascinating worlds. While adding to their conchological treasures, they can extend their hobby by collecting shells on stamps. More and more countries—at least fifty, according to one recent count—have been issuing stamps depicting members of the mollusk family, either as the main element in the design or in a supporting role, and the total of more than two hundred and fifty issues is enough to make shell-stamp collecting a challenging and rewarding pastime.

Although prepaid postage, through the use of postage stamps, is a comparatively recent development, postal services of one sort or another can be traced to antiquity. The Old Testament refers to a system that utilized swift runners and

Arms and heraldic standard of Lord Dacre of Gillesland, ca. 1525.

couriers on horses, camels, and dromedaries; Herodotus mentions "message-carrying" by relays six centuries before Christ; and the Persian kings Cyrus and Darius did much to refine and extend the ancient systems. Further improvements were added in later ages, and the postal service of antiquity reached its high point as the *cursus publicus* in Rome's Augustan age—aided not a little by the empire's network of paved roads. Succeeding centuries saw a variety of message-carrying systems, with payment for the service invariably being levied on the recipient of the message, except for the penny a letter charged by British sea captains to carry correspondence between the mother country and the American colonies in the first half of the seventeenth century.

This was the nearest approach to prepaid postage until the nineteenth century. Then came the invention of the adhesive label in 1834 by James Chalmers, a printer of Dundee, Scotland. A number of people, including Chalmers and Rowland Hill, a schoolmaster, recognized the possibility of utilizing the new labels in a long-overdue reform of the existing postal service, but it is generally to Hill that credit is given for making the reform work. His idea was revolutionary—a "Uniform Penny Post," which charged a flat rate of one penny for a one-ounce letter, no matter how far it had to travel.

After considerable debate, the British Parliament passed a bill in 1839 to establish universal penny postage, and put Hill in charge of the program. The treasury department instituted a competition for the design of the proposed stamps, and after more than two thousand entries were examined, the nod was given to Hill's original suggestion—a vertical rectangle bearing the likeness of young Queen Victoria in profile. The famous Penny Black, the world's first postage stamp, went on sale May 1, 1840, and was followed quickly by the Twopenny Blue.

The adhesive stamps were an immediate success. Switzerland and Brazil adopted the system in 1843, and by 1850 the custom had spread worldwide. In the United States, although several local postmasters had previously printed provisional stamps, the first official issue was not released until 1847. It is interesting to note that, when the Universal Postal Union, formed in 1874, decreed that a country's name had to appear on its stamps, Britain alone was exempted as a mark of honor for having invented postage stamps; to this day, the portrait of the reigning monarch on British stamps is considered identification enough.

On June 10, 1859, only nineteen years after the appearance of the Penny Black, the Bahama Islands, a British crown colony comprising more than three thousand islands, cays, and rocks in the West Indies, issued its first postage stamp. Purplish red and valued at one pence, it carried a portrait of Queen Victoria, as did all British stamps at the time. What makes it of special interest is the reproduction in the lower-right-hand corner of a queen conch, *Strombus gigas*. The shell is crudely drawn, but it is noteworthy as the very first mollusk to appear on a postage stamp. Since then, the conch shell has appeared somewhere in the design of most of the shells of the Bahamas, with those issued in 1902 being notable for the introduction of a somewhat more realistic and recognizable rendering of the shell. In 1959, to mark the centenary of Bahamian stamps, the Bahamas reproduced the original version of its first stamp, but substituted the likeness of Queen Elizabeth II for that of Victoria.

The queen conch has also been shown with regularity in the corners of the stamps issued by the Cayman Islands, another British West Indies colony. For its first featured appearance, however, it had to wait almost a century after its initial supporting role. That moment arrived on November 25, 1957, when Turks and Caicos

Islands issued a pictorial series prominently displaying the queen conch with a fishing boat in the background, an obvious tribute to the shell's commercial value not only in chowders and "steaks," but as a raw material for cameos, lime, garden ornaments, road paving, and porcelain-making.

The record for number of appearances on stamps may be held by *Turbinella pyrum*, the Indian chank, sacred shell of the Hindus and national emblem of the early Kingdom of Travancore. Between 1888 and 1951, the chank was shown in stylized form on three hundred and forty-five major issues of India's feudatory states of Cochin and Travancore, which have since become a part of Kerala state.

For the first bivalve to appear on a stamp we must go to the Somali Coast, at one time a French overseas territory in eastern Africa, where a 1915 series used the St. James scallop, *Pecten jacobaeus*, as a background for the stamps' figures of value. Somali stamps also have pictured the true pearl oyster, *Pinctada margaritifera*, the three-horned wing shell, *Strombus tricornis*, and the toothed top shell, *Tectus dentatus*. Another bivalve, the giant clam, *Tridacna gigas*, was first seen on a stamp in the upper corners of a 1938 three-shilling Cook Islands issue. It appeared the same way again in 1945, and then in a more oval manner in a 1949 issue, which used the outline of the clam as a frame around the central design, a map of the island of Aitutaki. A 1962 Comoro Islands one-hundred-franc airmail issue also featured the giant clam, while its cousin, *Tridacna squamosa*, the giant spined clam, has appeared on stamps issued by Somali and the Philippines. There have been others—Dubai, one of the emirates in the Persian Gulf, honored the edible cockle, *Cardium edule*, and one of the oysters in its first issue in 1963—but by and large bivalves have not been given equal time on stamps with gastropods.

The first fossil mollusk to appear on a stamp was the Berber ammonite, *Berbericeras sekikensis*, a fifteen-franc beauty issued by Algeria in 1952 to mark the meeting of the Nineteenth International Geological Congress in Algiers. Ammonites belonged to the early shelled cephalopods that flourished during the Carboniferous period and became extinct at the end of the Cretaceous. Their shells were chambered, much like those of the modern chambered nautilus, *Nautilus pompilius*, and some of them reached the extraordinary size of six and a half feet in diameter. Fossil ammonites have also found considerable favor with stamp designers in Cuba, Switzerland, and the Netherlands.

Living cephalopods have not been ignored by the stamp designers. In 1944, to honor the twelfth anniversary of the German Goldsmith's Society, Germany issued a stamp showing the chambered nautilus couched in gold and mounted as a goblet. The Ryukyu Islands in 1962 issued a flora and fauna set, with one stamp showing the nautilus, along with a banded sea snail and a map cone. Later that year, New Caledonia, located in the area of the Pacific where the umbilicate nautilus, *Nautilus macromphlus*, abounds, showed the shell alone, and in its natural state, on a twenty-franc airmail issue. Two other south Pacific islands followed suit, the Fiji Islands using the nautilus in the design of a one-and-a-half-pence stamp late that same year, and New Hebrides featuring it the following year on two thirty-centime stamps, one a British and the other a French version.

The argonaut, or paper nautilus, *Argonauta argo*, appears on stamps of Yugoslavia, New Hebrides, and Tunisia; the common octopus, *Octopus vulgaris*, on those of Uruguay, Togo, and San Marino; the cuttlefish makes the scene in Dubai. The chambered nautilus also is featured in a spectacular series of issues from Papua and New Guinea. Other

Shell stamps

shell-stamp collectors specialize in the anomalies and freaks—the sinistral specimens, the color variants, and other printing errors. Many right-handed shells have been shown in reverse; shell identifications have been given incorrectly; shells that have never occurred naturally in a country's offshore waters are included among indigenous species.

All these are collector's items. But for shell collectors, the most singular shell-stamp has to be the one "issued" in Uganda by the Rev. Ernest Millar, a missionary, in 1896. Devoid of illustration, the stamp is a square of paper on which the good reverend had typewritten a stipulated value of twenty cowries.

mollusks in the series include the glory-of-the-sea cone, *Conus gloriamaris*, at one time the most valuable of shells; the glistening white egg cowrie, *Ovula ovum*, popular for personal adornment in the Pacific and for decorating houses, canoes, and graves; the striking scorpion conch, *Lambis scorpius*, and the ever-popular Pacific triton, *Charonia tritonis*.

A shell-stamp journey around the world would lead us to many other fascinating ports of call: to Japan for the emperor's slit shell, *Perotrochus hirasei*; to Mauritius for the episcopal miter, *Mitra mitra*; to the Maldive Islands for *Conus aulicus* and *Distorsio reticulata*; and to Anguilla, Singapore, French Polynesia, Taiwan, Malagasy, Wallis and Futuna Islands, Togo, New Zealand, Kenya, Brazil, and Seychelles, Barbados, Morocco, Monaco, and other points north, south, east, and west.

Collecting shell-stamps has become even more popular since Lee and Stu Armington with their exhibit of seashells on stamps won the du Pont trophy, shelldom's major award, at the prestigious Hawaiian Malacological Society Shell Show in the autumn of 1972. Just as with shell hobbyists, many

Mankind's oldest use for mollusks is still the most important one. Oysters, clams, scallops, mussels, and other members of the family, among the first sources of protein for our food-gathering forebears, today provide the "harvest" for an industry that employs many thousands of men and women all over the world and represents the investment and turnover of millions of dollars every year. Fleets of specially equipped trawlers scoop huge quantities of oysters and clams from the bottom of bays and coastal shallows, while other ships head into open waters to dredge for deep-sea scallops. The countries with the most modernized shell fisheries, Japan, the United States, and the maritime nations of Europe, harvest well over 1 billion pounds of oyster meat a year, another 1 billion pounds of clam meat, and some 300 million pounds of scallops, the latter being not less desirable but less abundant.

Seafood lovers in this country have a smaller list of mollusk delicacies to choose from because they have not become familiar with some favorites of other lands, such as cockleshells, jingle shells, limpets, conchs, ark shells, and whelks. As a matter of fact, practically all mollusks are edible. Some may be so tough as to be indigestible, and others have a stomach-churning flavor, but no species is known to be of itself poisonous as food—except during reproduction periods, when the reproductive organs of some species become toxic. Large octopuses are capable of inflicting fatal bites, and the venomous cones of the Pacific have stung and killed at least ten people. But the sickness that sometimes comes from eating mollusks is often of an allergenic nature, or occurs because the animals have been taken from polluted waters and are contaminated with bacteria. Infectious hepatitis and typhoid outbreaks have been traced to oysters and clams collected in sewage-polluted areas; the more serious cases of gastrointestinal poisoning are almost always caused by typhus bacilli.

The mollusks most dangerous to health are those that have ingested *Gonyaulax*, microscopic dinoflagellate algae that are poisonous to man. Eating them can cause paralysis and even death. Most poisonings occur in the summer and early fall, for the algae—*G. tamarensis* on the Atlantic coast and *G. acatenella* on the Pacific—"bloom" in prodigious numbers when the temperature of the ocean rises. Fortunately, the special conditions that these algae require for development are comparatively rare, and when they do occur, do so in limited areas.

On the other hand, there are also exciting possibilities that mollusks and members of other marine clans will contribute generously to man's pharmacopoeia in the not too distant future. Researchers have discovered that raw abalone juice contains a substance that is effective against a number of penicillin-resistant bacteria, and are hopeful of finding in it a cure for poliomyelitis. Other scientists are seeking cures for cancer from certain land snails; for diabetes and allergies from seaweed; for gout from ray fishes; for tuberculosis from sea slugs and sea sponges; and for major heart disease and some types of mental illness from the octopus.

If all this sounds a little farfetched, keep an open mind. A substance called mercenine, extracted from the hard-shelled clam, has inhibited the growth of experimental cancers in mice. A local anesthetic rated as *one hundred thousand times* more powerful than cocaine or procaine has been made from mussels that have absorbed large amounts of toxic matter from polluted waters. And experiments have shown that raw oyster juice has antiviral properties—thus confirming the advice given by Pliny, so many years ago, to eat raw mollusks for relief of sore throats and wracking coughs. As a matter of fact, snails have been used for treating bad colds and consumption for centuries.

Even the empty shells of dead mollusks serve useful, if mundane, roles in our modern world. Tons of broken shells are used to pave roads in many coastal areas. More tons, burned and crushed, are shipped to poultry farms where they provide needed calcium to baby chicks and egg-laying hens. Cuttlebone is used not only to give caged birds their ration of calcium, but also in toothpaste and face powders. Iridescent abalone shells, hung on poles by farmers in the Channel Islands, off France's Normandy coast, swing in the wind and flash reflected light to frighten away hungry birds. Despite the inroads of plastics, mother-of-pearl shells are still used to make beautiful buttons, buckles, combs, teething rings, and fishing lures, and ground up into a powder impart to certain types of paints an otherwise unobtainable glowing luster. And now being imported into this country from the western Pacific is the remarkable windowpane oyster, *Placuna placenta*, whose translucent, almost flat valves have been used for centuries in the Philippines and East Indies as a substitute for glass in screens, windows, lamp shades, and ornaments.

No list of molluscan contributions to our

civilization would be complete without mentioning the jewels of the sea, pearls, which have been treasured for their beauty since 1500 B.C. in Egypt. Surely neither they nor their uses fall into the category of commonplace things, yet even that can depend upon one's point of view. In *Twenty Thousand Leagues Under the Sea*, for example, Jules Verne has Captain Nemo answer the question, "Sir, what is a pearl?" this way: "To the poet, a pearl is a tear of the sea; to the Oriental, it is a drop of dew, solidified; to the ladies, it is a jewel . . . which they wear on their fingers, their necks or their ears. But for the chemist, it is a mixture of phosphate and carbonate of lime with a little gelatin. And . . . for naturalists, it is simply a morbid secretion of the organ that among certain bivalves produces mother-of-pearl."

One of the oddest—and most oddly touching—stories of shell uses is told by Elva D. Sheets, a Midwestern grandmother, in *The Fascinating World of the Sea*. The popularity of chewing gum with American children, she writes, is matched among certain South Pacific children by a fondness for whistles made from the egg cases of five types of snails. After the larvae have been removed, the tough cases are dried, stained bright colors, and given catchy names: Sea Whistles, Snake Bottles, Sword Whistles, War Fans, and Pigtails. Known collectively as musical chewing gum for more than two hundred years, the mollusk whistles are so popular that Japanese entrepreneurs have developed a nice business raising the five types of snails in pens in order to produce the cases commercially. Which leads to the oddly touching part of the story: "In a Tokyo cemetery a granite monument has been erected in memory of the seashell egg case. On its back are the names of forty-three whistle merchants who had it erected because they became conscience-stricken over making their fortunes by killing snails."

A Taste for Collecting

Robert Louis Stevenson wrote in his *Lay Morals,* "It is perhaps more fortunate to have a taste for collecting shells than to have been born a millionaire." People today, faced with four-digit inflation, might not agree. But no one can argue with the satisfaction of finding a beautiful shell while strolling along the beach on a bright sunny day—especially since it is one of life's few remaining free pleasures.

As pleasant as it is, however, ambling along by the water's edge is not a very efficient way of developing a worthwhile shell collection. Your chances will be much better on the open flats, in trapped pools, and under rocks left exposed by the retreating tide, and for some species you'll have to become involved in deep-water diving or dredging, unless you choose to discover your specimen in a shell shop. But beach collecting is certainly the easiest, the least expensive, and the most common method of pursuing the hobby. It is the classic beginning for most serious collectors and collections, so let us begin there, too.

As you walk along slowly, head bent, eyes darting this way and that, most of the shells you'll see will be "dead." The animals that once wore them will be gone, devoured by predators, and they will have a beachworn look—bleached by the sun, broken and scarred by the tumbling waves and the roiling sands. These are worthless, and knowledgeable collectors look upon them with disdain. The better specimens do serve a valuable function for the beginning collector, however: they will help you to recognize and learn the names of various shells, and as you become more advanced you can replace them with finer samples.

If luck is with you on your beach stroll, you may come upon a "freshly dead" shell, cast ashore by the sea soon after its occupant's demise, or stranded by the outgoing tide and fallen on by hungry sea birds. Assuming it is in good condition, this find belongs in your permanent collection. But success depends upon skill as well as upon your luck, for you must know what to look for. Many beginning collectors make the mistake of expecting to spy on the sand or in the shallows shells as shiny and polished as those they've seen in display cases. They don't realize that most shells, in their live and natural state, are either covered by a dark, fibrous, and sometimes hairy skin called the periostracum, or are camouflaged with bits of algae, coral, and other marine growths. The trick to this kind of collecting is to look for drab and oddly shaped objects, to poke into piles of dead shells and soggy sponges, and to turn over and closely examine clumps of stranded seaweed, which often have shells clinging to them.

When is the best time for beach collecting? During or immediately after a violent storm, when high-riding waves usually litter the beach with a treasure trove of live shells, stands at the top of the list. Another excellent time is during the minus, or extremely low, tides that occur in late winter and early spring. With the change of the moon, the water recedes far out, exposing sections of beach, sandbars, and mud flats that normally are covered by water.

Under more ordinary circumstances, if you are shelling at mean tide, follow the tide line as you search in one direction and the high-tide line on your return. Most shellers congregate at the water's edge, so if you arrive at mean tide and find yourself crowded out—and competition at popular shelling beaches can be fierce—don't hesitate to go directly to the high-tide line; it probably has been neglected and your odds of finding something worthwhile will be better. Another way of beating the crowds is to move much more slowly than the rest of the eager traffic, giving shell piles a more thorough examination, and carefully turning over dead pens and other large shells to which such smaller species as boat shells and jewel boxes are often attached. As in much of life, success in the shell-collecting race is not always to the swiftest.

Since beach collecting is basically simple, you can get by with very little equipment. You'll need a bucket of some kind to carry back your catch, and it's wise to include some additional, smaller containers for fragile shells that might not survive the general accommodations. A long stick or cane is handy for poking into piles of beachdrift and turning over seaweed; some people use a toy garden rake lashed to a broomstick, and commercially produced aluminum devices equipped with mechanical hands are available at the more popular shelling resorts. And by all means provide yourself with tide tables for the area of your search.

As you become more involved in shell collecting, you'll want to move into a more advanced class—hunting shells in their own habitats. The best places for that are tidal pools, rock or coral reefs, and open flats exposed at low tide, preferably in quiet bays rather than oceanside beaches. Now the hobby and the equipment required become somewhat more complicated. A tide table is indispensable, not only for planning the hunt but for your own safety. Be sure to leave a mud bar, a rocky beach, or one backed by high cliffs well before high tide; it is a frightening—and potentially fatal—experience to discover that you have been so engrossed in your search that your route back to shore has been cut off by the quietly rising sea.

Never wade the flats barefoot. At the least, wear old tennis shoes to protect your feet; heavy-soled sneakers or shoes with thick, nonslip soles are better. Potential enemies of your feet include oyster shells, razor-edged barnacles, porcupine-spined sea urchins, stingrays buried eye-deep in the mud, jagged coral in tropical waters, and, on Australia's Great Barrier Reef, the ugly, highly venomous, and almost perfectly camouflaged stonefish. And if you miss all these natural hazards in your wading, you still have to worry about the ubiquitous bane of civilization—broken bottles.

Sliding your feet across the bottom rather than treading up and down will give a lurking ray notice of your approach and enable it to get out of your way; the same method of perambulation will prevent you from coming down four-square on the sharp spines of the sea urchin, which produce a painful and long-lasting sting. If these defensive measures fail and you are impaled, there are several recommended home remedies that you should carry in your kit: meat tenderizer is said to neutralize the pain; vinegar does the same, and is also said to dissolve the spine tips if they are not embedded too deeply. The poisons produced by the stingray and the stonefish are potentially lethal; get thee to a hospital.

Since you'll be turning over rocks in your quest, heavy work gloves are a must (some shellers even tape their hands), for barnacles, young oysters, and other marine creatures and growths can cut and scratch as keenly as razor blades and broken glass. (A word about conservation here: Always gently replace rocks exactly as you found them, and never remove all the animals you find underneath; leaving a goodly number of specimens behind to reseed the sea not only gives future collectors a chance for success in the hunt, but also helps guarantee the survival of the species. Selfish collectors are a greater menace to many mollusks than pollution and their natural enemies combined.) Even heavy gloves won't help if you invade the lair of a moray eel or the home of a spiny urchin, so be careful about poking your hands into cracks and crevices.

In addition to all these formidable hazards there are such minor discomforts as sunburn, windburn, blisters, and the bites of voracious mosquitoes, sand flies, and sand fleas, which always seem to turn out in force during the best shelling hours. Dress sensibly and protectively, therefore, and bring along a good supply of adhesive bandages and insect repellent.

What else will you need? Various experts recommend various pieces of equipment, and the list can get quite lengthy. Where you plan to do your shelling will shorten the general list, however, and some collectors manage with minimum equipment wherever they go. Here are some consensus "musts" and "should-also-haves":

• Some sort of prying and digging tool—a pinch bar if your search takes you to rocky coasts and tide pools; a small shovel or trowel and a clam hoe or rake if you'll be trekking over sand and mud bottoms, for the shells that dwell in these areas must be dug or raked out.

• A sturdy knife or a hammer and chisel to remove chitons and other rock clingers, and a spatula for frail limpets. In tropical waters you'll use the tools to get at the many types of boring mussels, clams, and snails that make their homes in dead coral. A word of caution: Please do not carelessly damage *live* coral; selfish and unthinking collectors can destroy in a few moments what it took nature years to build.

• Something to carry your catch: a plastic bucket or a "game bag" of plastic or net, and small capped bottles or plastic bags that will fit in your pocket for fragile specimens and those you want to keep alive. Angel wings, for example, contract so violently when dug up that they often shatter their fragile shells. Popping them immediately into a water-filled container substantially reduces this risk.

• If you are going to be hunting in water more than a few inches deep, a face mask or some sort of glass-bottomed bucket or box will eliminate surface reflections and wind-ripple distortion, enabling you to see shells and fish underwater almost as clearly as if they were in your home aquarium. Photographers find the looking-box invaluable for underwater shots. You can make your own by fitting a sheet of glass into one side of a wooden frame and caulking all around for a watertight fit; paint the wooden walls inside a dull black to reduce the sun's glare. If you aren't that handy, you can buy a commercially produced glass-bottom bucket, and if you'd like to do your shell-watching for hours in maximum comfort, you can invest in a rubber raft with a built-in see-through plastic window.

As you become a more serious collector, you'll discover other helpful items, such as a small kitchen sieve that you can use to screen sand for miniature shells or scoop up slow swimmers and crawlers; a notebook and pencil for recording the place and date of each catch; wooden tongue depressors for stretching out chitons; and a pair of long forceps or tweezers for capturing the residents of narrow clefts and crevices. In the cold waters of the north, some shellers clad themselves in armpit-high fisherman's waders, with heavy rubber boot bottoms and a large inside pocket at the top. On the coral reefs of the southern seas you'll be wise to wear long trousers of heavy denim, tied at the ankles, to protect your legs from live coral, beautiful to look at but nasty to brush against. A gig, or fish spear, comes in handy, too, not only to discourage barracuda and dislodge sea urchins, but to take a big lobster or crayfish for the pot. The gig, or some kind of stick, will also enable you to feel your way as you move about in the shallows, where the running of the water and reflections on the surface can make your vision of the bottom deceptive; to stumble into a deep hole is to risk a broken leg.

You won't use all these items on every expedition, of course, but it makes sense to keep them stored in the trunk of your car, available when you need them. The equipment you carry with you will depend upon where you are going shelling, what you hope to get, and how far you expect to wander from your car, vacation cottage, or other base of operations.

During low tide, naturally, is the best time for hunting in the shallows, not only because mollusks brought in on the high tide are left behind in pools and under rocks, but because you then have access to the wooden pilings and concrete supports beneath docks, wharves, and trestles—marine wonderlands, with many species of shells among the residents. Of the animals that dwell in the intertidal zone, the gastropods, generally speaking, hide themselves among and under rocks, awaiting the return of the waters; the bivalves burrow beneath sand and mud. Yet sandbars, just awash, may house big whelks and more than a half-dozen other gastropods as well as bivalves. Look for tracks—each animal makes a distinctive one that you will come to recognize—and start digging where the trail ends.

Bivalves don't leave tracks, but their siphons, stretched up to clean water, are telltale signs of their presence just below the surface of the mud or sand seabed. Approach slowly and carefully, for any jarring of the ground will cause them to draw in their siphons immediately. Since they must eject the water they contain in order to contract and snap their valves together, however, a miniature geyser of water spurting from a hole is a dead giveaway. Dig alongside the hole to avoid damaging the shell with your shovel (the same procedure holds true when digging at the trail's end for gastropods), and break through the side wall of the hole with your hands. The burrows of most shells range between a few inches and a foot, but be prepared for a race if you're going after angel wings or razor clams. They can burrow as fast as most of us can dig, and go down two feet or more. Angel wings, in fact, will keep on burrowing until something solid stops them. To capture them, look for huge siphon tubes protruding in the mud flats, mark the water spurt hole with a twig or stick, and bend to the task. Try to seize the siphon, if possible; it is so large the animal cannot fit it all back into its shell—which explains why the beautiful but delicate valves break with strenuous contracting. As mentioned earlier, plopping them quickly into a bucket of salt water may save at least the two shells; the animal is doomed in either case.

For some shell fanciers, an ideal way to spend an hour or two on a warm, sunny day is face down in a tidal pool, becoming almost a part of a fascinating miniature sea world. For this kind of exercise you will need goggles and snorkel tube, as well as a wet suit or protective clothing, unless your tan is deep and sure. The name of the game here is patience. Many shells look so much like rocks and sand, blending marvelously with their surroundings in nature's camouflage artistry, that a cursory glance will miss them entirely. Lie quietly and look, really look: eventually a "rock" will move or a little ridge or hump sticking up in the sand will come into focus—almost miraculously, for you will swear you saw nothing there before. Kathleen Yerger Johnstone speaks of the rich rewards of patience: crown shells, with "crowns" so like the jagged edges of the 'coon oysters on which they feed; cowries that resemble jellyish sea growths when their mantles are fully extended; hawk wings, overgrown with furry green moss, almost invisible in beds of eel grass; Caribbean vase shells so encrusted with powdery marl and coral that even the distinctive shape of the shell is disguised.

You won't see all of these species in one tidal pool, but you'll see plenty of others. And you may find the experience so interesting and educational that you spend more time watching than collecting—a highly commendable decision in the many over-collected areas of the world. R. Tucker Abbott wrote vividly of the watching game in *Kingdom of the Seashell:* "Trails in the sand tell a tale, and if you follow a furrow in the surface of a Florida tidal flat, you may find a hump in the sand caused by an olive shell, a venus clam or a small *Busycon* whelk. If whelk and clam happen to meet, you will see the snail envelop the bivalve in its black foot, press the edge of its shell between the clam's valves and slowly but surely pry open its victim. Equally fascinating, but seldom seen except by snorkelers or scuba swimmers, is the process of egg-laying by a whelk. The capsules are formed in a pore in the sole of the foot and pressed up by the oviduct, where several eggs are injected into each wafer-shaped case. When filled, the capsules, strung together like the segments of a rattlesnake's tail, are pushed up out of the sand."

Rocky shores are good hunting grounds for chitons, with limpets, winkles, top shells, and whelks hiding in pools and crevices among the rocks; mussels can be found here, too, as well as clinging to breakwaters and old boat hulks. On mud-and-gravel shores look for clams and bubble shells. Coral reefs offer a rich assortment of colorful cowries, cones, volutes, murices, and tritons. Mangrove clumps, often overlooked, are home to a number of snail species that not only live below water but cling to the aerial roots. Periwinkles thrive on high, rocky shorelines where the tide never reaches, satisfied by wind-driven spray and salty pools in which to lay their eggs. Some mollusks, the "dreaded" shipworms, bore into anything wooden; others drill their way into rock or coral—piddock clams of England, date mussels of the Caribbean, and elongate ark clams of South America's tropical Pacific coast, to name several.

In fact, mollusk representatives are found from high in the mountains to the ocean deeps, but to gather specimens of this latter group, many of which rarely, if ever, appear in the shallows or on the beach alive, you will have to go in for the ultimates in shell collecting—snorkeling, scuba diving, and dredging.

Ocean shallows teem with life, and as you swim about in mask and snorkel, marveling at the sights, don't be surprised to see a scallop, most proficient of the swimming bivalves, staring back at you with dozens of beady blue eyes. Experienced underwater collectors carefully search partially submerged wrecks for a potpourri of marine forms that consider man-made structures to be ideal habitats. Fishermen in some areas have built artificial reefs of old car bodies to attract fish, and the men who work on oil-drilling platforms in the Gulf of Mexico and other offshore fields have found the waters around their rigs abundant with life, including numerous mollusks.

Divers with scuba equipment—and the training and experience to use it safely—can descend to great depths to hunt in wrecks on the bottom. They also keep their eyes peeled for octopus dens, not out of fear of the animal—which, contrary to the mythology of the sea, is quite shy—but because they usually find around the doorway to the lair a treasure trove of empty shells once inhabited by creatures ranking high on octopus menus. Since octopuses collect mollusks for different reasons than their human counterparts, much of the take will be mundane; but, more often than not, a number of shells will be rare or unusual.

Diving collectors should carry, in addition to their normal underwater gear, a diver's sheath knife, a collecting bag of cloth or plastic, and, "just in case," a spear or sharpened metal rod attached to the wrist by sturdy line. Anything else, such as glass jars in which to keep specimens alive, can be conveniently stored in a homely, inexpensive, but wonderfully serviceable contraption—an ordinary bushel basket set into an inflated automobile inner tube. This also should be attached to the diver's wrist by a light but strong cord, of suitable length. An exceedingly practical outfit, the basket-*cum*-tube also serves as a floating game bag and is buoyant enough to double as a rest platform between dives. This hints at the subject of safety, and it goes without saying that snorkeling or scuba diving alone, for whatever purpose, is a risk no one should take.

For efficiency in gathering a wide assortment of life from the sea bottom, nothing beats dredging. Dredges come in a variety of sizes and types, both rectangular and triangular, and usually consist of a metal frame attached to heavy mesh screening or fishnet. The lower bar of the frame is sharpened and canted at a slight downward angle to dig into the sand or mud of the bottom. Most dredges are designed with a release that enables one arm to fold back, making it possible to retrieve the expensive device if it should snag on some underwater object. Dredges can be towed from any kind of craft, from rowboats to large cabin cruisers or charter boats. A rowboat or small outboard is certainly the most economical way to go, but the dredge will have to be a small one, with a capacity of about half a bushel and a frame of less than a square foot; anything bigger would be difficult to haul up and boat.

The rule for successful dredging is three to four times as much line out as the depth of the water in which you are dredging—at ten feet, for example, you should have thirty to forty feet of three-eighths-inch nylon or five-eighths-inch manila rope out. If you're working in one hundred feet of water, the three hundred to four hundred feet of line out will need to have weights attached to it; otherwise it will float and lift the digging edge of your dredge from the bottom. A couple of strong men can haul in by hand a small, rowboat-size dredge and rope from a depth of about one hundred fifty feet; depths greater than that call for wire cable, which means a bigger boat equipped with a winch.

Whatever the size of the boat, you'll also need a sorting board. Given enough hands and enough room to work, the dredge can be lowered for another pass along the bottom while the treasures that have been dumped on the sorting board are being examined, separated, and placed in buckets and cloth bags. It all sounds a lot easier than it really is, especially in a rowboat crowded with sorting board, storage containers, rope, miscellaneous equipment, and two or more people. It is also a dirty job and a smelly one—in many areas, the gunk that comes up from the bottom, said one veteran collector in a classic remark, smells like the armpit of the sea. Except that he didn't say armpit.

Similar to dredging, but simpler and cleaner, is the process called mopping, which utilizes an iron bar to which is tied a mass of unraveled rope strands of varying lengths. Attached by a bridle to a towrope and pulled across the bottom, this device, sometimes called a "tangle," works on the irritation principle—a bivalve will snap its valves shut on anything passing through that annoys it. Happy collectors reel in many scallops and pen shells this way, and often they receive a bonus when the rope threads become entangled in the spines of the thorny oyster, known also as the chrysanthemum shell and considered by many to be the most beautiful bivalve in the world.

There are several other ingenious ways of obtaining deep-water shells. If you can locate a kelp bed, row out and pull up some of the long fronds, and you may be rewarded with clinging top shells. If you go deep-sea fishing, check the stomachs of cod, halibut, flounder, sculpin, and other fish that feed on bottom-dwelling mollusks. Many valuable shells have been found this way, including the rare Fulton's cowrie of South Africa. If you can't go fishing, make a deal with someone who works in a fish factory; but the fish must be freshly caught, for its digestive juices will not be kind to calcareous shells. New England collectors will do well to cultivate the friendship of lobstermen, who often find deep-sea mollusks in their slat traps. Their counterparts in Florida use old oil drums for traps, and cowries find these particularly attractive. Many of the shells that end up on dealers' shelves come from sources such as these, for the toilers of the sea have developed a quick and appreciative eye for the rare, unusual, and valuable in the mollusk world.

Baiting and trapping are effective methods of capturing carnivorous shells, of which there are many. Olive shells respond to baited hooks left in the water overnight; in the Philippines, conch meat is the preferred bait, while crown shells find old fish heads irresistible. Crab cages can be adapted for mollusk trapping, or the bait can be left between squares of wire mesh, weighted down. Visiting the trap the next morning, you'll be able to take your pick of the various diners. Even simpler is a mix of crushed crab, dead fish, and entrails, placed in a cloth bag to thwart small fish. Dropped to the bottom with a stone for a weight, the bag's contents will send out a powerful message on the passing water currents, and by morning all sorts of guests should be clinging to the bag or nestled in the sand next to it. Another trick involves serving eviction notices on hermit crabs. Lay out a bait of rotten meat and fruit on the beach, and when the crabs arrive, all wearing their current shell abodes, chances are good there will be at least one you'll want to dispossess. Legend has it that the famous Edwards glory-of-the-sea cone, now in the Austrialia Museum in Sydney, was taken this way on the beach at Rabaul, New Britain.

In all your collecting endeavors, what you find will be determined by geographic location, by the habitat, by the time of day or night, by the tides, by the season, by violent storms, and perhaps even by spells of hot or cold weather. Chance and unknown natural factors also play a part—shells that have been found on a certain beach for years will suddenly disappear, only to return years later; other shells, foreign to that shore, will show up one morning, littering the sands, and just as abruptly leave, to be seen there no more.

If you go out looking for a particular kind of shell, therefore, you may be disappointed. On the other hand, since there are more than sixty thousand species of mollusks, most of them fitted with shells, there's really no way to anticipate exactly what treasures might turn up at any moment. And that, of course, is the thrill that makes shell collecting as much fun—almost—as being a millionaire.

Laboring for Posterity

Collecting shells can be hard work, but it is usually fun, especially if you engage in some snorkeling or scuba diving, or enjoy a particularly rewarding day. That's one side of collecting. The other side— cleaning the catch—isn't considered fun by anyone. But it's an inevitable next step and a very necessary one, as you will realize the first time you get a whiff of the vile stench arising from a batch of shells left untended for too long.

The sooner you get at the task, the better, especially if the shells have been out of water for several hours. By that time the animals inside the shells probably will have died, and once a mollusk's body begins to harden, it is much more difficult to remove. Keeping the shells in water solves the problem for a while, but acids from the dead animal's body will attack the finish of the shell unless you change the water often. All things considered, it is best to keep your shells alive until you are ready to process them. If you don't have access to a renewable supply of salt water, wrap the shells in wet rags or seaweed and they may survive for up to three days.

Over the centuries, collectors have developed a number of "easy" ways to clean mollusks, with the size and type of the creature usually determining the best method. Bivalves, for example, pose no serious problem, even though it is almost impossible, no matter how sharp your knife, to open a live bivalve without damaging the lips of its

valves. The simplest system is to soak them in a bucket of warm fresh water for a half hour or so, or pop them into boiling water for a few minutes. When the animal dies, its adductor muscle relaxes, leaving the shells agape. With your knife, cut and scrape the body away from the shell, working carefully so as not to scratch the lustrous inner lining. After giving the valves a good cleaning with a stiff vegetable brush or an old toothbrush, dry them, close them in their natural position, and bind them shut with a rubber band, thread, or string. After two or three weeks the hinge will dry out, and the valves should remain closed. If you want the valves to stay partly open, hold them in that position with a piece of wood until the hinge dries. Although open bivalves are a nuisance to store, some collectors like to show their bivalve specimens in pairs, one closed in the natural position, the other open to display the interior. A drop of pure glycerin on the hinge ligament will help to keep it from crumbling.

Separating gastropods from their shells is a somewhat more difficult matter, except for the very small ones. These, having so little meat to start with, can be left to dry out in a shady spot not *too* close to your house—or your neighbor's. The odor should wane quickly. The advantage of this method is that the animal's operculum, the trapdoor with which it closes off the opening in its shell, remains in its proper place, thereby enhancing the scientific

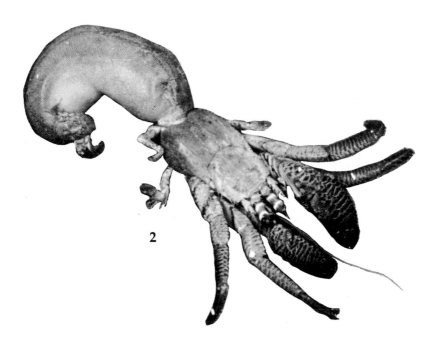

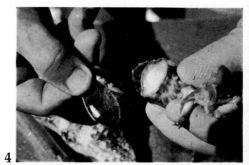

1: *Evicting a hermit crab from its home*

2: *The shell-less crab*

3: *Using an ice pick to remove the operculum*

4: *The operculum separated from the shell*

5: *Removing the animal*

174

value of the shell as well as its natural appearance.

An alternative method that gets rid of the smell problem entirely calls for soaking the tiny gastropods for a few days in an alcohol-water solution—70 percent alcohol if it is the drinkable grain or ethyl type, 50 percent if it's one of the poisonous forms—and then letting them dry in the shade. A 10 percent formaldehyde solution can also be used this way, but will damage some shells if they are left in it longer than three days. The drawback to this quick-cure method is that the animal's body may contract so much that the operculum shrinks out of sight. This will not happen if the animal is dead or almost dead before immersion; some experts therefore recommend killing the animal in an overnight fresh-water soak before the alcohol or formaldehyde treatment.

For larger gastropods, one of the quickest and most efficient ways of cleaning is by boiling. Dropping the mollusk into boiling water will kill the animal almost instantly, but it isn't always good for the shell. Glossy shells, such as cowries, olives, and marginellas, will fog, check, or craze if subjected to rapid temperature changes; other thin, delicate species will split. Prudent collectors protect these shells by using the alcohol soak, which does not affect the shells. Even for other shells, it is best to start with warm or cold water, preferably seawater, bring the pot to a boil slowly, then bring the temperature down gradually, either by letting the water stand for an hour or so or by dribbling in cold water. Similarly, time in the boiling bath is a critical matter for many species. Generally speaking, small shells should be boiled for no longer than a few minutes, while large ones can take up to a half hour. To keep the shells from banging around in the pot and cracking or chipping during the boiling process, some collectors put them in a mesh bag or in their collecting bag; others line the bottom of the pot with cloth to remove the shells from direct contact with the heat source.

Start the delicate business of removing the animals as soon as the shells are cool enough to handle—they will come out more readily while still hot. It makes sense, therefore, not to cook too many at one time. The tools you'll need for this operation will depend upon the size of the shell and the shape of its opening, and improvisation is often the road to success. In addition to tweezers of various sizes and long-nosed forceps, most collectors choose from an array that includes bent safety pins, metal skewers, ice picks, crochet hooks, bent wires, used dental picks and curved needles. Insert the tool of your choice in the siphonal canal, the notched end of the shell, drive it as far as possible into the thickest part of the animal's body, twist it a little to set it, if it's a hook, and pull gently until the animal comes free. This will work with some species, but for many gastropods you'll have to hold the shell in one hand, your tool in the other, and literally unscrew the animal from its shell. This is necessary because the creature's body conforms to the internal spiral of the shell, and fills it all the way. Undertake your corkscrewing turns gently, for you want to remove the body in one piece, and this is not always easy to do: the part of the body at the end of the coil is occupied by the stomach and liver, the softest portion and therefore the portion most easily torn away and left behind. If the body comes to a point when you remove it, you know you've got it all; if it doesn't, what you've got is a problem.

The same holds true if you use the most modern of removal methods—quick freezing—and don't succeed in a total extraction. Freezing takes longer than boiling, but is ideal if you can't get to work on your shells right away. The process is no different than the freezing of other things, except that you'd be wise to put your sealed plastic bag of mollusks in the refrigerator for a few hours before subjecting its contents to the deep freeze; this, of course, is to guard against the crazing and cracking that can result from rapid temperature changes, whether they be up the scale or down. Similarly, when you take the shells out of the freezer, let them thaw gradually in the refrigerator or in cool—never hot— water. The hoped-for result of freezing is that the animal will shrink to such an extent that the muscle attaching it to the shell will be pulled away; time in the freezer is important, therefore, so figure on at least three full days. If all goes well, when thawing is complete you should be able to remove the animal easily by using the same tools and techniques developed to serve the boiling method.

Many collectors consider the freezing method the best, for although it takes longer than boiling in terms of total time elapsed, actual work-time is no longer, and the shells do not lose any of their natural colors, always a danger in boiling. On the other hand, with both these methods there is a risk of leaving part of the mollusk in the shell, with unpleasant results sure to follow. There are methods of coping with this, and these corrective measures have a place on the list of possible alternatives to boiling and freezing.

One way is to bury the offending shell in sand or earth, and let nature take its course. This is one form of the "rotting out" method, and the shell should be stood on one end so that the liquids that develop during the putrefying process will drain away into the soil without injuring the shell. Rotting out can be used on shells of any size and condition if time is of no consequence, and if you choose your burial site well and put some sugar down as bait, ants and possibly blowflies will speed up the process considerably. But don't rush matters—give nature at least a week before you dig up the shells and wash them out. A reminder: If you are going to bury a shell with the animal intact, first make sure to cut off the operculum with a sharp knife and set it aside to dry. And if more than one shell is getting the

treatment, devise an identification system so that each operculum can be matched to its shell.

The other rotting out method is messy and disagreeable and not recommended for tiny apartments or people with weak stomachs. It involves soaking the shell in salt or fresh water until the body starts to rot and fall apart. You must change the water two or three times a day or, as mentioned earlier, acids from the decomposing flesh will eat into the shell's surface and turn it dull and chalky. With each water change, shake the shell vigorously and flush out as much of the deteriorating animal as possible until the shell is clean. Once again, a system for linking opercula and shells is important, especially if you soak a batch together rather than in individual glass, plastic, or enamel containers.

If all else fails and the last vestiges of the animal refuse to leave, you can try embalming them with formaldehyde. Modern advice warns against the old system of a few drops of the chemical followed by a wad of cotton to plug the opening, because the acids in formaldehyde can etch away the shell. Instead, dilute the standard 40 percent strength formaldehyde with sufficient water to make a 5 percent solution, buffer it with two tablespoons of baking soda per quart to neutralize the acids, and let the shell soak in it. If the leftover piece of animal isn't too big, this method may work. One expert— who doesn't like formaldehyde, because eventually the piece of cured meat, attracting insects, sifts out of the shell in the form of a dirty brown powder— has two alternate suggestions. First, stand the shell on end and fill it with full-strength shampoo or liquid detergent; in a few days the remnant may be loose enough to shake out. If that doesn't work, fill the shell as far as necessary with melted paraffin. Another expert swears by his water-jet dental hygiene device for flushing out smaller shells up to one-half inch.

1

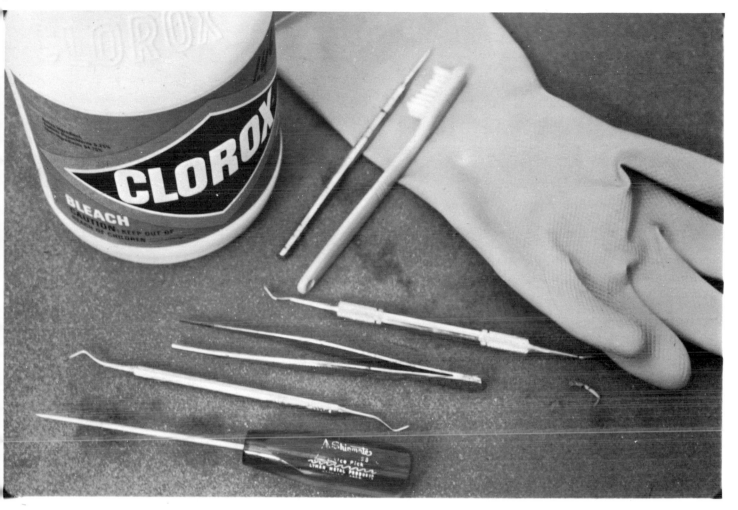

1: *Tools of the trade*

2: *Cleaning with a toothbrush*

3: *Soaking shells in a tub of warm water and detergent*

2

3

Opposite: *Even when snorkeling in the blue waters of Bermuda, collectors wear rubber suits, because although the water inside the coral reefs is warm, it chills off rapidly outside them—and the divers often spend two or three hours at a time floating face-down in the sea and peering through their masks for the telltale signs of movement on submerged rocks, coral, or the ocean floor.*

Above: *Face masks come in handy at shallower levels, too, and especially in tidal pools, where the patient watcher can observe a miniature marine world at close range, or find a snail by following its track across the sand until it disappears.*

An unusual and little-known method of removing the animal from large shells, used by natives in the West Indies, Central America, and the South Pacific, is reported by Stuart and Leni Goodman in their book, *Art from Shells*. Equipped with a piece of string or nylon fishing line with a slipknot at one end, you place a live shell in the sun and wait for the animal to emerge, seeking a way to escape into the shade or the water. "As he comes out," the Goodmans write, "gently slip the string around his foot . . . and pull tightly. He will immediately try to get back into his shell house, but if the string is tightly tied, he will be caught. Then tie the other end of the string onto a branch or a hanging ledge a few feet off the ground until the weight of the shell forces it to fall off, leaving the animal tied to the end of the string. . . . As the shell falls three or four feet in the process, make sure that the area below is cushioned in some way, so that the shell is not damaged when it drops."

Because it takes several hours for the muscles attaching the animal to the shell to finally weary and let go, this process is certainly not the most humane way of executing the creature. And there is no guarantee that the animal will come out in one piece; often the soft organs tear away and are left behind.

As all but the most naive of collectors know, shells that scurry around on several legs aren't mollusks at all, but hermit crabs in empty mollusk shells. There are several ways to convince a hermit crab to leave its shell, but seizing the animal and pulling it out is not one of them. Although the crab has only borrowed the shell and has no permanent attachment to it, at the first sign of danger it will zip far back inside and wrap its tail around the core of the shell in a death grip. Even if you were quick enough to catch a claw before it disappeared, you could pull until the claw broke off without budging the animal.

One recommended method of evicting the creatures is to place them in water to which chlorine bleach has been added; in a short time the crabs will vacate their shells and die. Another method is to submerge them in boiled water which has cooled to the point at which you can safely put in your hand, and leave them there. You definitely must not boil them, since quickly killed hermit crabs retain their death grip on their shells and usually have to be rotted out. Why boil the water, then? Because boiling removes the oxygen from the water, and the crab dies more slowly, by suffocation, and usually relaxes its tail grip, sometimes even slipping a little way out of the shell. Talk of slow and fast killing, or killing of any kind, may offend some readers. But these are the methods that have been developed over years of experimentation, and they will continue to be used for as long as people continue to collect and value shells—or at least until some better way is found.

Once your shells are clean on the inside, you have to turn your attention to the outside, which, under ordinary circumstances, will be overgrown with such things as sea moss, tiny worm tubes, miniature barnacles and oysters, mud, lime, coral, or other crustings and organisms. You will also have to decide what you're going to do about the often ugly epidermis known as the periostracum.

Scientists, and collectors of scientific bent, usually want to keep the periostracum intact because it is a part of the natural animal. Some collectors prefer to leave the growths on the outside of the shell alone, since in a sense they too are a part of the natural state of the animal. But if you're like most collectors, you'll want your shells to look their best, and that means removing all outer coverings and growths so that the beauty of the shell's sculpturing and coloring can be seen and appreciated. A compromise between the two approaches is the obvious solution: one shell of each species in the state in which it was captured—or with periostracum intact—and another cleaned and oiled to perfection.

Opinions among experienced collectors differ as to how to start the cleaning operation. One school believes in going over the shell first with a dull knife or old nail file, carefully scraping off worm tubes, barnacles, lime encrustations, and the like. Only if that treatment fails to remove all unwanted growths and dulling film do they move to sterner measures—immersion in chlorine bleach. The next step is to dunk the shell in warm water and detergent and give it a good scrubbing with a stiff-bristled brush.

Other collectors dump their shells into a chlorine solution right away and let them soak, sometimes for hours and sometimes overnight. Most recommend a solution of one cup of bleach to each two quarts of water, some use a stronger solution, and some even go full strength. If you decide to use the full-strength treatment, which you might for a particularly difficult shell, you would be well advised to keep a close watch on it. Normally, the bleach in solution, while loosening various deposits on the epidermis, will not harm the shells or their coloration, and may even enhance the latter. A strong solution is fine for white shells, but others left too long in it might emerge with colors faded; and carrier shells treated this way will lose the bits of shell and other camouflaging materials that they have cemented to themselves. Until experience gives you some guidelines to go by, you'll be sensible to use too little bleach for too short a time rather than too much for too long. And don't forget to rinse the shells thoroughly in fresh water after their chlorine bath. Russell Jensen, technical advisor for this book, offers this advice: To counter the effect and smell of chlorine bleach spilled on hands, rub in a drop or two of vinegar or pickle juice before washing with soap and water.

These methods should take care of most cleaning problems. For particularly stubborn stains or growths, caustic soda (lye) or muriatic acid will probably provide an answer, but these are extremely dangerous substances and should not be used without proper training and precautions. An overnight soaking solution of a pound of lye to a gallon of water will usually remove cemented-on barnacles and calcareous deposits, as well as the periostracum, and it will not adversely affect the shell's color, as bleaches can. Read the directions for use on the label carefully, follow them faithfully, and never forget that the chemical is every bit as damaging to unprotected hands and eyes as it is to metal containers—and containers can be replaced.

The same is true of muriatic acid. Although a very weak solution of the acid will bring out the color of many shells, it can also destroy delicate sculpturing and eat holes in the shell if it is not flushed away quickly or neutralized in a baking soda bath. One recommended method for cleaning is to dip a shell in full-strength acid for one second, then plunge it immediately into ice water. The shell must be sturdy, and it had better be held so that the acid drains out of the aperture the moment it is picked up; if it is trapped inside it can eat through the shell before the transfer from one bowl to the other.

If you must use the acid, it would be better to prepare a weak solution, about a teaspoonful to a pint of water, and with a watercolor brush paint one small section of the shell at a time. Rinse it immediately in a rinsing bowl or in running water, and, when you're all finished, in a strong baking soda solution. This is the only way to use muriatic acid on shells with thin lips and delicate spines, and the safest way for all shells. Things you must remember: muriatic acid burns through people as well as metal and other substances; mix it in a bucket of glass or hard plastic; wear rubber gloves and never handle the shell being treated or pick it

1: For the shell collector with limited space to sort and store his finds, micromollusks are an ideal solution. Basic tools and requirements include tweezers, microscope, small containers, a large quantity of beach drift or dredged material—and plenty of patience.

2: Equipped with snorkel, face mask, and wet suit, experienced collectors carefully search partially submerged wrecks for shells. Many mollusks— along with a variety of other marine forms—find man-made structures in the water ideal habitats. To attract fish, fishermen have built artificial reefs out of old car bodies, and the men who work on oil company drilling platforms offshore swear that the fishing is better there than anywhere.

3: Box screens with meshes of various sizes are a great help in sifting the sand for tiny shells.

4: To obtain specimens from deeper waters, the most rewarding method is to haul a dredge over the ocean bottom. Another, newer device is a deep-water trap, strong and efficient, designed by J. R. H. Lightbourn, assistant general manager of the Bank of Bahama and an ardent shell collector.

up with your fingers—use chemists' tongs; always work next to running water or a rinsing bowl; always have a strong baking soda solution near at hand—it is even faster than water in neutralizing the burning effects of the acid; follow the directions on the bottle religiously. One last reminder of the utmost importance: Never leave muriatic acid where it might by any stretch of the imagination fall into the hands of small children; the stuff is vicious.

As a matter of fact, try not to use it at all. Instead, invest in one of those small, light, hobbyist's drills fitted with little burrs and rasps, but practice with it before tackling your best shells. Another worthwhile investment is a set of used dental tools. The variety of shapes will enable you to clean out almost any crevice and safely scrape off almost any encrustation.

Now that your shells are clean and dry inside and out, you may notice that some of them aren't as shiny as you imagined they would be. This is because all the boiling, bleaching, and other processing tend to dry up the pigment-carrying oils that give the shell its color; time will do the same, and even the most beautifully colored shells will fade eventually unless treated. There are many collectors and craftsmen who make things out of shells, and they often coat their specimens with lacquer, varnish, or even nail polish to impart a brilliant gloss. Scientists and most serious collectors wouldn't dream of following such a practice, but many of them find nothing objectionable about rubbing the shell inside and out with an oily cloth. The oil not only protects the shell from further deterioration, but actually penetrates and replaces the lost natural oils, thereby restoring much of the shell's original luster. A coating of oil or glycerin will also prevent the perioscratum from drying up and flaking off those shells you want to preserve in their natural state.

The most commonly used oils are baby oil, mineral oil, and high-grade machine oil. As in other areas of shell collecting, it seems that each collector has his own preferred recipe, using one of these oils straight or in combination with such things as chloroform, cleaning fluid, mineral spirits, window cleaner, and, especially, lighter fluid. Cutting the oil with a liquid that will evaporate achieves the glossy effect without leaving the shell "greasy." A shell too heavily oiled, unless it is protected under glass or plastic, becomes a dust-catcher of magnetic qualities. Cutting the oil and treating the shell every three months or so achieves the desired ends and reduces the dusting problem to manageable proportions.

The final step in the cleaning and preserving process is to stuff the shell's aperture with cotton, if it is a gastropod, and glue the operculum to it in its proper position. You may prefer to wrap the operculum in tissue paper and store it inside the shell, using the cotton wadding to keep it from falling out and getting lost. To clean the operculum, soak it in warm, soapy water to which a little bleach has been added, scrub it vigorously, and then dry it. Once you've got it clean, you may be amazed at how much its beauty rivals that of the shell itself.

By now you may have reached the conclusion that cleaning and treating shells involve as least as much work and effort as collecting them. So far, that's true. But you are not finished with the unglamorous, noncollecting side of it yet.

"As a beginner," writes Kathleen Yerger Johnstone in *Sea Treasure*, "you may not appreciate the importance of labeling. But in time, if you continue to be interested in shells and your collection grows, you will realize how important it is to label and catalogue. Scientists feel that the value of a collection is in direct proportion to its labeling. It is more important to know when and where a shell was found, than to identify it properly. The proper name can be supplied at any time, but localities have a way of becoming lost in poor memories."

The next subjects, then, are labeling and cataloging—along with housing or storage—and although they may not be as exciting as collecting, nor as traumatic as cleaning, in their own way they can be just as interesting. If you belong to the large group of hobbyists whose main interest in collecting shells is to use them as raw materials for arts and crafts projects, such as shadowboxes and shell jewelry, your interest in labeling may be limited to learning a given shell's name, and your cataloging may be designed with that aspect of your hobby in mind. Similarly, if you're a once-a-year collector, you may not want to go to too much bother—until your shoeboxes of shells start to overflow or the bug finally gets you. But if you're a serious collector and you want to leave a collection that is valuable both scientifically and financially to your heirs and assignees, you should approach the business of labeling and cataloging in a businesslike manner.

Labeling and cataloging actually begin out in the field, a moment or two after you have gathered a specimen. It's at that moment that you whip out your pocket notebook and jot down such pertinent and important information as the date; the time of day; the geographical location; whether the shell was found on the beach, in shallow water, under a rock, or wherever; the type of bottom, such as mud or sand; the condition of the tide; the weather; whether the shell was dead, newly dead, or alive; if alive, what it was doing when captured—mating, hiding, feeding on a dead crab, or attacking another mollusk, for example. Add the name of the shell if you know it, but this is the least important piece of information at the moment; with the shell in hand, you'll always be able to get identification; the other information is at the mercy of your memory. Also necessary is a quick description of the shell or some code that will enable you to match your notes and

the shell later, especially if you have a good day in the field.

Later you'll transfer this information into a more permanent catalog—index cards, a ledger, or a loose-leaf notebook (for easy typing). Set up a numbering system and mark each shell accordingly with indelible ink, either on a small square of adhesive tape or, better still, on the shell itself in an inconspicuous place. Then, next to the corresponding number in your log, enter the data you have assembled. Don't be stingy—give a full report. For locality, merely writing "Gulf Coast, Florida," doesn't mean much. Be specific, as in "Sanibel Island, Florida, half-mile below lighthouse," or "Little Egg Harbor, New Jersey, one mile southwest of new bridge in two feet of water, mud bottom."

In addition to the catalog—or instead of it, say some collectors—you may want to prepare labels for your shells, especially those you are displaying. The type of label you choose will be determined largely by your storage and display facilities, and may include all the information in your master log or merely extracts from it. It should certainly contain the popular name of the shell, if there is one, as well as the scientific name—and here you can have a lot of fun if you don't know the shell's name and enjoy the challenge of working out puzzles and doing some detective work.

The process is one of elimination. Even if you are the veriest tyro, you shouldn't have too much difficulty in telling a bivalve from a gastropod. That in itself considerably narrows the field. The next step is to go to the library and borrow a few books on shells. Works like this one, which deal with shells and shell collecting on a broad scale, might help if you should happen to come across an illustration of one or more of your shells. But for purposes of identification you will be much better served by illustrated shell catalogs and field guides. Compare

1: *The best time to go hunting for shells on the beach is during or immediately following a heavy storm. The wave-lashed shore will usually be littered with all sorts of sea-borne debris, including not only old, beach-worn shells, but some newly dead specimens, and even some live ones. After a high tide is a good time, too; the material left behind as the tide begins to ebb is known as beach drift. Gathered and dried, it will bring back many a warm summer memory if you wait until a cold, wintry day to take it out and sort it.*

2: *Remember to bring a knife and hammer on collecting expeditions, for many types of boring mussels, snails, and clams make their homes in dead coral, and the only way to get at them is to break off a piece. Be careful, however, not to damage live coral; selfish collectors can destroy a lot faster than nature can rebuild.*

3: *Early morning beach walkers make their way carefully around a stranded Portuguese man-of-war whose long tentacles bear large stinging cells that can inflict painful injuries on the unwary.*

4: *Bearded periwinkles, Tectarius muricatus Linné, less than an inch high, abound in rocky shores from southern Florida and Bermuda to the West Indies. Also called knobby periwinkles, they are usually found on rocks well above the high-tide limits, and can survive long periods without water. The naturalist Henry A. Pilsbry recorded a specimen that revived after being kept in a cabinet drawer for a year. Periwinkles and related chink shells appear to be a transitional stage between true marine snails and land snails: they are not fond of being submerged, and in an aquarium with but a single stone sticking out of the water will all converge on that one dry spot.*

your shell to those in the illustrations, and when you find one that seems to fit, read the description. If it says that the illustrated shell is found off the southern coast of Japan and you found yours off South Carolina, you obviously have to look further. But if the general appearance, form, and sculpturing are similar, continue looking in that family or genus: some shells have representatives scattered over most of the world.

As a general rule, bivalves are considerably more difficult to identify than gastropods. It's easy enough to tell the difference between the general run of scallops and the general run of clams, but within a single genus the differences may be so slight that only a close identification of the hinge will lead to an accurate identification. This brings the problem into the area of professional expertise, so if all else fails, seek the help of a conchologist or museum curator. Most of them will be happy to share their knowledge with another collector—if you don't ring their bell too often and if you are willing to follow the unwritten custom of sharing one or two shells from your catch; this is one way museums build their collections.

Shell collections range from the simple—that old shoebox filled with the take from a weekend at the shore—to the professional—hundreds of steel cabinets and cataloged trays stored in museums. Most collectors fall in between these extremes in the manner in which they display and store their treasures, depending not only on the number and variety of shells they have accumulated, but on how much money they can afford to spend on their hobby. Basic requirements for any collection, however, are organization and protection. Those able to afford it can have custom-designed cabinets with drawers of varying heights to accommodate shells of different sizes, along with handsome glass-topped display cases. Others have to make do with less. Throughout the history of collecting, a wide variety of containers and storage bins has been pressed into service: matchboxes, cigar boxes, glass tubes, pill bottles, plastic-lidded sweater boxes and thread cases (you've seen them in clothing stores and sewing centers), glass-topped coffee tables, and all sorts of secondhand furniture that can be adapted and compartmentalized. Lack of ventilation and high humidity are dangerous to shell collections because they provide conditions for the growth of a shell-destroying fungus, which usually shows up as a white crust.

Popular among collectors today are plastic boxes of varying sizes that can be arranged geometrically. Specimens are cushioned inside the boxes on beds of cotton or foam plastic; if you use cotton, lay a sheet of waxed paper or tissue over it to prevent the fine fibers from catching on any irregularities the shell might have. Clear plastic boxes are ideal because you can slip the identification label under the bedding, face out, so that it is readable from one side, while the shell is visible from the other. If you use glass vials or bottles you can also put the label inside, facing out. Stopper them with cotton batting only, not with corks or airtight caps, because condensation could affect the shell.

Collectors used to glue shells to a sheet of stiff cardboard, along with the label, but this practice is dying out, except when someone is willing to use duplicate shells to make a nature chart for a school or library. The disadvantages to gluing shells to a backing are several: only small shells can be treated this way; you can see only one side of the shell; and the glue is often difficult to remove if you should want to do something else with the shell, or perhaps trade it.

How you categorize your collection is up to you. Some collectors arrange their shells by families, some keep shells from one beach or country together, and some create elaborate habitat groups by including rocks, dried seaweeds, and other

Sea gulls and seascape

appropriate elements. Whatever systems of housing, storage, and display you decide on, remember that the main objectives are organization and protection. You want to be able to put your hands on any given shell with a minimum of searching. You want to protect your shells from becoming chipped, from dust, and, especially, from sunlight, which will fade them in time. And you want to be able to provide pertinent information about the circumstances of the shell's capture, since this could add to your fund of knowledge, if not to science's.

Shell collections range from the simple to the professional, from an old shoe box filled with the take from a weekend at the shore to the hundreds of steel cases and cataloged trays stored in museums. Basic requirements for any collection—assuming the shoe box isn't gathering dust in the back of a closet—are organization and protection. Many collectors use plastic boxes of varying sizes, but capable of being arranged geometrically, to hold their specimens. Cushioned by cotton or plastic foam, the shells are numbered, and identification labels carrying collecting information can be pasted on the box or slipped inside. Thus the shells can be seen and admired, but are protected from dust and the danger of being chipped.

Name Conus au

(= aura

Locality

The History of a Hobby

In the spring of A.D. 40, as reported by the Roman biographer Suetonius in his lives of the Caesars, Emperor Caligula stood on the banks of the English Channel with his legions massed for an invasion of Britain. Instead of embarking on that stormy and formidable stretch of water, however, the demented emperor decided to declare war on Neptune. He set his battle-ready veterans to gathering shells along the French coast, and when the booty wagons were filled led them back to Rome to parade through the city, triumphantly displaying "the spoils of conquest."

Mad Caligula may have been the most colorful of the shell collectors of antiquity, but by no means was he the first. People have been gathering mollusks for food and for ornamental, religious, and other purposes since prehistoric times. But nobody, so far as we know, collected shells for the sake of knowledge until the fourth century B.C., when Aristotle, the first of the Greek philosophers to formulate an orderly approach to the physical sciences, wrote a detailed account of mollusks. It is unlikely, however, that Aristotle wandered the shores of the Aegean seeking shells like any ordinary collector. When Alexander of Macedon, who had been one of the philosopher's pupils, became ruler, he presented his old tutor with the world's first zoological and botanical gardens, and had his soldiers and hunters keep them well supplied with flora and fauna specimens from all over his vast empire. Alexander himself was so interested in marine life, legend tells us, that he had a large glass barrel made in which he sealed himself and visited the bottom of the sea.

The first shellers who collected for the sheer pleasure of it may have been two Roman consuls of the second century B.C. who whiled away their leisure hours between military campaigns and intellectual pursuits at a favorite seaside resort south of Rome. Wrote Cicero: *"Laelius et Scipio conchas apud Caietam animi relaxandi causa legere solebant."* ("Laelius and Scipio, for the sake of relaxing their minds, used to collect seashells at Gaeta.")

A more famous Roman, Julius Caesar, was at least a onetime collector. According to another Suetonius—Suetonius Paulinus, the general who defeated Queen Boadicea after the Iceni revolted in Britain in A.D. 61—the island's reputation as a source of pearl mussels was one of the inducements that drew Caesar across the choppy waters that stopped his infamous successor some years later. His take of pearls was a disappointment in terms of quality, noted Pliny the Elder, but he made good use of the jewels by encrusting a buckler with the best of them and dedicating it to Venus.

Pliny himself, a naturalist of note, was a collector. His one extant work, a thirty-seven-volume encyclopedia of natural history, included a large section on mollusks. In A.D. 79, Pliny died of asphyxiation while investigating the eruption of

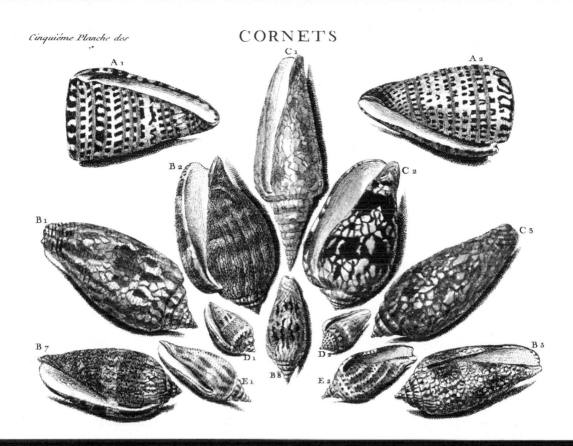

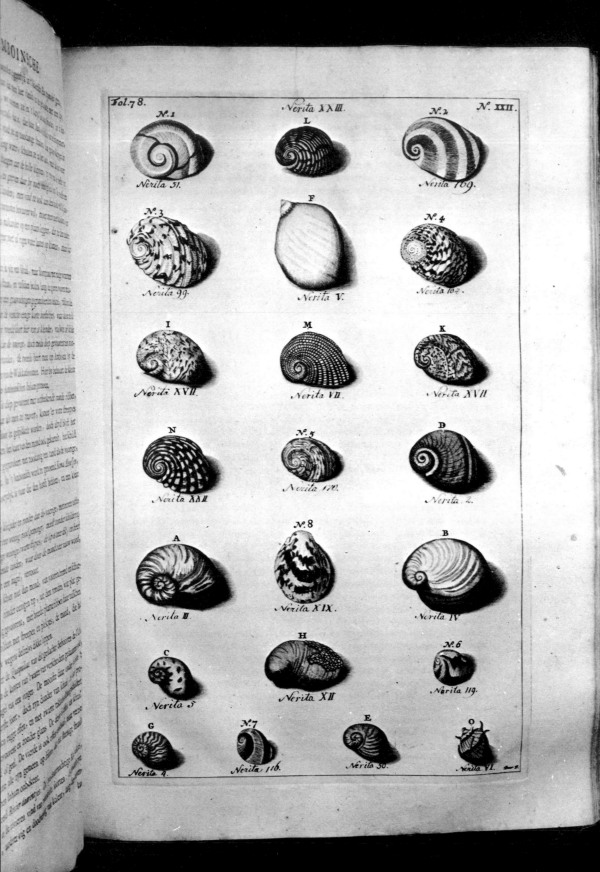

A page from Rumphius's Amboinsche Raritekamer

Vesuvius, and when a magnificent collection of ancient shells was unearthed from the ashes of Pompeii seventeen centuries later, ownership was attributed to him. Most of the shells in the collection were of Mediterranean origin, but some came from the Red Sea, and a few, including a rare textile cone, came all the way from the Indian Ocean.

There must have been other collectors and collections in ancient times, for shells were often found in the accumulations of relics and curiosities assembled in churches and monasteries during the Middle Ages. It wasn't until the Renaissance, however, that interest began to revive in the work started by Aristotle two thousand years before. Da Vinci, whose conception of the spiral staircase was inspired by a shell, had a collection, as did the German artist Albrecht Dürer, the French potter Bernard Palissy, and the Dutch scholar and theologian Erasmus.

The voyages of discovery by Columbus and later explorers did much to stimulate a growing fascination in Europe with the natural world, especially when the intrepid adventurers returned from over the oceans with hard-to-believe tales backed up by strange and exotic plants and creatures, including beautifully sculptured and colored shells from tropical seas. A veritable collecting mania swept through the Continent during the seventeenth and eighteenth centuries as the merchants followed on the heels of the explorers, opening trade routes to strange lands. It became fashionable for royalty, the aristocracy, wealthy traders, and men and women of cultivated tastes to assemble "cabinets" (entire rooms, often enough) crammed with curiosities from the new lands: stuffed birds and animals, fish, shells, minerals, tools, weapons, and primitive works of art.

Few collectors in those days did their own collecting. In 1625, for example, the Englishman John Tradescant wrote to a friend in Virginia, one Edward Nicholas, and told him that he had been taken into the service of the Duke of Buckingham, and that it was the duke's pleasure for him to deal with merchants from all places, but especially from Virginia, Bermuda, Newfoundland, Guinea, the Amazon, and the East Indies, and "to furnishe His Grace With All manner of Beasts & fowells and Birdes, shells, Bones, Egge-shells. . . ." It was a marvelous opportunity; by the time Tradescant was finished collecting for the duke and, one presumes, other gentlemen, he had amassed a collection of curiosities of his own. He filled his house in South Lambeth with his treasures, including a "physic" garden of rare plants, and named it "Tradescant's Ark." Through the efforts of his son, also named John, the collection was considerably enlarged, and in 1656 this younger Tradescant published a catalog called *Museum Tradescantianum*, "a rare collection of rarities presented at South Lambeth near London." Elias Ashmole, astrologer, alchemist, and antiquarian, assisted in the cataloging and later obtained possession of the collection, which in time became the cornerstone of the famed Ashmolean Museum at Oxford.

The British Museum in London got its start in a similar way when Sir Hans Sloane, who had collected shells from all over the world, investing some sixty thousand seventeenth-century pounds in them, willed his cabinet to the nation. A big assist came later from the outstanding collection put together by Elizabeth Bligh from shells gathered by her famous husband Capt. William Bligh of H.M.S. *Bounty*, during his wanderings in the far Pacific.

Credit for the largest European collection of the period goes to the Duchess of Portland, Margaret Cavendish Bentinck, a wealthy dowager for whom collecting shells and other objets d'art became an addiction. Distinguished visitors to her crowded

Recreatio Mentis et Oculi
in Obseruatione Cochlearum

cabinets (one in each of her two mansions) included King George III; the celebrated Swedish botanist, Carolus Linnaeus, whom we shall meet shortly as the originator of the modern scientific classification of plants and animals; Capt. James Cook, who picked up many novelties for the duchess on his voyages; and Sir Joseph Banks, the naturalist who accompanied Cook on his first voyage around the world. Dr. Daniel Solander, Cook's botanist and a student of Linnaeus, was employed for a time as curator of the collection. Having exhausted her considerable fortune on her cabinets, the duchess died in 1785 and her collection was put up for auction. The task of compiling the sales catalog for the vast collection—and naming a number of mollusks in the process—was performed by Rev. John Lightfoot, the duchess's librarian and chaplain for many years. The sale, which lasted for thirty-seven days, included more than four thousand separate lots, with winning bids ranging from nine shillings for lot number 2, a partitioned box containing a variety of small shells for making flowers and other artistic subjects, to 1,029 pounds for the Portland Vase, considered the prize of the collection.

In Great Britain, cabinets were largely the playthings of the well-to-do. But on the Continent, almost everyone was a collector. Holland had

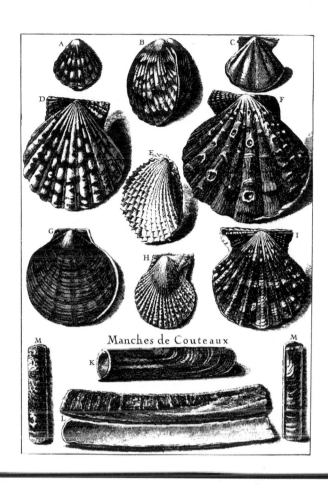

Manches de Couteaux

Opposite: *The first extensively illustrated book devoted to shells,* Recreation for the Eyes and the Mind through the Study of Shells, *by Philippo Buonanni, a Jesuit priest, appeared in Rome in 1681.* **Above right:** *The first semipopular book on conchology, published in 1757, was written by Antoine J. Dezallier d'Argenville, secretary to the King of France, Minister of the Accounts, and avid conchologist. It was called* La Conchyliologie ou Traité Général de Coquillages de Mer. **Right:** *One of the earliest known books to include mollusks among the illustrations was Belon's* La nature & diversité des poissons (The Nature and Diversity of Fishes), *published in Paris in 1555.*

contracted the collecting mania like no other country, feeding on its rich Indies trade and Pacific island colonies. Most of its famous cabinets, therefore, were located in Amsterdam and other ports served by the Dutch East India Company. Glass-fronted cupboards followed one after another, filling huge rooms, this one packed with butterflies, that one with snakes, frogs, rats, and even human embryos in preservative jars; and, of course, at least one section devoted to shells. Little attempt was made at scientific classification, the shells usually being arranged with an eye to aesthetic elegance or, too often, in grotesque combinations caricaturing human and animal forms.

On the other hand—and on the other side of the world—a representative of the Dutch East India Company based in the East Indies became famous as the first outstanding scientific shell collector. Born in Holland in 1627, George Eberhard Rumphius, botanist and conchologist, spent most of his seventy-five years in the Indies on the island of Amboina, where the Dutch operated a trading post. In his travels over the area he collected a vast store of knowledge about the shells of the Indo-Pacific, drawing on it to create what has been called a masterwork of natural history based on observation, *Amboinsche Raritekamer* (Amboinese Curiosity Cabinet). His efforts and work were beset by adversity: In middle age he lost his sight; in 1687 he lost his wife and the drawings for his work in a great fire; the first copy of his manuscript was lost at sea; and he died before a second copy reached Holland. The work received great acclaim when it was finally published, however, and Rumphius was soon being toasted posthumously as "the Pliny of the East Indies." Even greater tribute came half a century later, when Linnaeus adopted and "made official" many of the names Rumphius had originated for Pacific shells.

While Rumphius's classic chronicle was the first

extensive written account of molluscan natural history, it was not the first book devoted exclusively to shells. That honor goes to Philippo Buonanni, a Jesuit priest of Rome who published in 1681 a lavishly illustrated book called *Recreation for the Eyes and the Mind through the Study of Shells*. Although it was nonscientific and afflicted in areas with mysticism, the book served as a worthwhile introduction to the budding study of conchology, and its woodcuts of shells from distant seas proved valuable to scientists.

Four years later, in England, Martin Lister produced the first practical, systematic work on conchology, *Historia Conchyliorum*, a book containing more than a thousand copperplate engravings of shells. His two daughters, Susanna and Anna, engraved all the plates from their own drawings, a labor that must have taken them, it has been estimated, at least seven years. The first semipopular book on conchology was written in 1742 by the French naturalist Dezallier d'Argenville. It was called *La Conchyliologie ou Traité Général de Coquillages de Mer*, and in it, among other things, he described the famous cabinets of Europe, all of which he had visited.

The first scientific iconography of shells, the *New Systematic Conchological Cabinet*, was begun by a Hamburg physician, Friedrich Martini, in 1769. The first multivolume work illustrated by hand-colored woodcuts was issued over the years between 1760 and 1773 in six parts by Georg W. Knorr, a Nuremburg painter, and was called *Delights of the Eyes and the Soul*. One of the saddest experiences in the history of shell books occurred to Edgar Allan Poe in 1839, when he agreed to write the foreword for a textbook by an Englishman, Thomas Brown. To boost sales, the American publisher attributed authorship of the book to the popular Edgar Allen (Brown's name was left off the title page), and the literary world rose in rage to accuse poor innocent Poe of plagiarism.

In all, more than four thousand books and ninety-one thousand shorter works have been devoted to shells since the invention of the printing press. Many of these have been scholarly works and textbooks, and many in more recent years have been "popular" books, such as this one, written for the ever-growing audience of shell collectors. And some have combined both popular appeal and scientific weight with a surefire attention getter—adventure. These books resulted from some of the great sea voyages of the eighteenth and nineteenth centuries. Many of these voyages were undertaken for trade and empire-building purposes, but others had natural history knowledge and specimen-collecting as their main goals. The three exciting and scientifically profitable voyages of Captain Cook to the South Seas between 1768 and 1779 showed the way, and soon the oceans were churning with the comings and goings of natural history expeditions.

A chronological sampling:

1799: German naturalist Alexander Von Humboldt and botanist Aimé Bonpland begin a five-year exploration of virgin areas in northern South America.

1826: Alcide d'Orbigny leads a Paris Museum expedition to southern South America and returns with a huge work on mollusks.

1846: The *Samarang*, British registry, brings back from the Pacific "great conchological treasures," vividly described by Arthur Adams, ship's surgeon.

1860: The British vessels *Lightning* and *Porcupine* pioneer deep-sea dredging for specimens of marine life.

1872: Sir Charles Wyville Thomson leads the *Challenger* on a four-year voyage that has been called one of the greatest scientific deep-sea expeditions of all time, covering sixty-nine thousand miles and bringing back nineteen hundred species from depths of up to twenty-nine hundred fathoms.

Through the years there have been numerous other scientific voyages, many of them under the aegis of national governments, and many others sponsored by private citizens who happened to be shell enthusiasts. The most famous of the latter was Hugh Cuming, an Englishman "of humble birth" who, says R. Tucker Abbott, "was to conchology as Henry Ford was to the automobile industry. No man has ever equaled the amount of material he personally acquired nor discovered a larger number of new species."

After making his fortune in Chile, Cuming built a yacht, dubbed it *Discovery*, and between 1827 and 1840 covered thousands of shell-collecting miles in the Pacific—along the coasts of Central and South America, to the islands of Polynesia, and through the Philippines. From his first expedition, 1827–1831, he brought back to London some two thousand new species; from his last and greatest expedition, 1836–1840, to the Philippines, three thousand more, along with thirty-four hundred different plants and twelve hundred birds. Cuming single-handedly revolutionized descriptive conchology, commented S. Peter Dance, eminent British shell expert, and "as a result of his remarkable collecting activities, some of the great classics of conchological literature came into being, most notably the twenty-volume *Conchologia Iconica* of L.A. Reeve." In fact, it would be no exaggeration to state that Cuming's molluscan contributions kept many of the greatest conchologists of the time busy for years writing descriptions. Most of his collection is now in the British Museum of Natural History in London.

The greatest twentieth-century collector, and an outstanding conchologist in his own right, was Belgium's Philippe Dautzenburg, who during his lifetime accumulated, by personal collecting as well as by purchase of rarities and old collections, more than thirty thousand species and a magnificent library of works devoted to shells. Dautzenburg's collection holds an impressive place in the Institut Royal des Sciences Naturelles in Brussels.

Among the foremost present-day collectors is John E. du Pont, director of the Delaware Museum of Natural History, in Greenville, Delaware, who ranges the world in expeditions designed to add to the museum's treasury of 1.25 million shells. Also on that exclusive list is Emperor Hirohito of Japan, whose training as a marine biologist explains his deep interest, and who is said to have the largest collection of shells in his island country, if not in all Asia. And not to be forgotten is the Smithsonian Institution in Washington, D.C., with an unrivaled collection of 10 million specimens.

Another chapter in the historical background of shell collecting remains to be told—how shells are named.

What's in a name? To paraphrase the famous answer to that question, a shell by any other name would still be one of nature's most inspired creations. Knowing that a certain shell is called the paper moon scallop may enhance our appreciation of the symmetry of its form, but it is not necessary. Neither do we have to know that another is called the comb of Venus to take pleasure in its one hundred or more perfectly shaped and curved spines.

Because human beings have been blessed with imagination, however, they take pleasure in giving fanciful names to objects, such as shells, that titillate that imagination. But since fancies differ from person to person, where one sees in a shell a comb for Venus, another might see a rake. Because of this it is possible that a single mollusk could be known by a different name wherever it is found.

This was not a problem when people collected shells merely to use as tools, as ornaments, in bartering, or as religious symbols. But when the early scientists began examining and describing shells—and later the fascinating animals themselves, how they lived and reproduced and formed their wondrous stonehard coverings—it became a different matter. For what one scientist discovered in his study of a certain bivalve or gastropod would have little meaning to other scientists unless they knew which animal—or related group of animals—he was writing about.

For a long period, the situation was very confusing. In early books on natural history, some authors used local common names of plant and animal species, sometimes in their native tongue, sometimes in a Latinized version, and sometimes both, side by side. Others developed scientific names, rendered in Latin, which described the shell or flower in such meticulous detail that they became unmanageable, indigestible sentences—with the longest and most difficult of names usually bestowed on the tiniest of specimens. Using Latin was a step in the right direction, for as a "dead" language it could be trusted to say and mean the same thing to scientists all over the world. But what was needed along with this universal language of science was a universally accepted system of nomenclature.

Order was brought out of chaos in the middle of the eighteenth century by the great Swedish naturalist mentioned previously, Carolus Linnaeus (which spelling is the Latinized form of Karl Linné). In his *Systema Naturae*, which was published in twelve editions between 1735 and 1768, Linnaeus presented his system of binomial nomenclature for animals, and did the same for plants in *Species Planatarum* in 1753. He did not originate the idea of two-name identifications, one generic and the other specific; a Swiss botanist named Gaspard Bauhin had suggested it more than a century before, in 1623, and early herbalists had already put a similar system to use. But Linnaeus gave it its first definite form and substance, and it was quickly accepted by most of the international scientific community as an idea whose time had come. For his contributions, the king of Sweden in 1761 ennobled Linnaeus, making it retroactive to 1757, whereupon the naturalist formally adopted the name Karl von Linné.

Many people are unnecessarily frightened of Latin words and names. Unlike English, Latin is pronounced pretty much as it is spelled; no matter how long the word, take it syllable by syllable and you'll have it. Many English words come directly from Latin and practically translate themselves. For example, you probably mentally translated the titles of Linnaeus's books mentioned above as you read along, without a second thought. Similarly, you should have no trouble converting *Conus nobilis* to noble cone, and even such longer species names as *longispina* and *brevispina*, which look imposing at first glance, break apart nicely into long-spined and brief or short-spined. Other descriptive Latin words popular in shell names that more or less announce themselves include *gigantea*, *bicolor*, *corona*, *pugilis*, *musica*, *contracta*, *rosea*, *pyramidalis*, *radiata*, *corrugata*, *globosa*, *triangularis*, *volcano*, and *nodosa*.

The binomial system using Latin is a precise and simple method of naming plant and animal species. The first word in the name tells us the genus, or "family," to which the shell belongs. This is the generic name, the first letter of which is always

Beginning of the section on murices from d'Argenville's La Conchyliologie.

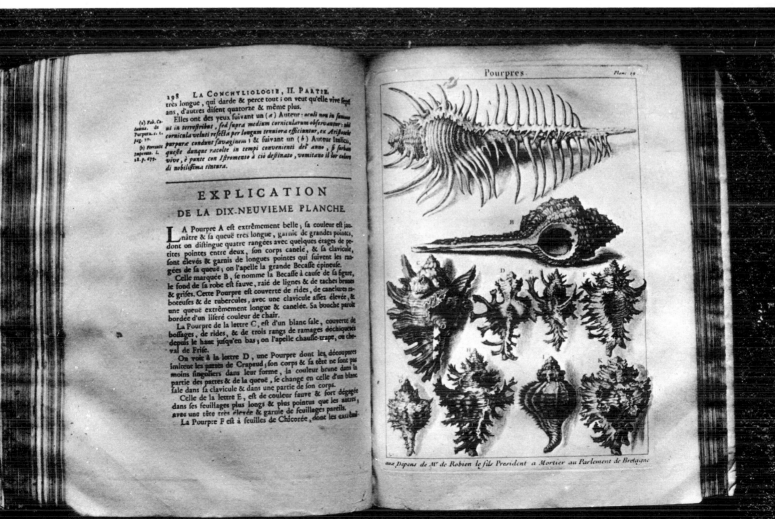

capitalized. The second word is the name of the species, comparable to a person's given name, and refers to one particular kind of shell. This is the specific name, sometimes referred to as the "trivial" name, and it is never capitalized. Occasionally a third word is added to designate a variation in a certain species; this is called the subspecific name, and it also is never capitalized.

It is valuable to remember that a generic name cannot be used for more than one group, or genus, of animals, and a specific name cannot be used for more than one species in that group. A specific name can, however, be used for a species in *another* group. Thus, there can be only one species of cone shell called *Conus nobilis,* but there can also be a species of volute called *Voluta nobilis.* Incidentally, when two or more species of one genus are being discussed in close proximity, the author usually will give the full name of the first one, as in *Strombus canarium,* and then abbreviate the generic name of the others, as in *S. gigas* and *S. gallus.*

After the Latin name of the shell, which is always italicized, comes the name of the "author" of the shell, which may or may not appear in italics. Popular books and shell handbooks often do not include the name of the author, but scientific works always do. The author of a shell is the person who first discovered it or first published a valid description of it and gave it a name. This recognition in the record books is the author's reward for adding new information to "the sum of human knowledge," but if his name is too long, he gets shortchanged—it will be abbreviated in the various shell catalogs and only other malacologists will know who is being honored.

Once an author has properly identified the genus of a new species, whether it be *Pecten* (scallops), *Busycon* (whelks), *Cypraea* (cowries), or another, he has the privilege of dubbing it with any specific name he chooses, so long as that name is not already

in service within the genus. There are many possibilities. He may try to describe the shell: *pygmaea* if it is very small, for example, or *undosa* if it is undulating or wavy. He may choose to describe where it was found, Latinizing geographical areas into such forms as *floridanus* or *bermudensis.* He may name it for his wife, or she—there are plenty of female malacologists—may name it for her husband. Or the malacologist who is describing the shell may name it for the amateur collector who discovered it and brought it to him. Sometimes the shell is named for a scientist whom the author wants to honor, as in *stimpsoni* or *perryae.* The "i" ending signifies that the honored person is a man; the "ae" denotes a woman.

Authors of shell books (not to be confused with authors of shells) are fond of telling the story of the malacologist who named a new shell after his sweetheart, whose name was Maria. A little while later he received some good news and some bad news. The bad news was that his girlfriend had broken their engagement and run off with another man. The good news was that the International Commission for Zoological Nomenclature, arbiters in such matters, deemed *mariae* unacceptable as a name because of a scientific technicality. Given a second chance, the spurned malacologist had his revenge: he named the shell *inconstans.*

Occasionally an author will give a name to a shell that seems to be not only obscure, but downright inappropriate or misleading. Most people, for example, cannot understand how Linnaeus could possibly have called a popular shell from the Pacific and Indian Oceans *Cypraea tigris* (tiger cowrie), since the shell is marked beautifully not with stripes, but with spots! Similarly, the zebra cowrie (*C. zebra* Linnaeus) has more the appearance of a leopard than a zebra. Did Linnaeus have spots before his eyes?

Not really, says A. Hyatt Verrill in his *Shell*

Collector's Handbook: "In some cases, such inappropriate names resulted from a mistake. . . . Like many other species of *Cypraea* this shell [zebra cowrie] when immature has broad bands of light and dark color, but when adult is covered with light spots on a dark ground. When Linnaeus named the shell *Cypraea zebra* he described an immature specimen. Later he described an adult specimen as *Cypraea xanthema,* the measly cowrie. For many years the shell was known by this name, but as the name *Cypraea zebra* had priority the name *xanthema* was discarded, although far more appropriate than *zebra.*"

The matter of priority is important, for it is the rule in the science of taxonomy that the name by which a species is known is the oldest available one. Sometimes several scientists will discover a new species at about the same time; there have been occasions in the past when widespread species have been given a dozen or more names. The law of priority holds that the name used by the first scientist to describe and name the shell is the one that stands. The rule prevails even if a shell name has been in use for a long time and an earlier name comes to light. This causes understandable confusion, and results in the same shell being called by one name in one book and by a different name in a later book. As a concession to common sense, a number of the best-known shells have now been put on a protected list—the names by which they have been known for scores or hundreds of years cannot be changed even if a prior naming is discovered.

A shell's name can change for other reasons, however. Perhaps it has been found that a generic name has already been applied to another group of animals. When someone discovered that a type of salamander had first claim on the name *Tritonia,* a group of triton shells had to be renamed *Charonia,* even though they may still be called tritons in the vernacular. Or perhaps scientists with today's modern laboratory equipment and facilities will determine that a given mollusk's physical characteristics ally it more closely with a genus different from the one in which it has been placed. A change is made, and later reference books once again will offer a different name for the same animal. When this occurs, the original author's name is retained, but is placed in brackets. If you come across this situation in your attempts to identify a shell, the sensible rule-of-thumb is to check the dates of publication and go along with the latest book.

Familiarizing yourself with the Latin names of shells can be rewarding in several ways: You'll know better what the experts are writing and talking about; you'll know immediately to which group each animal belongs; you'll be able to trade shells and know exactly what you're getting in return, something you are never sure of if you use only popular names, which vary from country to country and even from locality to locality. And if you go a little deeper into the subject, putting a Latin-English dictionary to work, you can pick up a lot of interesting information about shells, geography, history, and social customs, and have some fun in the bargain.

However you approach this ancient hobby, it's plain to see that there's more to being a shell collector than just collecting shells.

A Shell Galaxy

Part II

1, 2: Rudicardium tuberculatum *Linné, the knobbed cockle, 2 to 3 inches, Mediterranean and eastern Atlantic. Cockleshells, or heart shells, are generally swollen and heart-shaped, particularly when viewed from the side. One of the larger bivalve families, they are extensively used for food, especially in Europe.*

3: Gafrarium pectinatum *Linné, the pectinate*

Venus, 2 inches, Indo-Pacific. One of the large family of Venus clams, which has representatives in all seas and at all depths.

4, 5: Mactra corallina stultorum *Linné, the fool's mactra, 2 inches, Europe. The Mactridae, surf clams, are found all over the world. They are usually fairly large but often fragile, and generally inhabit shallow water.*

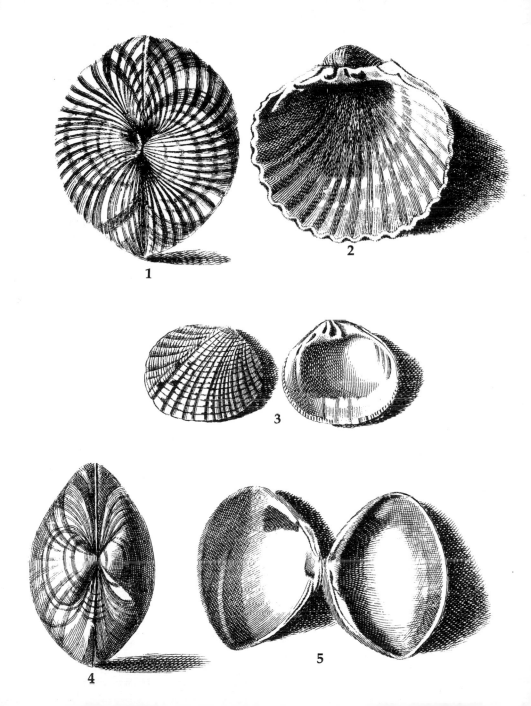

1, 2: Glycymeris pectunculus *Linné, the comb bittersweet, 1 inch, North Carolina through the Caribbean to Brazil. These dog-cockle clams are related to ark shells but have more colorful, compressed, oval shells. They are usually found in sandy, shallow areas. The comb bittersweet has a brown-splotched gray shell with twenty to forty raised ribs.*

3, 4: Acanthocardia echinata *Linné, the northern spiny cockle, 3 inches, northern Europe. The large cockle family, divided into numerous genera, can be found all over the world.*

5–7: Cardium costatum *Linné, the costate cockle, 4 inches, West Africa. Considered the true cockle and often called the ribbed cockle, Cardium costatum is the culmination of a family with strong, deeply ribbed shells.*

8–11: Venericardia pectinata *Linné, the comb cardita, 1 to 2 inches, Indo-Pacific. The family Carditidae, the little heart clams, consists of about two dozen species. The thick-shelled Cardita are heavily ribbed and usually spin a byssus, while the Venericardia are more rounded in form and do not produce a byssus.*

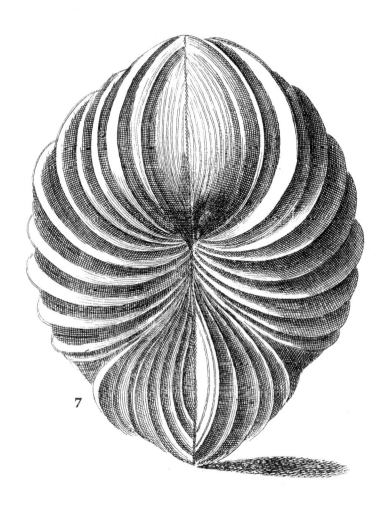

7

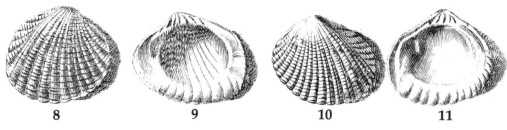

8   9   10   11

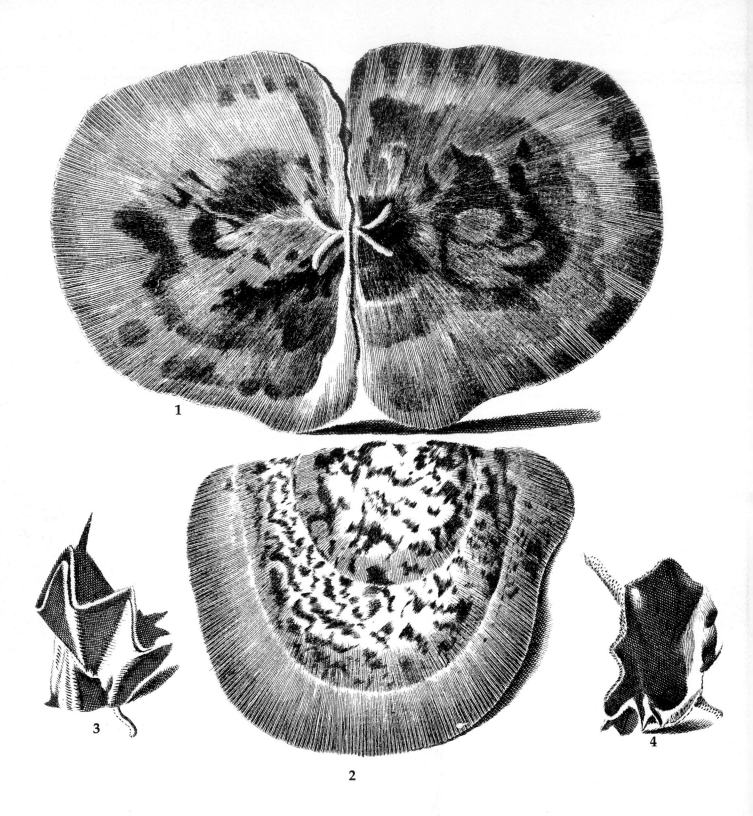

1, 2: Placuna sella *Gmelin, the saddle oyster, 8 inches, western Indo-Pacific. These thin animals are related to the windowpane oysters,* P. placenta, *of the Philippines.*

3, 4: Lopha cristagalli *Linné, the cock's comb oyster, 4 inches, Indo-Pacific.*

5: Spondylus princeps *Broderip, the Pacific thorny oyster, 3 to 6 inches, from California to Panama. Sought by collectors for its rich colors and the fantastic long spines growing out of its ribbed surface. The live shell normally is so encrusted with marine growths that its bizarre beauty is hidden.*

1, 2: Acanthocardia ciliare *Linné, the ciliated spiny cockle, 1½ inches, Mediterranean.*

3–5: Acanthocardia aculeata *Linné, Mediterranean spiny cockle, 3 inches, Mediterranean Sea. Cockles, like scallops, are active animals, and have a long, powerful, sickle-shaped foot that enables them to leap several inches off the bottom. All have solid shells with radial ribs ornamented with scales and spines; these trimmings are often worn off the sand-dwellers, however. Cockles are adaptable, and thrive equally well in high-salinity lagoons and the diluted*

waters of estuaries. They are said to be the only marine mollusks to have made their way into the Black and Azov seas, and, even more remarkably, into the salty Caspian, the largest inland body of water in the world.

6, 7: Glycymeris undata *Linné, the Atlantic bittersweet, 2 inches, North Carolina to Brazil. Also known as the wavy bittersweet, this species differs from the comb bittersweet by having a smoothish shell, with very fine concentric and radial scratches giving it a ''silky'' look.*

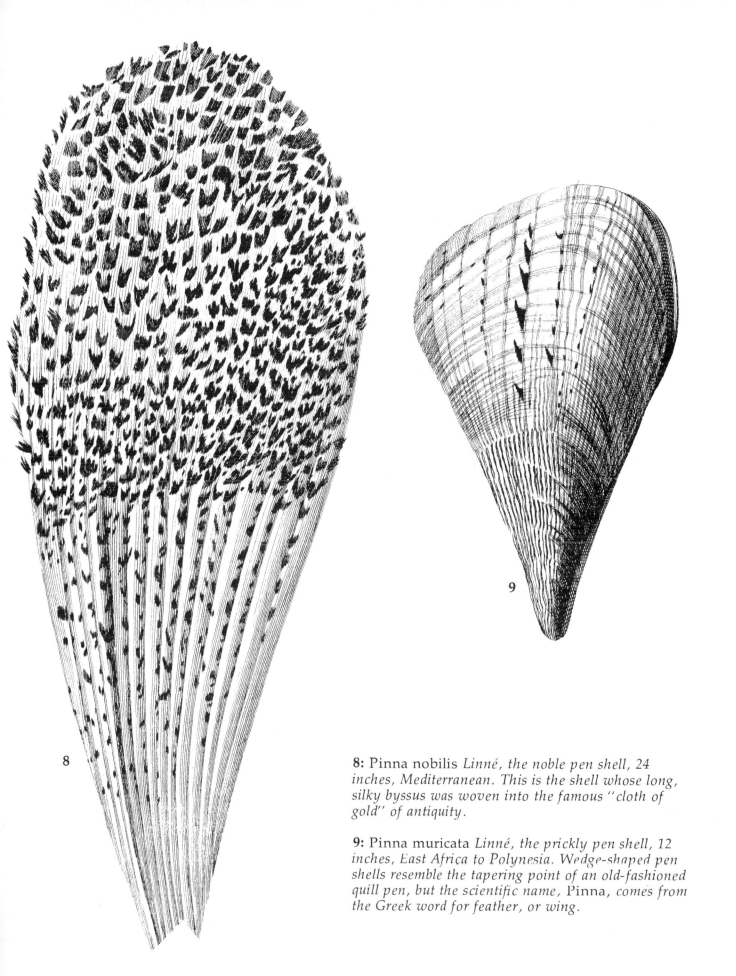

8: Pinna nobilis *Linné, the noble pen shell, 24 inches, Mediterranean. This is the shell whose long, silky byssus was woven into the famous "cloth of gold" of antiquity.*

9: Pinna muricata *Linné, the prickly pen shell, 12 inches, East Africa to Polynesia. Wedge-shaped pen shells resemble the tapering point of an old-fashioned quill pen, but the scientific name,* Pinna, *comes from the Greek word for feather, or wing.*

1: Pecten ziczac Linné, the zigzag scallop, 5 inches, North Carolina through the Caribbean to Brazil. This once fairly common shell, sometimes called the sharp-turn scallop, has been over-collected and is now protected. Zigzag scallops are numbered among the best swimming bivalves, darting this way and that in typical scallop fashion, but their name more likely came from the zigzag lines of black ornamenting the crowded ribs on the flat upper valve.

2

4

2 left: Lophocardium cumingii *Broderip,* Cuming's cardium, 1 ½ inches, Acapulco to Colombia.

2 center: Laevicardium attenuatum *Sowerby, the weak cardium, 2 ½ inches, eastern Africa and Indian Ocean.*

2 right: Nemocardium bechei *Reeve, Beche's cardium, 2 ½ inches, Indo-Pacific.*

7

8

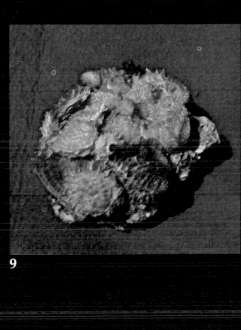

9

3: Chlamys swifti *Bernardi, 3 to 5 inches, Japan.*

4: Lioconcha castrensis *Linné, tented clam, 1 to 2 inches, Indo-Pacific. This is a cream yellow clam marked with a variety of angular blackish lines in shapes that explain its common name.*

5: Cyrtopleura costata *Linné, the angel wings, 4 to 7 inches, Massachusetts to Brazil. This is one of the amazing boring clams that are capable of penetrating wood, coral, and even some types of rock by using their thin, brittle shells as drill bits.*

6: Penicillus giganteus *Linné, the giant watering pot shell, Indo-Pacific. This is a picture of the lower end of this strange bivalve, showing the two embryonic clam shells from which it grew.*

7: Lopha cristagalli *Linné, the cock's comb oyster, 4 inches, Indo-Pacific. This is a tropical species that often exhibits a shell edge with wildly haphazard angles; there are other specimens, however, that have a lip as regular as any other oyster. Color also can vary, from slate gray to a deep but dusty blue.*

8: Siliqua patula *Dixon, the Pacific razor clam, 3 to 4 inches, Pacific coast. Although clams are more important to sportsmen and individual clam-diggers than to marine commerce on the West Coast, the industry is growing.*

9: Chama macerophylla *Gmelin, the jewelbox shell, 2 inches, North Carolina to the West Indies. These pastel-colored, frilled shells attach themselves to rocks, coral, and sturdy plants so firmly that, on rocks, at least, they must be removed by hammer and chisel.*

1, 2: Asaphis deflorata *Linné, the gaudy sand clam, 2 inches, southeast Florida to Brazil. It is the only member of its genus in North America, but, curiously, also occurs in the Indo-Pacific. It is variably colored in white or yellow tinted with shades of red, blue, or purple.*

3, 4: Americardia media *Linné, the Atlantic strawberry cockle, 2 inches, North Carolina to Brazil. This thick shell has thirty-three to thirty-six strong radiating ribs; its color is white, well-mottled with reddish brown. Also called the American cockle.*

5–9: Lioconcha castrensis *Linné, the tented clam, 2 inches, Philippines. This is a cream yellow clam marked with a variety of angular blackish lines in shapes that suggest its common name.*

10–17: Corculum cardissa *Linné, the heart cockle, 1 to 3 inches, Indo-Pacific.*

18, 19: Modiolus barbatus *Linné, the bearded modiolus, 2 inches, Mediterranean. One of the widespread family of sea mussels, found all over the world but most prolific in cool waters.*

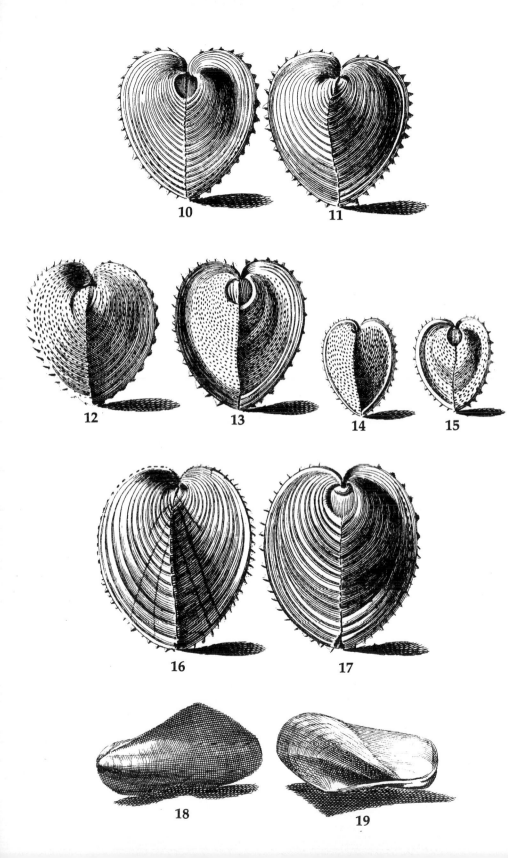

1

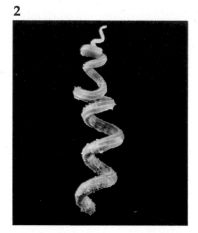

2

3

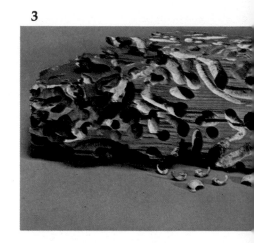

4

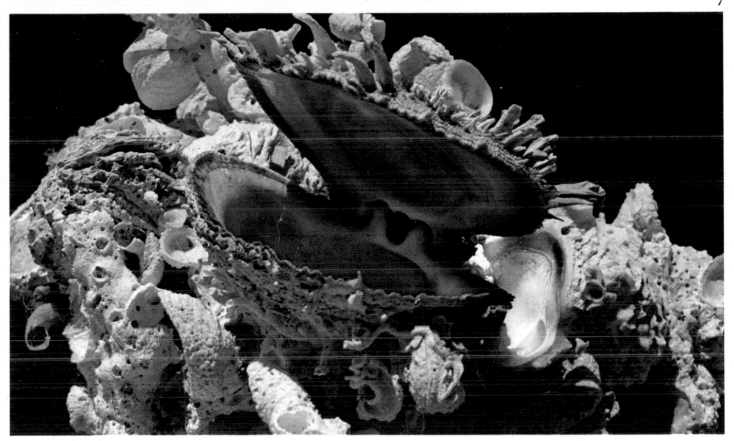

1: Dentalium formosum *Adams and Reeves, a tusk shell, 2½ inches, Japan.*

2: Siliquaria squamata *Blainville, a slit worm shell, 3 to 5 inches, western Atlantic.*

3: *Wooden piling destroyed by* Teredo navalis *Linné, the "shipworm," a type of clam that is distributed worldwide.*

4: Vermicularia spirata *Philippi, the common worm shell, 7 inches, Massachusetts to the West Indies. The shell's whorls, after the first few, are unpredictable.*

The animal is a true gastropod, although it looks more like a worm—in fact, its shell has been likened to a petrified angleworm.

5: *A denuded test, or shell, of the sharp-spined sea urchin, which attains a diameter of 6 inches. Not a mollusk but an echinoderm.*

6: Modiolus americanus *Leach, the tulip mussel, 3 to 4 inches, North Carolina to the West Indies.*

7: Spondylus americanus *Hermann, the Atlantic thorny oyster, 4 to 6 inches, western Atlantic.*

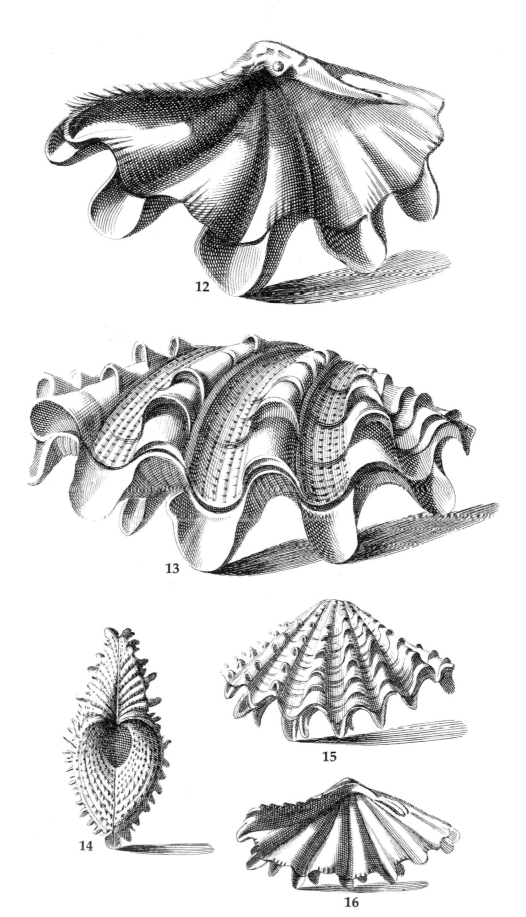

1–4: Tridacna crocea *Lamarck, the crocus giant clam, 4 to 6 inches, western Pacific. The Tridacnidae, or giant clams, include the largest of living shelled mollusks,* T. gigas, *one specimen of which tops the record list with a pair of valves 4½ feet long and a weight of 579½ pounds. The clams on these pages, while members of the giant clam family, hardly fit that image. But they are interesting enough in their own right.* T. crocea *is one of the true boring bivalves. Twisting back and forth on a byssal anchor, it hollows out a groove or basin in hard coral blocks until it is almost completely buried, and maintains its position through constant grinding movement.*

5–16: Tridacna squamosa *Lamarck, the fluted giant clam, 5 to 8 inches, Indo-Pacific. Widely distributed from the Red Sea to Polynesia, this is one of the most highly sculptured of the giant clams, with beautiful elongated fluted scales and a wide range of pastel colors.*

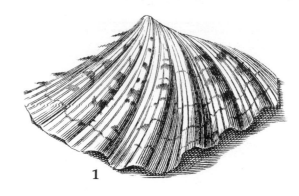

1

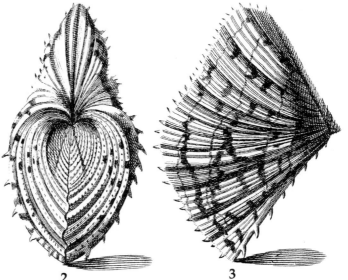

2   3

4

1–3: Hippopus hippopus *Linné, the bear paw clam, 10 to 12 inches, western Pacific. Found mostly in the seas from the Malay Peninsula to Japan and eastward as far as Samoa, the beautiful and abundant bear paw clam is highly prized all over the world by shell dealers, collectors, and creators of shell art and novelties. It is known for subtle variations in shape and markings, for gracefully curved ridges and scalloped edges, and for an eye-pleasing mixture of white, beige, and brown tones. Single valves become attractive salad bowls and centerpieces for fruits, nuts, and flowers. The scalloped edges of matched*

bear paw clam valves usually fit so neatly together that spectacular jewel boxes can be made from them.

4: Tridacna squamosa *Lamarck, the fluted giant clam, 5 to 8 inches, Indo-Pacific.*

5, 6: Tridacna maxima *Roeding, the large tridacna, 4 to 8 inches, Indo-Pacific. There are six species of Tridacnas, with a huge variation in size, but all alike in some things—all from the Indo-Pacific and all living partially buried upside down, or hinge-side down, in sand or coral blocks.*

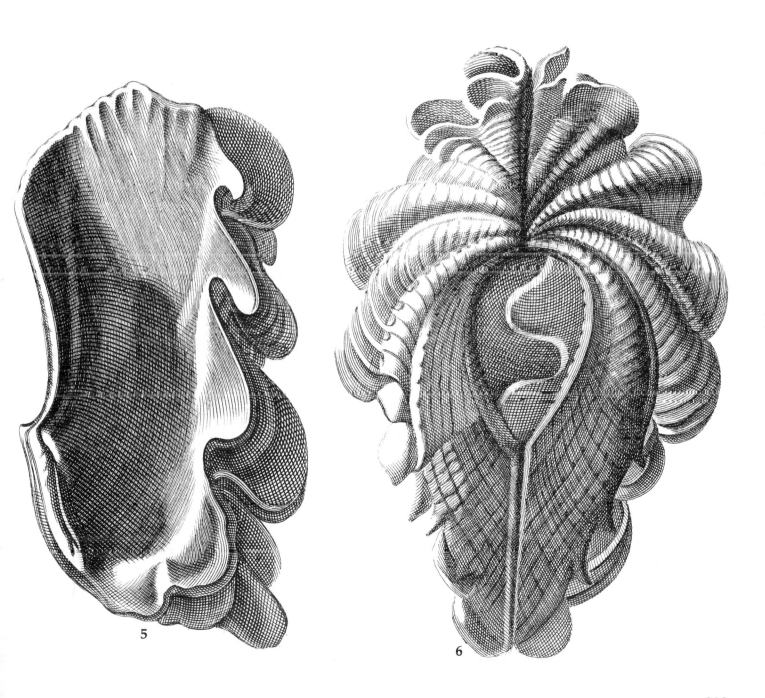

5

6

Marine crabs on coral

Clump·of madreporan coral

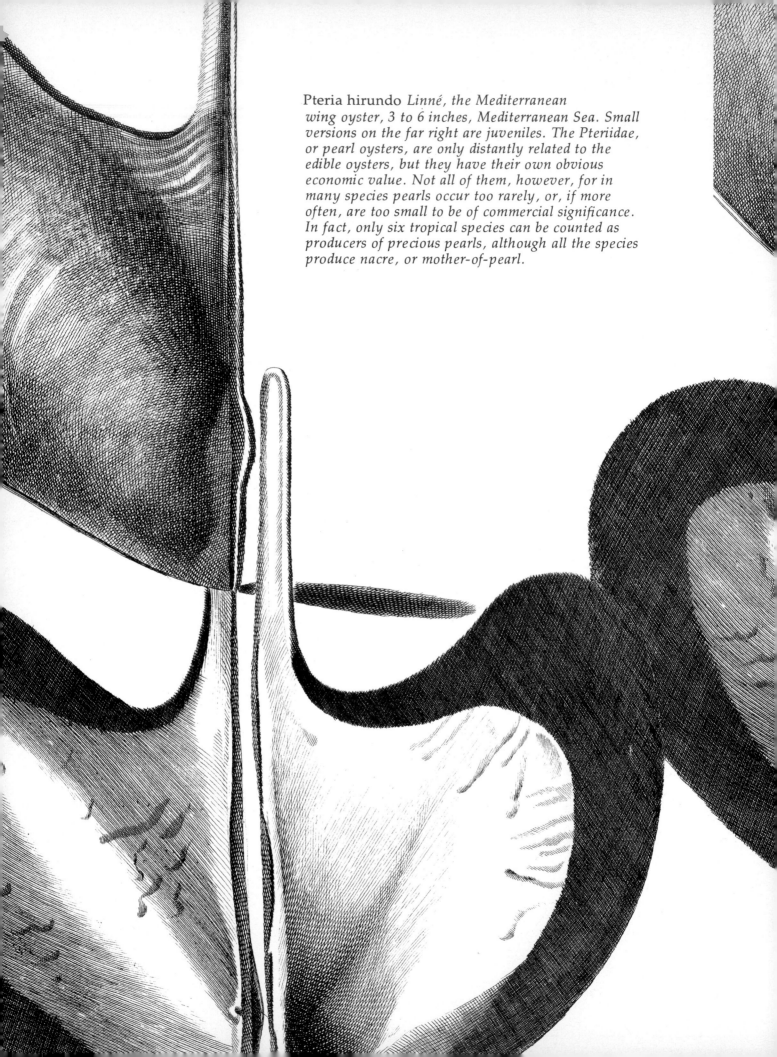

Pteria hirundo *Linné, the Mediterranean
wing oyster, 3 to 6 inches, Mediterranean Sea. Small
versions on the far right are juveniles. The Pteriidae,
or pearl oysters, are only distantly related to the
edible oysters, but they have their own obvious
economic value. Not all of them, however, for in
many species pearls occur too rarely, or, if more
often, are too small to be of commercial significance.
In fact, only six tropical species can be counted as
producers of precious pearls, although all the species
produce nacre, or mother-of-pearl.*

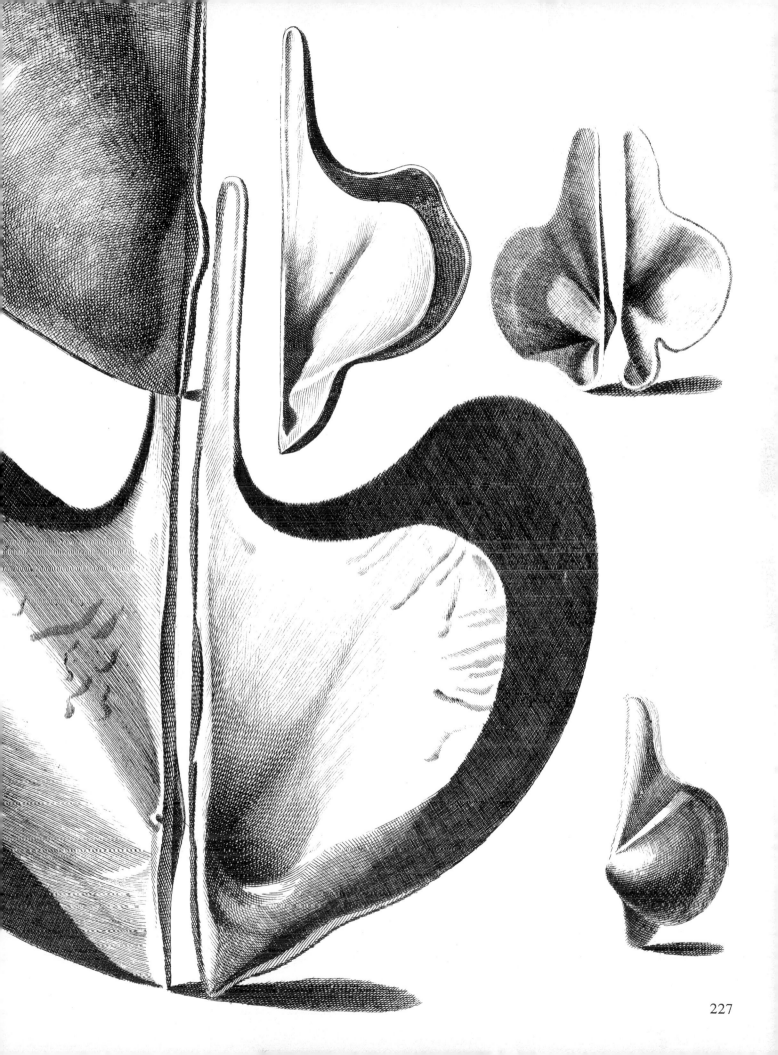

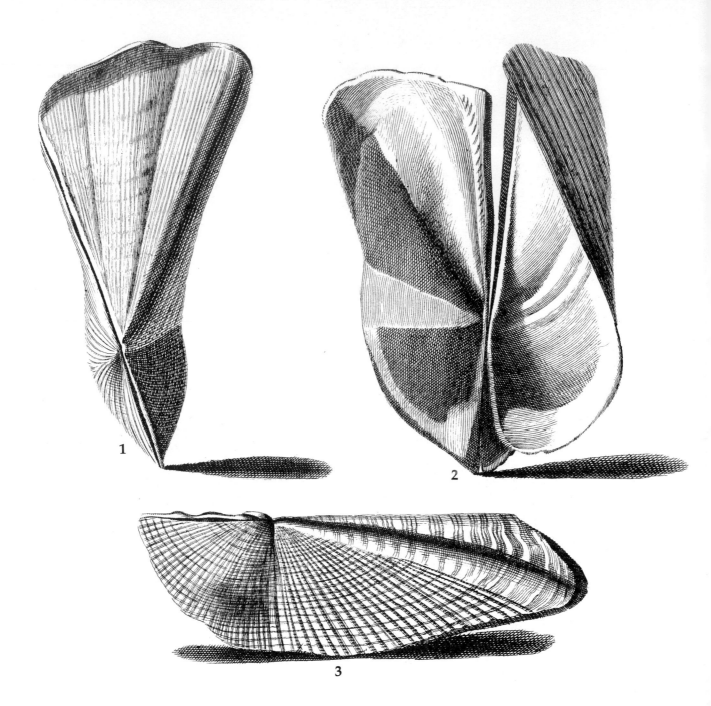

1–3: Trisidos tortuosa *Linné, the twisted ark shell, 2 to 4 inches, western Pacific. Of some two hundred species of ark shells, only two dozen are natives to the Americas, and these are mostly tropical shells marked by a long, straight, many-toothed hinge. But* T. tortuosa, *if only by name, could not be considered straight—and its peculiar twisted shape is unique among ark shells.*

4–6: Malleus malleus *Linné, the common hammer oyster, 4 to 7 inches, Indo-Pacific. Hammer oysters are so called because of their obvious resemblance, especially when closed, to a hammer. The common hammer oyster has a black exterior and a nacreous interior. A close relative, the white common hammer,* M. albus, *has a white shell, and was so rare in the eighteenth century that dealers who could not obtain sufficient specimens for their customers resorted to shell forgery.*

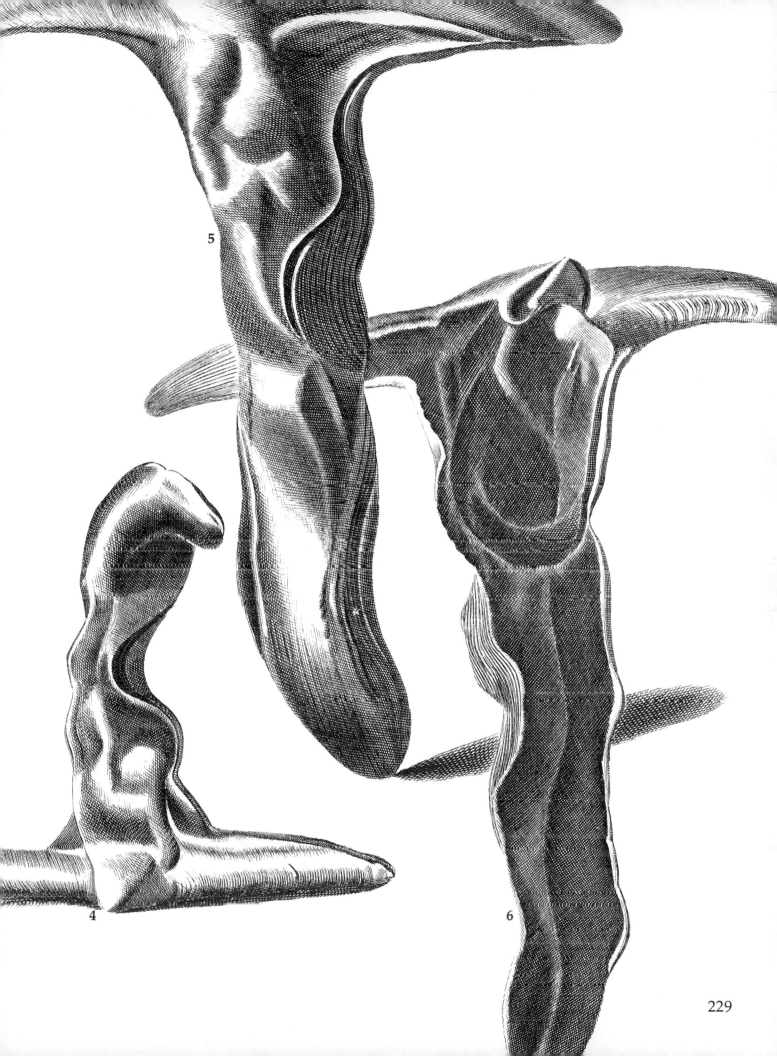

1, 2: Lyropecten nodosus *Linné, the lion's paw scallop, 3 to 6 inches, Florida and the West Indies. This striking bivalve, also known as the knobbed scallop, can be bright red, deep orange, or even purplish red in color. It is marked by numerous riblets and seven to nine large ribs armed with large, hollow blisters or nodes (the knuckles of the paw) into which the Aztecs of Mexico worked nuggets of gold, turning the shell into a pendant worth a king's ransom. These scallops thrive among deep-water sponge beds, and at one time were brought to market in perfect condition by sponge divers. With the decline in demand for natural sponges, however, the supply has fallen off, and collectors are driven more to accepting a single valve, washed up on the beach after being knocked about a bit, but still available.*

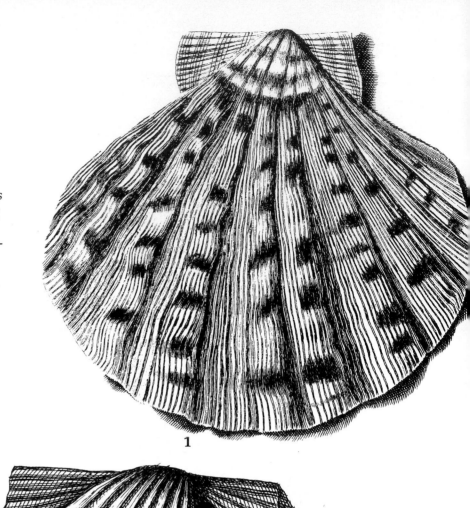

1

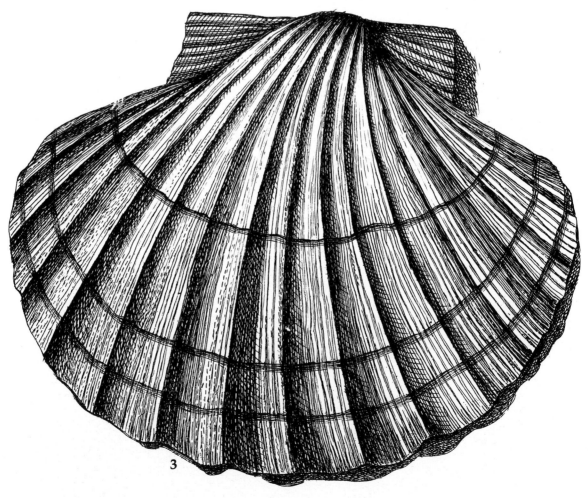

3

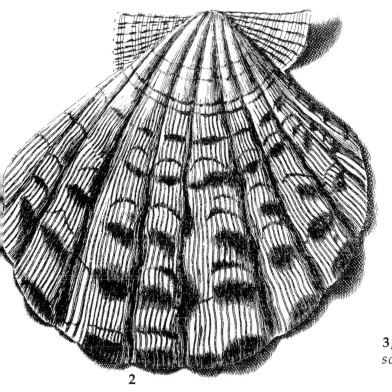

3, 4: Pecten maximus *Linné, the giant scallop, 6 inches, northeast Atlantic.*

2

4

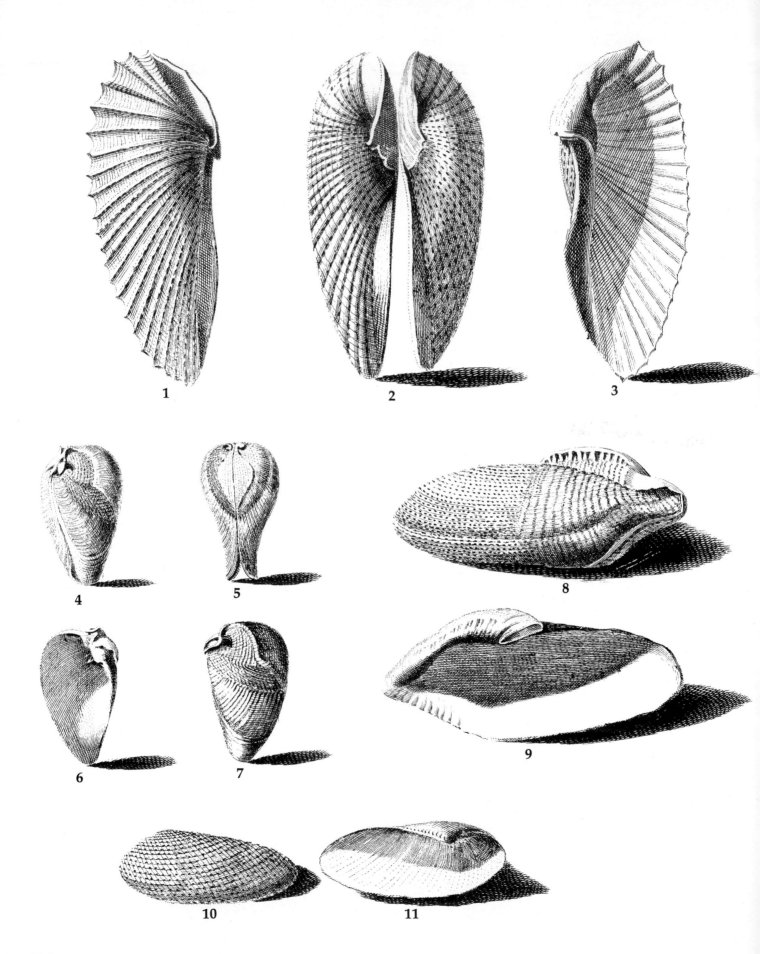

232

1–3: Cyrtopleura costata *Linné, the angel wing, 7 inches, Massachusetts to Brazil. This beautiful white shell is the most popular of the family Pholadidae, the angel wings and piddocks. It lives in colonies in mud flats, and its valves are extremely fragile, as you might expect angel wings to be. A sad story is told of a bed of angel wings on Florida's Gulf Coast, where shell collectors could always find specimens and local residents in need of money could dig up a few and sell them for a dollar a pair. Then some fool in search of a killing came in with a suction dredge and dug up the entire bed. There were so many shells the price dropped to fifteen cents a pair, and the bed never recovered.*

4–7: Martesia striata *Linné, the striate piddock, 1½ inches, North Carolina to Brazil; bores into wood.*

8, 9: Pholas dactylus *Linné, the European angel wing, European waters. Pholas comes from the Greek, pholeo, to bore. Most malacologists now agree that the ability of such fragile shells as angel wings and piddocks to bore into rock is aided by a powerful chemical solution which they exude.*

10, 11: Barnea candida *Linné, the white angel wing, 4 inches, northern European waters.*

12: Hyotissa hyotis *Linné, the honeycomb oyster, 4 inches, worldwide distribution.*

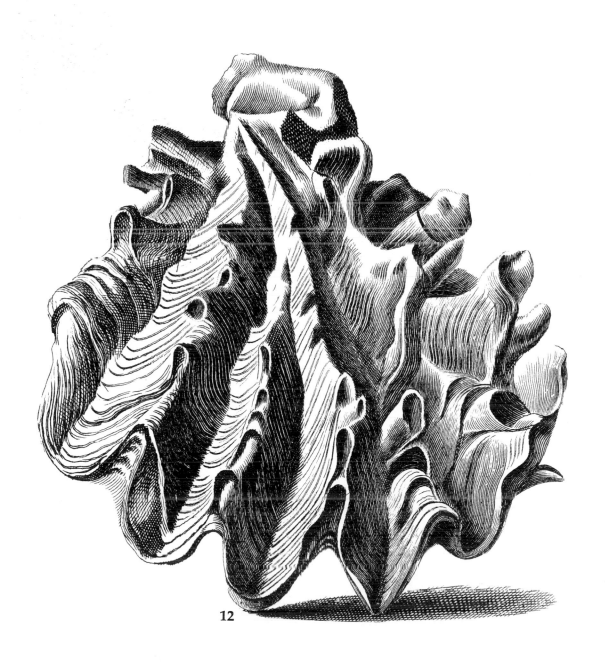

12

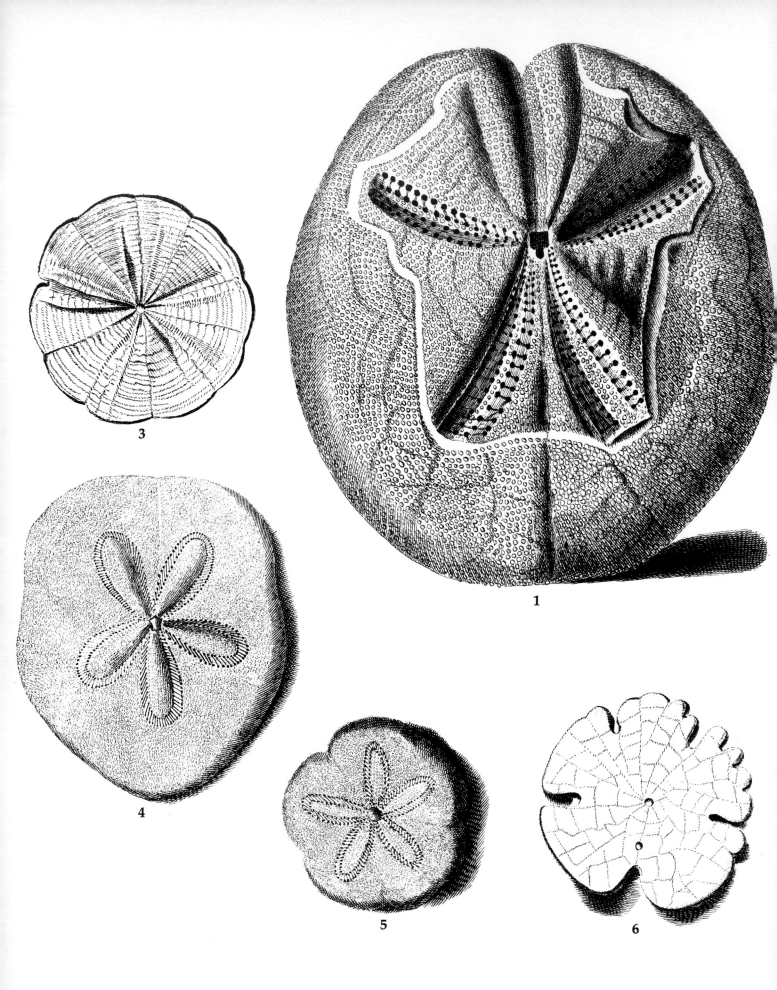

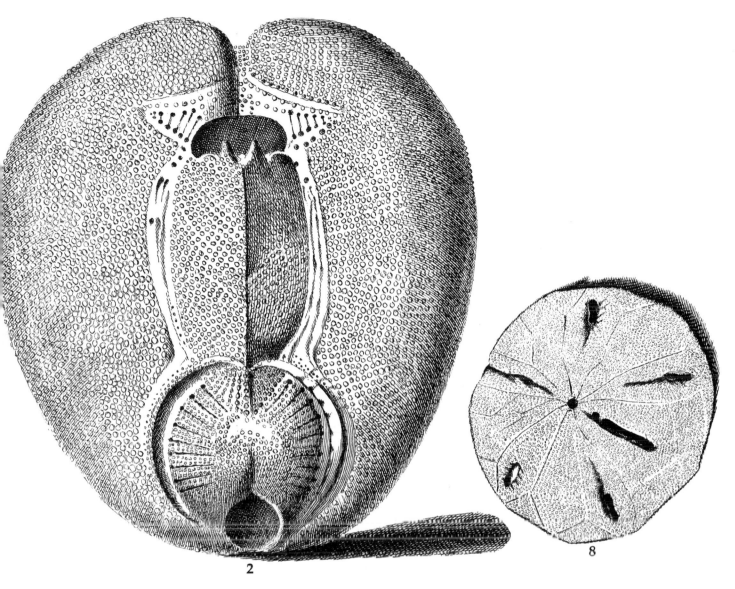

1, 2: *Tests, or shells, of heart urchins.*

3–8: *Tests of sand dollars. Sea urchins and sand dollars are members of invertebrate animals known as echinoderms, and are related to starfish and sea cucumbers.*

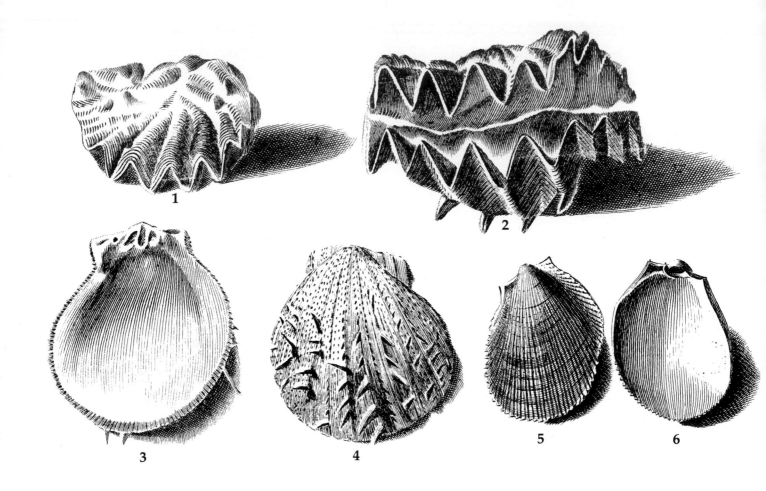

1, 2: Lopha cristagalli *Linné, the cock's comb oyster, 4 inches, Indo-Pacific.*

3, 4: Spondylus gaederopus *Linné, the European spiny oyster, 3 inches, Mediterranean.*

5, 6: Lima lima *Linné, the spiny file shell, 2 inches, Bermuda to Brazil. Like scallops, file shells can swim by beating their valves in the water. Many species construct nests of byssal threads, but will swim away if disturbed. The mantle edge is lined with long, waving tentacles, which in some species secrete a fluid that apparently turns off would-be predators.*

7, 8: Tellina planata *Linné, the flattened tellin, 3 inches, Mediterranean.*

9, 10: Siliqua radiatus *Linné, the rayed penknife clam, 3 inches, Indian Ocean.*

11: Mya truncata *Linné, the truncate soft-shell clam, Arctic seas down to Massachusetts, Japan, and Europe. The Indians introduced soft-shelled clams to the Pilgrims, and a list of local animals prepared in 1634 by John Winthrop of Plymouth included this entry: "Clams—white. Their broth is most excellent in all intermitting fevers, consumption, etc. These clams feed only on sand."*

12–14: Tellina radiata *Linné, the sunrise tellin, 4 inches, Bermuda to Brazil. This is perhaps the most spectacular of all the tellins, a creamy white, highly polished shell with wide rays of pink or yellow, a bright red stripe on the beak, and an interior flushed with yellow. Sometimes, instead of rays, areas of pink or yellow will appear near the beak.*

15: Phaxas cultellus *Linné, the penknife clam, 3 inches, Indian Ocean to Australia.*

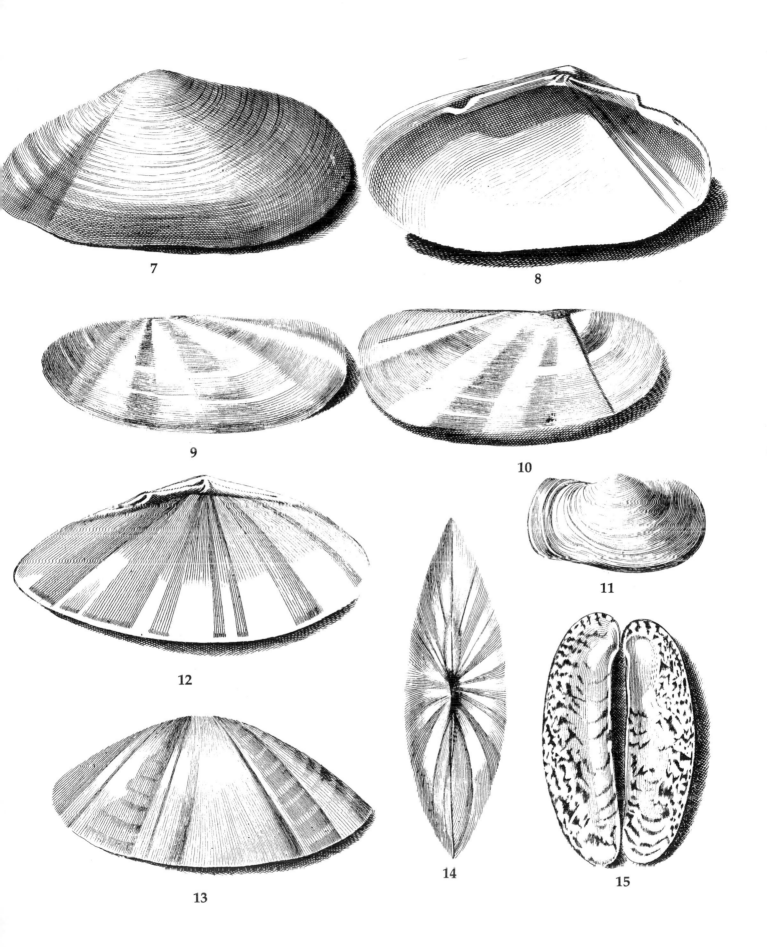

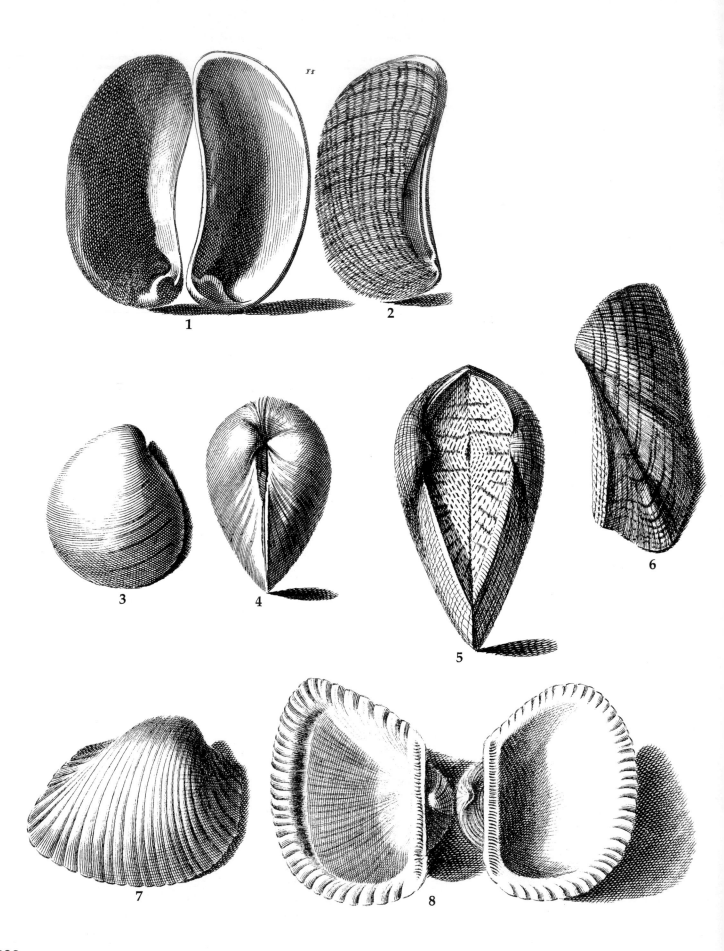

1, 2: Vulsella lingulata *Lamarck*, *the tongue vulsella, 3 inches, Indo-Pacific.*

3, 4: Laevicardium laevigatum *Linné, the egg cockle, 2 inches, Bermuda to Brazil. Quite common, this is a thin and rather smooth shell, although the surface often has about sixty radiating ridges that are so fine they cannot be felt. The color is usually whitish, with brown, orange, yellow, rose, or a pinkish purple.*

5, 6: Arca noae *Linné, the Noah's ark shell, 3 inches, Mediterranean. This is one of the best-known of the ark shells, a family of more than two hundred species found in all the world's seas.*

7, 8: Anadara antiquata *Linné, the antique ark, 2 inches, Indian Ocean.*

9–11: Fragum fragum *Linné, the wedge cockle, 1 inch, Indo-Pacific.*

12–14: Pitar dione *Linné, the royal comb Venus, 2 inches, West Indies and western coast of Central America. This somewhat uncommon variety of Venus clam should not be confused with the glamorous comb of Venus,* Murex pecten, *which is a univalve.*

15, 16: Trachycardium magnum *Linné, the large cockle, 3 ½ inches, Bermuda to Brazil.*

17, 18: Macrocallista maculata *Linné, the calico clam, 3 inches, North Carolina to Brazil. This common shell is sturdy, smooth, and egg-shaped, with a fawn base color and irregular brown checkerboard markings. It was introduced into Bermuda in 1962.*

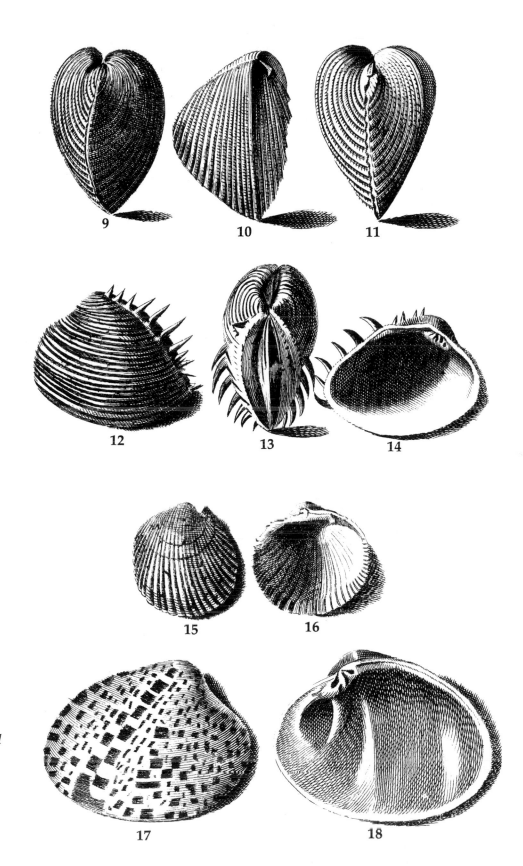

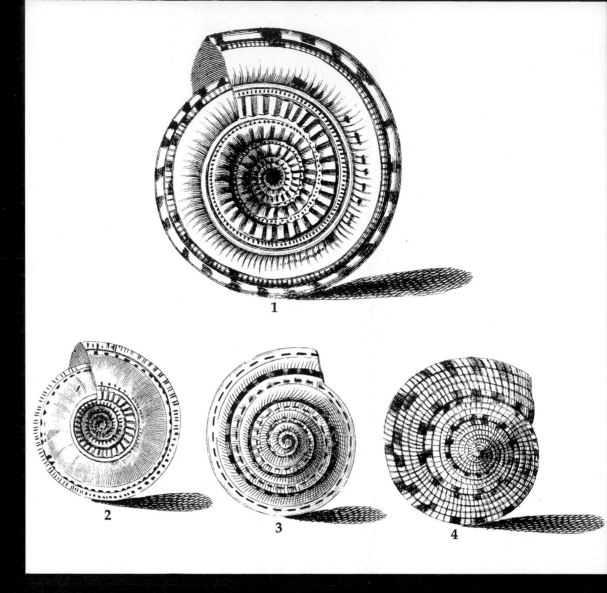

1–4: Architectonica perspectiva
*Linné, the sundial shell, 2 inches, Indo-Pacific and Australia. There are some
forty species of sundials, all natives of
tropical waters and all small, low,
conical shells decorated with netlike
spiral bands.*

5, 6: Glossus humanus *Linné, the ox
heart, 4 inches, Mediterranean. This
edible cockle can also be found along the
Atlantic coast of Spain, Portugal, and
North Africa.*

7: Amusium pleuronectes *Linné, the
Asian moon scallop, 3 to 5 inches,
Southeast Asia.*

8: Gloriapallium pallium *Linné, the
mantle scallop, Indo-Pacific.*

9: Chlamys glabra *Linné, the smooth
scallop, 3 inches, Mediterranean.*

10, 11: Ostrea edulis *Linné, the edible
oyster, 4 inches, European seas.*

241

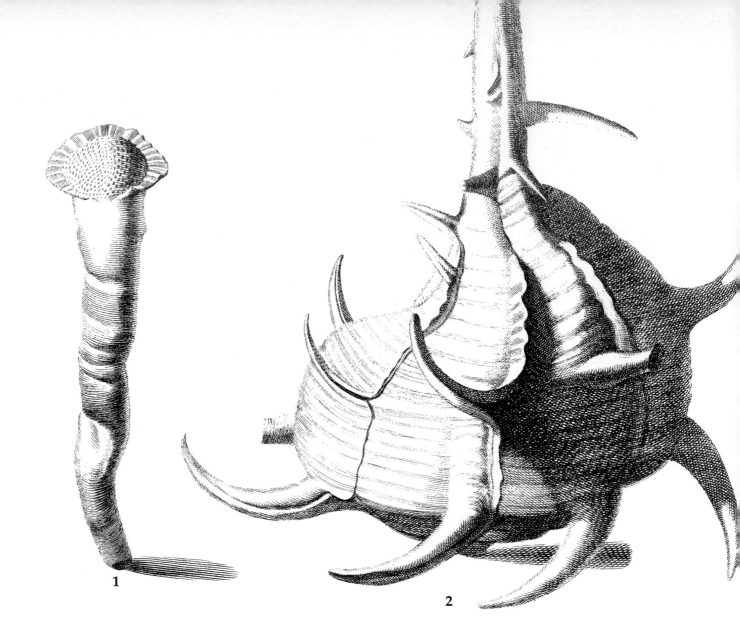

1: Penicillus penis *Linné, the watering pot shell, 6 to 10 inches, Indo-Pacific. Shaped like the spout and nozzle of a gardener's watering can, this odd, immobile clam can be recognized as a bivalve only by the minute nucleus of two clam valves on its lower end, not visible here.*

2: Murex cornutus *Linné, the horned murex, 4 to 10 inches, West Africa.*

3, 4: Telescopium telescopium *Linné, the telescope shell, 3 to 5 inches, Indo-Pacific.*

5, 6: Natica canrena *Linné, the Atlantic natica, 2 inches, Caribbean.*

7, 8: Nerita polita *Linné, the polite nerite, 1 inch, Indo-Pacific.*

9, 10: Trochus maculatus *Linné, the spotted top shell, 2 inches, Indo-Pacific.*

11, 12: Tectarius pagoda *Linné, the pagoda periwinkle, 3 inches, western Pacific.*

13: Natica stercusmuscarum *Gmelin, the fly-specked natica, 1 inch, Mediterranean Sea. The* Natica *moon snails, also called cat's-eye shells, rank close to starfish as bivalve enemies. Fastening itself to the shell of its prey with a huge, flatiron-shaped foot, the snail drills a circular hole with its radula and sucks out the soft parts through its proboscis.*

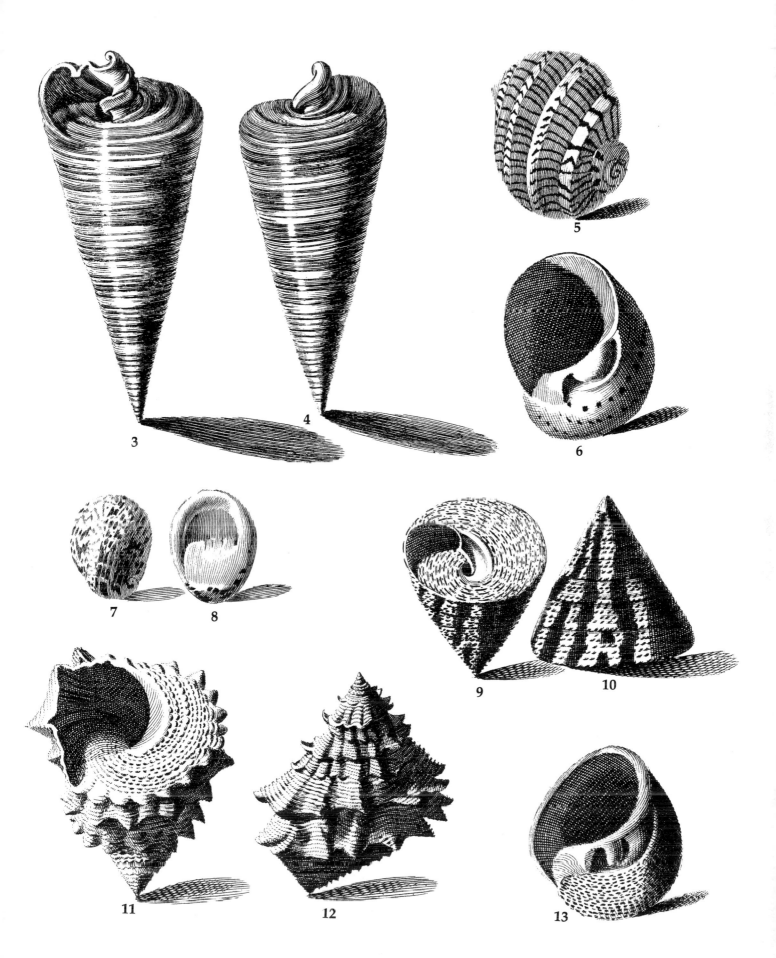

Bibliography

Abbot, Charles Greeley, editor. *Shelled Invertebrates of the Past and Present.* New York: Smithsonian Institution Series, 1931, 1934.

Abbott, R. Tucker. *Seashells of North America:* A Golden Field Guide. New York: Golden Press, 1968.

————. *Kingdom of the Seashell.* New York: Crown Publishers, 1972.

Allcock, Hubert. *Heraldic Design.* New York: Tudor Publishing Co., 1972.

Angeletti, Sergio. *Color Treasury of Sea Shells,* adapted from the Italian. English Edition, London: Orbis Publishing Limited, 1971, 1973.

Cameron, Roderick. *Shells.* London: Octopus Books, 1972.

Clayton, J. M. *All Color Book of Seashells.* New York: Bounty Books, a division of Crown Publishers, Inc., 1974.

Cox, Ian, editor. *The Scallop.* London: Shell Transport and Trading Co., 1957.

Cox, James A. *The Mollusk,* Volume 17 of *The Illustrated Encyclopedia of the Animal Kingdom.* Adapted from the Italian, *Gli Animali e il loro mondo,* Antonio Valle, editor. English Edition, New York: the Danbury Press, a division of Grolier Enterprises, 1970, 1971.

Critchley, Paula. *The Art of Shellcraft.* New York: Praeger Publishers, 1975.

Dance, S. Peter. *Shells and Shell Collecting.* London: Hamlyn, 1972.

————. *The World's Shells.* New York: McGraw-Hill Book Co., 1976.

Emerson, William K. and Jacobson, Morris K. *The American Museum of History Guide to Shells.* New York: Alfred A. Knopf, 1976.

Goodman, Stuart and Leni. *Art from Shells.* New York: Crown Publishers, Inc., 1972.

Graham, E. C. *The Basic Dictionary of Science.* New York: The Macmillan Co., 1966.

Hoyt, Murray. *Jewels from the Ocean Deep.* New York: G.P. Putnam's Sons, 1967.

Johnstone, Kathleen Yerger. *Sea Treasure.* Boston: Houghton Mifflin Co., 1957.

Lindner, Gert. *Field Guide to Seashells of the World.* New York: Van Nostrand Reinhold Co., 1978.

Logan, Elizabeth D. *Shell Crafts.* New York: Charles Scribner's Sons, 1974.

Lynch-Robinson, Sir Christopher and Lynch-Robinson, Adrian. *Intelligible Heraldry.* New York: D. Van Nostrand Co., 1948.

Major, Alan. *Collecting World Sea Shells.* New York: Arco Publishing Co., 1974.

Miner, Roy Waldo. *Field Book of Seashore Life.* New York: G.P. Putnam's Sons, 1950.

Morris, Percy A. *A Field Guide to Shells of the Atlantic and Gulf Coasts and the West Indies,* 3rd edition. Boston: Houghton Mifflin Co., 1973.

Pine, L. G. *The Story of Heraldry.* Rutland, Vt.: Charles E. Tuttle Co., 1966.

Potter, Piet. *World Treasury of Shore Life in Color.* New York: Galahad Books.

Ritchie, Carson I. A. *Shell Carving.* New York: A.S. Barnes and Co., 1974.

Rogers, Julia E. *The Shell Book.* New York: Doubleday, Doran & Co., 1931.

Scott-Giles, C. Wilfrid. *The Romance of Heraldry.* New York: E.P. Dutton & Co., 1929.

Sheets, Elva D. *The Fascinating World of the Sea.* New York: Crown Publishers, 1974.

Simon, Helen. *Snails of Land and Sea.* New York: Vanguard Press, 1976.

Stephens, Cleo M. *Shellcraft.* Radnor, Pa.: Chilton Book Co., 1974.

Stix, Hugh and Marguerite and Abbott, R. Tucker. *The Shell: Five Hundred Million Years of Inspired Design.* New York: Harry N. Abrams, 1968.

Travers, Louise Allerdice. *The Romance of Shells in Nature and Art.* New York: Avenel Books, a division of Crown Publishers, 1962.

Verrill, A. Hyatt. *Strange Sea Shells and Their Stories.* Boston: L.C. Page & Co., 1936.

————. *Shell Collector's Handbook.* New York: G.P. Putnam's Sons, 1950.

Webb, Walter Freeman. *A Handbook for Shell Collectors,* 1948 revised edition. Wellesly Hills, Mass.: Lee Publishing Co.

Index

In most cases, common names are indexed under the last, or generic, part of the name, without reference to family classification. Page numbers in italics indicate caption references.

Acknowledgments

All photographs are by F. H. Roberts with the following exceptions.

Ravi Ari: 101 top
Jerry Harasewych: 190–91
Historia Conchyliorum, by Martin Lister (1685): 29, 65
Index Testarum Conchyliorium, by Nicolaus Gaulterius (1742): 48, 50, 51, 54, 55, 58, 59, 62, 63, 68, 72, 73, 76, 77, 80–96, 98, 99, 102, 103, 106, 107, 110, 111, 113–19, 205–08, 210, 211, 214, 215, 218, 219, 222, 223, 225–43
Robert Lipe: 39 (3 pictures at right), 74 top, 75
Manuel de Conchyliologie et de Paleontologie Conchyliologique, by J. C. Chenu (1859): 17–20, 23, 24, 27, 30, 121, 126, 145
National Gallery of Art, Washington, D.C.: 140
Pictorial Museum of Animated Nature (1845): 44
Shell Oil Company—Enrico Ferorelli: 60 top
Stedelijk Museum, Amsterdam: 144
Hugh Stix and Werner Wolff: 112, 130–31
Uffizi Gallery, Florence: 132
Helen Coolidge Woodring: 142–43

Special thanks to Diane Andersen, Ravi Ari, Reg Barker, Mildred Camille, Colette Coman, Susan Eno, Jerry Harasewych, Renate Luebge-Kraus, Eric Marshall, Pamela Park, and Lori Stein.